THE PETER PAN SYNDROME

A Chicago-based psychologist who is well-known for his
advice on family relationships, Dr. Dan Kiley has
treated hundreds of PPS cases during his professional
career. His first clinical case came when he was working
with young military personnel in the Air Force, and the
ensuing years of counselling adolescents, university
students and young married couples taught him even
more about "the trials and tribulations of coming of age
. . . It slowly dawned on me that an alarming number of
men *weren't* coming of age. Something was wrong.

"This book focuses on adult males who have never
grown up, how they got that way, and what can be done
about it . . . Whether you're a victim, a lover, a parent,
a grandparent, or just a friend, you can help the victim,
no matter what his age. As you try to understand him,
remember: love the child, for he does not love himself;
believe in the man, for he does not believe in himself;
and, most of all, listen to him, for he does not listen to
himself. To overcome this affliction, he must travel the
greatest distance in the world – the one between his
mouth and his ears."

From the *Preface*

The Peter Pan Syndrome
Men Who Have Never Grown Up

Dr. Dan Kiley

CORGI BOOKS

THE PETER PAN SYNDROME

A CORGI BOOK 0 552 12554 7

First publication in Great Britain

PRINTING HISTORY
Corgi edition published 1984

Copyright © 1983 by Dr. Dan Kiley

This book is set in 10/11 Souvenir

Corgi Books are published by
Transworld Publishers Ltd.,
Century House, 61–63 Uxbridge Road,
Ealing, London W5 5SA

Made and printed in Great Britain by
Cox & Wyman Ltd., Reading, Berks.

To my wife, Nancy,
a Tinker who makes every day an adventure

Acknowledgments

My deepest appreciation goes to the following people: Evan Marshall, senior editor at Dodd, Mead, whose enthusiasm is outdone only by his brilliant editing; Kay Radtke, publicity director, and her able staff; Howard Morhaim, my literary agent, who could have been a great psychotherapist; and Donald Merz, Ph.D., friend and colleague, who has guided my investigation throughout the years. These persons have made this book infinitely better than I, by myself, could ever have done.

Contents

Author's Note

The case histories presented in this book are intended for instructional purposes. To protect those who have labored to confront and overcome the Peter Pan Syndrome, I have fictionalized ancillary information and made composites of individual cases. The resulting stories represent the real-life struggles of PPS victims while obscuring the identity of any one person.

Any similarity between these stories and an actual family or individual is purely coincidental.

To live would be an awfully big adventure.

Peter Pan

Preface

It's not life-threatening, so it's not a disease. But it endangers a person's mental health, so it's more than an inconvenience. Its symptoms are well known, so I can't call it a discovery. But the condition itself has never been disclosed, so this book is more than a rehash.

"It" is a novel psychological phenomenon. It doesn't fit into any recognizable category, but there's no denying its presence. In my business, we call such an anomaly a syndrome. In standard jargon, a syndrome is a collection of symptoms that is expressed by some type of social pattern. I want to tell you about a syndrome in our society that is causing a lot of problems. We all know it's there, but until now nobody has labeled or explained it.

I've been studying this syndrome for many years, trying to make sense out of a complicated maze of cause-and-effect. I suspect that it has occurred in isolated cases for a long time; only in the past twenty or twenty-five years, however, have the pressures of modern life exacerbated the causative factors, resulting in a dramatic increase in the frequency of the problem. And there's every reason to expect it to get worse in the coming years.

My first clinical case was a victim of the syndrome, though I didn't realize it at the time. I was working with military personnel, counseling young adults who were struggling to come of age in the Air Force.

His name was George. He was twenty-two going on ten. His emotional expressions were exaggerated, ill-timed, and silly. He talked a lot, but he didn't say much. It was time for him to move on with his life, yet he longed for his carefree high school days. I thought he would outgrow his fear of manhood. To this day I don't know whether he did.

Many years of counseling adolescents, university students, and young married couples rounded out my knowledge of the trials and tribulations of coming of age. It slowly dawned on me that an alarming number of young men *weren't* coming of age. Something was wrong.

This book focuses on adult males who have never grown up, how they got that way, and what can be done about it. By the time you've finished the first two chapters of this book, you will have identified someone you know as a victim of this affliction. I expect that you will have an "Ah-haa" reaction as the behaviour of this person suddenly makes sense.

During their late teens and early twenties, these men indulge in an impetuous lifestyle. Narcissism locks them inside themselves, while an unrealistic ego trip convinces them that they can and must do whatever their fantasies suggest. Later, after years of poor adjustment to reality, life seems to reverse itself. "I want" is replaced with "I should." Pursuit of other people's acceptance seems their only way to find self-acceptance. Their temper tantrums are disguised as manly assertion. They take love for granted, never learning how to give it in return. They pretend to be grown-ups but actually behave like spoiled children.

It takes time for a bright, sensitive child to become an immature, angry adult. Parents have many chances to reverse the process; hence this is a book for parents. But wives and lovers have the greatest opportunity to turn "never" into "someday", that's why this book is especially for women who have a special relationship (married or otherwise) with the victim. Friends and relatives who have an influence on the victim's life can offer aid; therefore, this is a book for concerned adults in general. Finally, it's never too late for a man to grow up through his own efforts; that's why this also is a book for the victim himself.

Whether you're a wife, a lover, a parent, a grandparent,

or just a friend, you can help the victim, no matter what his age. As you try to understand him, remember: love the child, for he does not love himself; believe in the man, for he does not believe in himself; and, most of all, listen to him, for he does not listen to himself. To overcome this affliction, he must travel the greatest distance in the world – the one between his mouth and his ears.

PART 1
INTRODUCTORY

1 Do You Know This Man-Child?

CAPTAIN HOOK: 'Have you another name?'
PETER PAN: 'Ay, ay.'
HOOK *(thirstily)*: 'Vegetable?'
PETER: 'No.'
HOOK: 'Mineral?'
PETER: 'No.'
HOOK: 'Animal?'
PETER *(after consultation with a friend)*: 'Yes.'
HOOK: 'Man?'
PETER *(with scorn)*: 'No.'
HOOK: 'Boy?'
PETER: 'Yes.'
HOOK: 'Ordinary boy?'
PETER: 'No!'
HOOK: 'Wonderful boy?'
PETER *(to Wendy's distress)*: 'Yes!'

Do you know this person? He's a man because of his age; a child because of his acts. The man wants your love; the child wants your pity. The man yearns to be close; the child is afraid to be touched. If you look past his pride, you'll see his vulnerability. If you defy his boldness, you'll feel his fear.

You think you know this person well, but you don't know him at all. The contradiction is disturbing. The answers are elusive. Even the questions are hard to find. But look to your children or to the child of a friend and ask yourself: 'What would happen if his body grew up, but his mind didn't?'

This man-child is the victim of a serious affliction. If he is

11

not helped, his life will slowly turn sour. He is not mentally ill, nor is he incapable of functioning in society. He is, however, very sad. He sees life as a waste of time. He tries hard to camouflage his sadness with gaiety and sporting fun. In many cases his trickery works, at least for a few years. Eventually, the people who love him become discouraged with his immaturity. Their disappointment seems unwarranted and their disgust a bit premature. But once you see what they see, you understand their wish to be rid of this person.

Your task is to identify this man-child. The sooner you know who he is, the better your chances of helping him. He may be your son, your husband, an uncle, or a cousin. Then again, he could be a friend, a neighbor, or a co-worker. Or, if you are a man, he could be you! Whoever he is, he thinks he doesn't want your help. He doesn't want it, because he doesn't know he needs it. He's so accustomed to viewing life as an empty cavern that his 'I don't care' attitude seems normal. If he dares to care about someone else, the dissonance turns him inside out. He prefers the peace and quiet of bland indifference.

Chances are you won't be able to identify this man until he's older. The disparity between his age and his maturity will be your first clue. Once you've identified his problem, you can take steps to offer help, or at least avoid contributing to his difficulties. Once you understand the complexities of his affliction, you can spot the early warning signs. If you happen to be the parent of a child who might be heading for trouble, you can learn how to stop this monster dead in its tracks.

The affliction begins to grow early in a man's life. Chances are, some child in your immediate environment is moving toward the crisis stage right now. He could be the neighbor boy, one of your friends' children, the president of the church youth group, or even your own son. The closer you are to this boy, the greater the opportunity for you to stop the development of his affliction.

Identifying this man-child is a three-step process. It is designed to be objective; consequently, it has a rather impersonal quality, much like a psychology textbook used to learn about *the* classic case.

First, define your *observational ground*. This ground includes your home, your neighborhood, your work place, and anywhere else you spend a significant amount of time. Wherever you come in close contact with other people is where you will ultimately see this person. You might see him at a party, at a neighborhood gathering, at a family picnic, or in the office next to yours. If you are a sensitive parent, you may see a miniature man-child at the dinner table. If you are a woman in love, you might see him in your bed. If you are a thoughtful male, you may even spot him in the mirror.

Second, assume the role of *social detective*. Gather preliminary evidence using this social profile of the classic case:

The Victim's Social Profile

Sex: Male

Age: 12 to 50

Symptomatic chronology:

Ages 12 to 17: Four fundamental symptoms develop in varying degrees: irresponsibility, anxiety, loneliness, sex role conflict.

Ages 18 to 22: Denial flourishes as narcissism and chauvinism dominate behavior.

Ages 23 to 25: Acute crisis period during which victim may seek help, complaining of a vague but all-inclusive dissatisfaction with life. Often interpreted as normal by doctor/therapist.

Ages 26 to 30: Victim settles into chronic stage, acting out the 'grown-up' adult role.

Ages 31 to 45: Victim is married, has children, keeps a steady job, but suffers bland despair that makes life dull and repetitious.

Beyond 45: Depression and agitation increase as menopause approaches. Victim may rebel against an unwanted, meaningless lifestyle, attempting to recapture his youth.

Socioeconomic level: Middle to upper class.

Appearance: He is seen as personable and likable by people who don't know him very well. He has an ingratiating smile and gives an excellent first impression.

Financial status: Younger victims are rarely self-supporting. In their early twenties they still live at home or live hand-to-mouth, getting money from parents or other sources. Older victims may be financially secure but not feel as if they are. They are often stingy, except when it comes to their own indulgences.

Marital status: Younger victims (under 25) are usually single. They date women younger than they are or whose actions suggest immaturity. Once married, these women often find themselves having to keep the victim on the straight and narrow. The victim usually prefers his buddies to his family.

Education: Younger victims flirt with a college education, finding it difficult to decide what they want to study. They rarely finish college in the usual allotted time. Older victims have achieved some education but are dissatisfied. They believe they should have done more. Victims are usually seen as underachievers.

Work history: Younger victims have a very shaky work history. They work only when under pressure. They want a career, but don't want to work at it. They're easily offended by jobs that they see as 'beneath' them. They get into employment difficulty because of severe procrastination. Older victims go to the opposite extreme. They become workaholics in an attempt to prove their worth. They have unrealistic expectations of themselves, their co-workers, and their bosses. They are nagged by the thought that they haven't found the 'right' job.

Family: The victim is usually the oldest male child of a traditional family. His parents have stayed together and are well-off financially. The father is most likely a white-collar worker, while the mother considers her main task to be keeping the house and raising children.

She is not a career person, but may work to provide
more money for the family.

Interests: The one consuming interest of younger victims is parties. Older victims work hard to have fun at
parties, and also tend to push themselves beyond
reasonable limits in participative sports.

The third step in the identification process is assuming the
role of *psychological detective*. Once the social profile has
helped you recognize the victim's outer life, use this
psychological profile to evaluate his inner life:

The Victim's Psychological Profile

Seven psychological traits dominate the PPS victim's life.
They are present at each stage of development but are most
noticeable during the crisis period. In the chronic stage the
victim tends to hide these traits behind a mask of maturity.

Emotional paralysis: The victim's emotions are
stunted. They are not expressed in the same way they
are experienced. Anger often comes out as rage, joy
takes the form of hysteria, and disappointment
becomes self-pity. Sadness may manifest itself as forced
gaiety, childish pranks, or nervous laughter. Older victims say they love or care for you but can't seem to
remember to express their love. Ironically, although
they started as extremely sensitive children, these men
often appear to be self-centered to the point of cruelty.
Eventually they reach a point at which they seem to
refuse to share their feelings. In truth, they have lost
touch with their emotions and simply *don't know* what
they feel.

Procrastination: During the developmental stage, the
young victim puts things off until he is absolutely forced
to do them. 'I don't know' and 'I don't care' become his
defense against criticism. His life goals are fuzzy and
poorly defined, mainly because he puts off thinking
about them until tomorrow. Guilt forces the older victim to compensate for past procrastination by becoming a person who must always be doing something. He
simply does not know how to relax.

15

Social impotence: Try as they may, victims cannot make true friends. As teenagers they are easily led by peers. Impulses take priority over a true sense of right and wrong. Seeking friends and being friendly to mere acquaintances take precedence over showing love and concern for the family. The victim desperately needs to belong; he is terribly lonely and panics at being alone. He may even try to buy friends. Throughout their lives, victims have difficulty feeling good about themselves. False pride constantly interferes with the acceptance of their own human limitations.

Magical thinking: 'If I don't think about it, it will go away.' 'If I think it will be different, then it will be.' These two quotes reflect the 'magical thinking' of the victims. Mental magic prevents the victims from honestly admitting mistakes and makes it almost impossible for them to say 'I'm sorry.' This irrational process shields the victims from having to overcome their social impotence and emotional paralysis, because they are proficient at blaming others for their shortcomings. It often leads them to drug abuse, because they believe that getting high will make their problems disappear.

Mother hang-up: Anger and guilt cause an overwhelming ambivalence toward Mother. Victims want to pull free of her influence but feel guilty every time they try. When they are with their mothers there is a tension in the air, punctuated by moments of sarcasm followed by moments of reactive sweetness. Younger victims elicit pity from their mothers to get what they want, especially money. They will argue with flashes of rage and then apologize with sustained silliness. Older victims feel less ambivalence and more guilt because of the pain they caused their mothers.

Father hang-up: The victim feels estranged from his father. He longs to be close to Dad, but has decided that he can never receive Dad's love and approval. The older victim still idolizes his father, never understanding Dad's limitations, much less accepting his faults. Much of the victim's problem with authority figures stems from his father hang-up.

Sexual hang-up: The victim's social impotence carries over into the sexual arena. Soon after puberty he begins to search desperately for a girlfriend. However, his immaturity and silliness tend to drive most girls away.

The victim's fear of rejection causes him to hide his sensitivity behind a cruel and heartless 'macho' attitude. In most cases the victim remains a virgin until his early twenties, a situation that embarrasses him and about which he lies – often to the point of 'rape talk,' in which he boasts of how he has forced, or plans to force, himself on girls.

Once he breaks the virginal barrier, the victim may go to the opposite extreme, having sexual intercourse with any girl who is willing, in order to prove to himself that he is potent. When he does settle on one girl, he attaches himself to her completely. His jealousy is outdone only by his ability to elicit pity from her.

The victim is provoked to anger or even rage by a woman's assertiveness or independence; he needs a female to be dependent upon him so that he can feel he is protecting her. In truth, he feels impotent to deal with an assertive female on equal footing, so he puts her beneath him. He longs to share his sensitivity with a woman, but denies this side of his personality for fear that his friends will see him as weak and unmanly.

By now you've probably identified at least one male in your environment as a victim of this affliction. It's unlikely that he fits perfectly the objective description I've offered. More than likely he has some, but not all, of the attributes described. Rarely does the *classic* case exist in reality. In the next chapter we'll move away from the objective and into the subjective, out of the classroom and into the lab, so to speak. That's when you may have to confront the fact that, to one degree or another, this affliction could be touching your daily life.

This brings us to the next step: personalizing the identification process. To do this you must address the question: To what degree does the man in my life exhibit this affliction? Your answer will guide you in deciding what, if anything, you wish to do about your personal reality.

Summary Profile

Identification: Men who have never grown up.
Code name: The Peter Pan Syndrome (PPS).

2 The Adult PPS Victim: A Test

PETER: 'What is your name?'
WENDY *(well satisfied)*: 'Wendy Moira Angela Darling. What's yours?'
PETER *(finding it lamentably brief)*: 'Peter Pan.'
WENDY: 'Is that all?'
PETER *(biting his lip)*: 'Yes.'
WENDY *(politely)*: 'I am so sorry.'
PETER: 'It doesn't matter.'
WENDY: 'Where do you live?'
PETER: 'Second to the right and then straight on till morning.'
WENDY: 'What a funny address!'
PETER: 'No, it isn't.'
WENDY: 'I mean, is that what they put on the letters?'
PETER: 'Don't get any letters.'
WENDY: 'But your mother gets letters?'
PETER: 'Don't have a mother.'
WENDY: 'Peter!'

The affliction has a simple name, and its objective identification is relatively simple. Yet discovering the whereabouts of any one victim's life space can be as confusing as trying to decipher the location of 'second to the right and then straight on till morning.'

You have to be careful in labeling an adult male as a victim of the Peter Pan Syndrome. In the investigative arena you always run the risk of 'true negatives' (the affliction appears to be present, but it really isn't) and 'false positives' (the affliction appears *not* to be present, but it really is).

To complicate matters further, many adult males possess one or two *attributes* of the Peter Pan Syndrome without actually having the syndrome itself: a rich imagination and a yearning to stay young at heart. Cannot these traits be portals to brilliance and serenity?

The presence of one or two attributes of the PPS doesn't make a man a victim any more than being unconscious makes a person dead. You must look beyond your first impression. A man becomes a victim of the PPS only when his attributes interfere with his daily functioning and the development of productive relationships with other people. Or, said another way, the PPS attributes become a problem when a man is no longer behaving in a childlike manner, but is just plain childish.

A simple test will help you decide whether or not the man in your life is a victim of the PPS. For those men who dare to examine themselves, this test can be very revealing. But I warn you: If you are a PPS victim, you'll find the test silly, irrelevant, and dumb. You might even get angry. If that happens, I suggest that you are threatened by the truth and try to dismiss it as you do other things that hit too close to home; that is, you slip into a cynical attitude in which you laugh on the outside but are scared to death on the inside.

The PPS Test

The test is simple. Read each behavioral description and rate the degree to which it applies to the person under consideration. A rating of 0 signifies that this behavior *never* occurs; 1 signifies that this behavior occurs *sometimes* (for instance, that it has happened once or twice but not very often); and 2 signifies *always* (or you can barely remember it *not* happening).

Since this test is designed for wives and lovers, it is written from the point of view of a female observing her man. If you have a different relationship to the potential victim, change the wording of the statement where appropriate to facilitate your evaluation.

0   1   2   When he makes a mistake, he overreacts, either

exaggerating his guilt or searching for excuses to absolve himself of any blame.

0 1 2 He forgets important dates; i.e., anniversary, birthday.

0 1 2 At a party, he ignores you but does his best to impress other people, especially women.

0 1 2 He finds it almost impossible to say 'I'm sorry.'

0 1 2 He expects you to have sexual intercourse when *he's* ready, giving little thought to your need for foreplay.

0 1 2 He goes out of his way to help his buddies but fails to do the little things you ask him to do.

0 1 2 He expresses concern for you and your problems and feelings only after you've complained about his indifference.

0 1 2 He initiates an activity or outing only if it's something *he* wants to do.

0 1 2 He seems to find it extremely difficult to express his feelings.

0 1 2 He yearns to be close to his father, but any conversation (present or past) with his dad is stilted, ceremonial, and lacking in depth.

0 1 2 He doesn't listen well to opinions that differ from his own.

0 1 2 He has uncalled-for flashes of rage during which he refuses to calm down.

0 1 2 He is intimidated by the wishes of his mother to the point that you become upset with her for being so demanding.

0 1 2 He believes he is employed in the wrong capacity, but fails to do anything about it except complain.

0 1 2 He is devoid of sincerity and warmth in relating to other people, especially his oldest son (if applicable).

0 1 2 He has a problem with alcohol; when he drinks, his personality seems to change; he demonstrates a hair-trigger temper, false bravado, or exaggerated gaiety.

0	1	2	He feels that he must not miss any fun or event with the boys, and goes beyond rational limits in order not to be left out.
0	1	2	He expresses chauvinistic attitudes; e.g., 'I want my wife to work as long as the house is clean.'
0	1	2	He appears to have unexplained fears and lacks self-confidence, but refuses to talk about it.
0	1	2	He accuses you of getting too emotional, while he appears to be above it all. When you get angry, he sits there like stone.

Now add up the numbers you have selected for each behavioral description. Use the following guide to judge the degree of affliction.

0 to 10   Not a PPS victim. His problems tend to be isolated and are not very serious. If there is a bothersome situation, talk with him about it. Most likely it can be resolved in a spirit of love and cooperation.

11 to 25   The PPS is definitely a threat. Follow the instructions outlined after this test and, if you are a woman, be prepared to evaluate yourself (see Chapter 13). There are steps you can take to improve the situation, but the higher the score within this category, the harder you must be willing to work.

26 to 40   The Peter Pan Syndrome is functioning. If the man won't seek help for his problems, you should probably talk with a professional about what you can do to cope with the situation. See Chapter 13 for an evaluation of your own role in this situation.

BLUEPRINT FOR CHANGE

Take another look at the test. The higher the score, the more carefully you should evaluate the seriousness of each trait you felt was present. Even if the Peter Pan Syndrome is functioning to a great degree (say a score of 30), there is still hope. You can use a thorough review of the test as a blueprint for future change.

Here's your next step: on a piece of paper set up three columns with the headings 'Never,' 'Sometimes,' and 'Always.' Now go through the test again, only this time, think back over the past six months and, as accurately as possible, place each trait in the appropriate column. Here's how a thirty-three-year-old wife completed this blueprint for change:

Never
Flirts
Doesn't listen
Flashes of rage
Cold relationships

Sometimes
No foreplay
Forgets dates
Selfish about outings
Drinking problem
Won't miss fun
Chauvinistic
Denies having fears

Always
Overreacts to mistakes
No 'I'm sorry'
Helps buddies
Told to care
Intimidated by mom
Underemployed
No feelings expressed
Distant from dad
Above it all

According to the person who should know, this man scored a 25 on the test. When I first talked with her about her husband's score, contradictions seemed apparent (he had honesty and warmth in relationships but never expressed his feelings). Such inconsistencies suggested that, try as she might, she could never be totally objective. Although there definitely seemed to be a problem, it was likely that she was misreading some situations. She did, after all, love this man, and would therefore, be biased in some of her judgments.

Thus, this woman's blueprint for change could guide her efforts in dealing with her mate's PPS while also serving as a reminder that, whenever she judged her husband, she had to consider the influence of her own personal thoughts and feelings.

If you're serious about helping a potential PPS victim, you'll need such a blueprint to guide you. Once you have it, hold onto it while you decide what your next step will be.

You can make that decision by asking yourself three questions and selecting the one you most want answered. These three questions are:

How did he get this way?

What is he thinking about?

What can I do to help?

If 'How did he get this way?' is most important to you, you will want to read Chapters 4 through 9. Here you will learn the complicated details of the PPS victim's development— how a child retreats from reality to the safety of Never Never Land.

If 'What is he thinking about?' concerns you most, I turn your attention to Chapter 7, especially the last section. It is with the development of the sex role conflict in late adolescence that a Jekyll/Hyde personality begins to form.

If 'What can I do to help?' is your primary question, I direct you to Chapter 13. There I will challenge you to confront not only the traits you find most distressing in your mate, but also to take a critical look at yourself. You probably won't be surprised to learn that you could be unconsciously supporting the Peter Pan Syndrome.

Whatever your next step, I suggest you take a few minutes to acquaint yourself with the overview of the Peter Pan Syndrome contained in the next chapter. A general understanding will help you keep your feet on solid ground and resist the temptation to fly away from reality by pretending that nothing is really wrong.

3 The Peter Pan Syndrome: An Overview

PETER: 'Would you send me to school?'
MRS. DARLING *(obligingly)*: 'Yes.'
PETER: 'And then to an office?'
MRS. DARLING: 'I suppose so.'
PETER: 'Soon I should be a man?'
MRS. DARLING: 'Very soon.'
PETER *(passionately)*: 'I don't want to go to school and learn solemn things. No one is going to catch me, lady, and make me a man. I want always to be a little boy and to have fun.'

We all remember the compelling story of happy-go-lucky Peter Pan, right? The soft, effeminate boy who wouldn't grow up? It was Peter who showed us the glory of eternal youth. It was the Pan who bedeviled Captain Hook. His song and dance broke the cruel pirate's heart and sent him on a self-destructive passage over the ship's side and into the waiting jaws of the 'clocked' and carnivorous crocodile.

Peter Pan symbolizes the essence of youthfulness. The joy. The indefatigable spirit. As Peter captures the *Jolly Roger* and cavorts with Tinkerbell, he awakens the child inside all of us. We are drawn to him. He is wonderful. He offers us the hand of an everlasting playmate. When we allow Peter Pan to touch our heart, our soul is nourished by the fountain of youth.

But how many people realize that there is another side to the classic character created by J.M. Barrie? Are there skeptics among us who would look deeper into this haunting tale? Have you stopped to consider why Peter wanted

25

to stay young? Sure, it's tough to grow up, but Peter Pan avoided it vehemently. What made him reject all things adult? What was he really after? Is it as simple as it sounded? Was not Peter's desire to stay young actually a militant refusal to grow up? If so, what was his problem? Or problems?

A careful and thoughtful reading of Barrie's original play opened my eyes to a chilling reality. As much as I want to believe the contrary, Peter Pan was a very sad young man. His life was filled with contradictions, conflicts, and confusion. His world was hostile and unrelenting. For all his gaiety, he was a deeply troubled boy living in an even more troubling time. He was caught in the abyss between the man he didn't want to become and the boy he could no longer be.

Forgive me for using a psychological claw to unearth a story line that the faithful have buried. But I do feel justified. A close examination of the fictional account of Peter Pan not only becomes an instructional allegory of youthful whims, but also gives modern-day professionals insight into a ghastly reality. Unknown to many parents and others who love them, many of our children are unwittingly following in the footsteps of Peter Pan.

With increasing frequency, the little-known side of the famous Pan has captured the heart and soul of a significant segment of our children. If they're not freed, they will endure endless emotional and social turmoil. I feel certain that Peter wouldn't mind if I use his story to help others. In fact, I'm not sure he would even care.

Today's children live in troubled times; it's not unlike the turbulence that surrounded Peter and his serene Never Never Land. But unlike our impish hero, our children are unable to fly off and stay young forever.

Like Peter's contemporaries, our male children are suffering the most. All across our land, young men are refusing to grow up. Thousands, maybe even hundreds of thousands, are moving toward a manhood that frightens them. In a state of fear, they rush to join the ranks of the legion of the lost boys. Sooner or later many overcome their fears of adulthood and drop out of the legion. But many others surrender to their fear and pledge allegiance to the cause of being lost. The legion of lost boys has members of all ages. Many 'successful' adult men still behave like lost children.

The younger members are easier to identify. They are a study in contrasts. There is nothing outwardly wrong with them. On the contrary, they are absolute gems—bright and beautiful, sensitive and sincere, the joy of any parent's hopes and dreams. However, if they stay in the legion very long, their behavior becomes a bit bizarre. They fly away from reality, get high on the natural herbs of the land, cavort with fairies, and cop out on mature responsibilities.

These reincarnations of the Pan would quickly echo his passionate rebellion expressed at the beginning of this chapter. They don't want anything to do with school, work, or anything else that smacks of adulthood. Their desire is to do whatever they must to remain just what they are: little children who won't grow up.

Most of us have flirted with this attitude at one time or another. It's perfectly normal to sprinkle a little magical dust on your head, especially during your younger days. Then you can fly away to Never Never Land by joining your pals in childish pranks or simply soar away from reality on the wings of your own fantasies. There's certainly nothing wrong with having the desire to join Peter and his frivolous fellows. Nothing, that is, *provided you return from Never Never Land when it's time to deal with the real world.*

I remember my own encounter with Peter and his magical dust. I wasn't invisible to adults as Peter was, but I did try to fly away one day by jumping off the chicken shed like my feathery friends. Nature gave me a down-to-earth (and painful) lesson in reality. I also told my grandma that I wasn't going to grow up. She was kind and compassionate as she said, 'That's nice, Danny. Now get out in the garden and hoe the tomatoes.'

Reality neutralizes the powers of the magical dust. If parents, teachers, and other concerned adults help the child deal with reality, the effects of Peter and his legion will fade fast, remaining a source of pleasant memories. But if children enter their adolescence in full pursuit of eternal youth, monumental problems develop as reality becomes clouded. And if they reach the beginning of their third decade with the same outlook, a serious identity crisis will consume them sometime during their early twenties.

There are many flesh-and-blood young men whose flirtation with Peter turns sour. They start out like the rest of us, enraptured by the excitement of eternal youth. But, for a combination of reasons, they reach a point where the day-dream of Never Never Land turns into a disastrous nightmare. Some recover; an increasing number do not. Your son might be a victim; so might your husband.

Children who follow in the footsteps of Peter Pan eventually experience a serious psychological problem that usually leads to social maladjustment. Many of them are emotionally crippled and interpersonally inept. Feelings of isolation and failure abound as they encounter a society that has little patience with adults who act like children. But these people see no reason why they should feel so bad. Viewing the problem as temporary, they do their best to forget about it. Needless to say, it gets worse.

Because the problem mirrors the fictional life of a classical hero, thereby facilitating explanation and understanding, it didn't take me very long to label this condition the Peter Pan Syndrome—PPS for short.

The PPS has its roots in early childhood. It doesn't begin to manifest itself, however, until puberty, at age 12 or thereabouts. From ages 12 through 18, four symptoms slowly develop in boys who have yet to forgo the pursuit of eternal youth. Each symptom is a product of the stresses that modern society places upon the family and, ultimately, upon the child.

From ages 18 through 22, two more symptoms emerge, both of which are fostered by the four basic symptoms. These two intermediate symptoms cement the problem in place and set the stage for a crisis period. During this crisis, the young man must confront and resolve many years of magical thinking and marginal ego development. If he fails in this process, he is likely to be trapped in the PPS for an extended period of time, possibly the rest of his life.

Below, I briefly review the six symptoms and the social stress that acts as a catalyst in the development of each symptom.

IRRESPONSIBILITY

Permissive attitudes have permeated our literature, media, and educational philosophies for over thirty years. They have given parents the notion that, in raising their children, they must avoid authority and punishment and never establish or enforce limits on a child's growth space.

The parents who adopt this approach nurture the development of irresponsibility. I speak not of laziness or minor procrastination, but of full-fledged irresponsibility in which the child believes that rules don't apply to him.

When such irresponsibility goes unchallenged, children fail to learn basic self-care habits. Failure in the little things (cleanliness, orderliness, proper manners) can build into an avalanche of slothful activity that buries self-confidence. The child believes, 'I'll never handle the big things if I don't even know how to handle the small ones.'

ANXIETY

PPS victims are filled with anxiety. Early in life, tension begins to pervade the atmosphere of the home. It grows every year. It surrounds the child, eventually becoming the background to every life scene. The cause of this free-floating anxiety is parental unhappiness.

Parents of PPS victims are dissatisfied with their marriage and themselves. Reasons for this discontent are varied and complicated. Some of the more prominent are: lack of emotional warmth and sharing, an imbalance in work and play, poor self-discipline, and an upheaval of traditional roles and values.

Each parent's unhappiness has a different effect on the child. Dad camouflages his pain with the tough-guy image and uses trite phrases to express his concern ('C'mon, don't be feeling sorry for yourself,' or 'Oh, you'll be okay.'). The result is an estrangement between father and son in which the son views Dad as an enigma and a person whose love and approval will never be forthcoming. The anxiety is like a dull ache.

Mom tries to suffer in silence but fails. She wears her martyrdom like a battle ribbon and feigns satisfaction at the prospects of sacrificing her life for the children ('I never really wanted anything for myself except your happiness.'). The son perceives the isolation and distress. He's tempted to blame his father but doesn't, because he needs Dad's love. So he blames himself, figuring that his mother has good reason to reject him. This irrational conclusion haunts him continuously and causes an anxiety that is akin to a deafening roar.

In most cases the parents pretend to be happy. They are afraid to confront their feelings and face the truth. Their avoidance is facilitated by the fact that they aren't terribly disturbed, just blandly miserable. So they put on false smiles and participate in forced and fitful family outings while uttering plastic words that have a million-dollar sound but aren't worth a plug nickel.

To the casual observer, nothing is wrong with these families. They appear well adjusted and are often the envy of the neighborhood, but this outward appearance is illusory. In truth, the specter of discontent spreads like an emotional cancer, devouring the children's security and peace of mind. The parents usually don't say it, but they are staying together for the sake of the children. They shouldn't. The children suffer.

LONELINESS

Families of PPS victims are usually too affluent for their own good. The parents give their children money instead of time. They don't help the kids learn how to earn. The youngsters take their food, shelter, and safety for granted and concentrate their efforts on finding new ways to purchase pleasure.

Affluence without restraints creates a falling domino effect in the children. The value of work is the first to tumble as children take pleasure as a right rather than as an earned privilege. Then, with too much time on their hands and too little security in the home, they search for group identity. They desperately want to find a place where they belong.

In a state of near panic, the children are seduced by the profit-seekers who use dazzling media displays to promise kids that the key to belonging is to do what 'everybody' else is doing. Consequently, peer pressure invades every aspect of their lives, compelling them to belong, no matter what the price. The stampede toward sameness tramples their spirit of freedom and deprives them of what little self-confidence they have. They work so hard to avoid rejection that they have little or no time to enjoy the comfort of belonging. The result is loneliness.

Loneliness is the worst problem in our country today. It affects both adults and children, the latter paying the biggest price. PPS victims, anxious and irresponsible, are dealt a crushing blow by loneliness. It thrusts them into an emotional quicksand. They desperately need friends; yet the more they struggle, the worse they feel. Many of them turn to drug abuse, sexual promiscuity, and other vices in a fruitless search for rescue.

Loneliness and affluence tend to go hand-in-hand. Children who don't appreciate the value of work don't have much of a chance to feel proud of their accomplishments. Without honest pride, they are more apt to be crushed by peer pressure than are the children whose day-to-day survival cannot be taken for granted.

Inner-city poor kids have a crying need to belong, but belonging must share time with concerns for physical shelter and safety. This deprived condition retards the development of the Peter Pan Syndrome.

Farm boys have more opportunity to learn good work habits, which in turn frustrate the growth of the PPS. If you can accept the premise that affluence contributes to loneliness, then you can see why I call the Peter Pan Syndrome a suburban affliction. With rare exception, the PPS affects middle- and upper-class children. In a moment you'll see why these kids are exclusively male.

SEX ROLE CONFLICT

During the past ten or fifteen years, political events and media strategy have thrust our male children into a monumental sex role conflict. A gross imbalance in sexual expectancies has resulted as our kids hear these messages:

Boys and girls must grow up immediately. Sexual prowess is the key to this achievement. You can make the leap from diapers to dates quickly if you try hard enough. If you fail, you won't belong to the 'in' group.

Girls may now actualize any and all traits that have been traditionally viewed as masculine. These include but are not limited to: toughness, endurance, assertiveness, demand for sexual satisfaction, and financial independence. When you do these things, you are politically and socially approved of. In fact, if you don't do these things, you are a failure.

If boys are to belong to their group and be accepted, they must stay in the strict macho role. Therefore, you must not act like a girl. This means you must not: express feelings, admit weaknesses, be sensitive, forgo the possibility of sexual conquests, or ever be dependent upon a female. If you dare cross the line into feminine traits, your peers will reject you. You will be labeled a 'fag' and will no longer belong.

Girls have a license to actualize both the masculine and feminine sides of their personality. They are often pressured to do both simultaneously whether they want to or not. Girls are no longer considered 'butches' or 'dykes' if they want to participate in bodybuilding or basketball.

Boys don't have this same license. Despite the rhetoric, the majority of boys still do not have the right to cry, at least in front of their peers. But, if they have strong family ties, they can break the mold, cross over into traditionally feminine territory, and eventually find other males like themselves.

Kids who don't have family support are left with two choices: Either they can give into the blackmail of possible group rejection and suppress tenderness, sensitivity, and any other trait construed as a weakness, never admitting that they feel estranged and lonely; or they can drop out of the heterosexual derby and actualize the feminine side of their personality by joining certain segments of the gay community that foster this attitude. I don't, of course, mean to imply that *all* gay men are gay because of PPS (although some gay men *do* fit the description of the PPS victim).

It's ironic and sad that there is considerable political support for the feminist and gay rights movements, but nothing to boost the morale of the man who wants permission to cry in the arms of a woman he loves.

NARCISSISM AND CHAUVINISM

These are the two intermediate symptoms that emerge in the latter stages of the Peter Pan Syndrome. Narcissism usually precedes chauvinism, giving the victim a systematic method of projecting his insecurities upon other people. Magical thinking flourishes during this period, taking the victim away from reality and toward attitudes that border on the bizarre. Narcissism locks the young man inside his own fantasies and prohibits the personal growth that comes from meaningful relationships with other people.

The chauvinism associated with the PPS is much more subtle than the highly visible variety commonly espoused by bullies and braggarts. It protects the narcissistic victim from heartache and disappointment, giving him an 'adult role' that promises acceptance, however shallow, from his peers. The women who fall in love with the older PPS victim are absolutely dumfounded when they finally become aware of the chauvinism. It is so surreptitious that the female thinks that *she* has the problem.

Narcissism and chauvinism, in concert with irresponsibility, anxiety, loneliness, and sex role conflict, complete the structure upon which the crisis period of the Peter Pan Syndrome will develop.

A PIRATICAL LIFESTYLE

In carefully reading Barrie's comments I found the concept I was looking for to sum up the behavior pattern of the PPS victim. At the end of Act V, Scene I, we learn that Peter has thoroughly defeated Captain Hook. The evil pirate commits suicide by throwing himself overboard and into the jaws of the crocodile. The author then comments:

> *The curtain rises to show* PETER *a very Napoleon on his ship. It must not rise again lest we see him on the poop in* HOOK'S *hat and cigars, and with a small iron claw.*

Barrie suggests that Peter's alter ego is a pirate. Given enough time and space, Peter could become as heartless and uncaring as his nemesis Captain Hook. I find this quite plausible. That's why I summarize the lifestyle of the PPS victim in one word—piratical.

Peter Pan Syndrome victims are jolly, happy-go-lucky rogues. They have a penchant for uproarious laughter and a pint or two of whatever ale is available, and they are forever seeking to regale themselves with a bevy of lovely wenches.

They are capable of unconscionable foul deeds and can sing and dance as they are stealing your life's treasures. If they feel that you have wronged them, they can call upon instant rage to run you aground or skewer your heart with a promise and a lie. They'll cross into your territorial waters and take insult from your displeasure. Cross them a second time and they'll make your soul walk the plank. Then, after pillaging your trust and concern, they will sail off into the sunset pretending to have neither worry nor care.

People who have been ravaged by the piratical behavior

of the PPS victim often conclude that this pretentious pirate has no misgivings about what he does. And that's what he would like you to think. But stop and consider: pirates have no home. They yearn for a place to call their own. They are consumed with a wanderlust that forces them on a never-ending journey to find peace of mind.

Hence, although the PPS victim steals your trust, he can't use it. Trust has no meaning without self-love; and that is the crucial item that is missing in the victim's life. His piratical behavior is only a temporary relief from an otherwise stormy life.

Captain Hook, reflecting on the pain and pleasure of his dastardly deeds, says it better than I:

> The children on this boat [are] about to walk the plank. Split my infinitives, but 'tis my hour of triumph! And yet some disky spirit compels me now to make my dying speech, lest when dying there may be no time for it. All mortals envy me, yet better perhaps for Hook to have had less ambition!
>
> [after a slight interruption]
>
> No little children love me. I am told they play at Peter Pan, and that the strongest always chooses to be Peter. They would rather be a Twin than Hook; they force the baby to be Hook. The baby! That is where the canker gnaws.

The despondency is unmistakable, as are the sounds of regret. But it is not a regret born of an understanding of the nature of the foul deeds. Rather it is a sort of bewilderment, springing from a vague sense that things are not going as planned. Conspicuous is the absence of personal accountability. The pirate and the PPS victim both find it nearly impossible to surmise that they may have caused their own misfortune. Rather than cast aspersions upon themselves, they simply accede to the remorse that accompanies not being able to find anyone else to blame.

If you know a PPS victim, your first reaction is to reject this piratical analogy. You cling to the notion that he is just a little immature for his age. It's tough to face the possibility that anyone so vital could be a thief, a con man of the first order. Better he should swipe your wallet than steal your trust. But he's not a crook, nor is he mentally ill. He's a modern-day pirate cast adrift on a sea of loneliness.

THE PETER PAN SYNDROME: A REMEDY?

PPS is not a fatal affliction (although some victims commit suicide). It is, however, devastating to the emotional well-being of the individual and his family. When the PPS is in its fully developed form, the victim's path to adulthood is blocked by fatalistic procrastination, irrational and magical thinking, and a denial system that borders on the bizarre.

The people who love these men are frustrated beyond belief. PPS victims desperately want to get out of their rut. Yet if you reach down to give them a hand, they will smite you with emotional abuse. They cry for attention; but when you give it, they snicker at the folly of your caring. Older victims have insight into their condition, but steadfastly refuse to seek or profit from help. Many of you will recognize a friend or loved one as a victim of the Peter Pan Syndrome. You will also empathize with the frustration. You don't know whether to hug'em or hit'em.

I've worked with these men for many years. I've seen the Peter Pan Syndrome in its early stages and witnessed the destruction during middle age.

As you might expect, it's tough to get the victims into meaningful psychotherapy. Their spirit is so flighty that I'm often tempted to close and bar all my office windows to prevent them from flying away. Indeed, if they had access to magical dust, they would soar away to a Never Never Land of their own making.

My first exposure to the PPS victim is usually when he is in his early teens to mid-twenties. Typically, he lives at home and is going to school or working part time with only marginal success. He professes to be an accomplished heterosexual but, in truth, feels very inadequate around women. His partying and disrespect cause his parents to be gravely concerned about his future.

For a reason you will understand later, it is the victim's mother who is successful in coercing her son to seek help. The threat is vague but demanding. 'You'd better get your life together or else.'

Mom usually doesn't spell out exactly what she means by 'or else,' but the kid gets the message. 'Go or else your free ride is over.'

It's a good bet that Mom won't follow through with this threat, but the guy doesn't want to risk it. He also doesn't want to take the chance of hurting his mother's feelings. So he shows up at my office at least once. He's hostile, but he comes.

No sooner does he sit down than he starts complaining about Mom's squeeze play. 'I don't need a shrink. I'm not crazy. But if I don't show up, she'll just keep bitching and nagging till I do.'

Rarely will the victim admit to sponging off his parents long after he should be making a life of his own. Nor does he appear willing to talk about his loneliness and irresponsibility. The prognosis is not good. The cornerstones and intermediate symptoms are firmly entrenched.

When I react to the complaint about Mom, he has a knee-jerk guilt reaction. In a state of near panic, he apologizes. 'I didn't mean anything by that. Don't get me wrong. My mom is great. It's just that . . . well, I guess she worries about me. You know how moms are, don't you?'

When I reflect on his defensiveness, he gets even more nervous. The hostility starts to creep out. 'Hey, I didn't know what I was saying. Just forget about it. Talk about something else, will ya?'

So I change the subject, for all the good it does me. No matter what topic I select, the young man 'ices' me, using shrugs, one-word answers, and other negative responses to cool my inquisitiveness. He figures that if he is cold and noncommital, I'll give up my questioning and he can tell Mom that, yes, he went, and the doctor couldn't find anything wrong.

Most younger PPS victims are involuntary participants in psychotherapy. This being the case, the process is over before it begins. However, there are cases in which a persistent reflection on the young man's unrealistic attachment to his mother leads to a productive outcome. The progress is slow and tedious.

If a potential victim can be reached before the sex role conflict is fully manifested, the chances of constructive change are good. But once sexual inadequacy is repressed, narcissism and chauvinism follow so methodically that confrontation usually results in increased hostility and withdrawal.

If they are successful in resisting help, most victims eventually leave home and get married. The magical dust of Never Never Land clings to their soul. They pretend to be happy with their wife and family. They tell themselves that they are satisfied with their job. They deny painful evidence that their bodies are growing more fragile. They have many friendships that are seen as lasting but in truth are shallow and fleeting. And, as they did as teenagers, they continue to party. For many of them, alcohol abuse is dismissed as social drinking. Others pursue sexual affairs compulsively. Recklessness is excused as the need to unwind. Despondency becomes a constant companion as loneliness grows into a vicious monster.

Preventing the Peter Pan Syndrome is relatively easy. The earlier the potential victim is reached, the better. Once you understand the final picture of the Peter Pan Syndrome, I'm certain you'll be moved to help in any way possible. For with all their rage, denial, and procrastination, the lives of the PPS victims are filled with sadness.

There's no other word for it. It is indeed sad that these beautiful people start out as kids who fly away from reality and pretend to live in a perpetual state of youthful bliss. If they don't become dropouts, their Never Never Land turns into a stark, deserted wasteland. If permitted to stay there, they grow into adults whose Never Never Land turns into a prison from which escape is almost impossible.

In this prison they are ravaged by loneliness but pretend

to have friends; they are trapped in self-doubt but pretend to be confident; they scream for happiness and pretend to be gay; worst of all, they are consumed by isolation and pretend they are loved.

I ask you not to believe their pretense. Like their fictional leader, the victims of the Peter Pan Syndrome are alone, terribly alone. As for their words—'I don't want to go to school and learn solemn things. No one is going to catch me, lady, and make me a man. I want always to be a little boy and to have fun.'—don't believe them. They are lying to themselves.

PART 2
THE PETER PAN
SYNDROME

In this section I will explain the development of the Peter Pan Syndrome. Parents will find implications for possible changes in child-rearing strategies. Wives and lovers will better understand why the man they love is both frustrating and fulfilling. Friends will discover empathy and more readily offer a helping hand. The victims themselves may gain the insight and courage to escape their trap.

The bulk of my explanation centers on the second decade of life, give or take a few years. Struggling to help young people grow up has taught me that this period starts at puberty—say, age eleven or twelve—and ends at or near age twenty-four, a time when most young people have settled into an adult life. I call this period of life the 'Coming of Age' age.

As indicated earlier, six major symptoms comprise the Peter Pan Syndrome. I will review one of them in each of the next six chapters. I've arranged the chapters and symptoms chronologically according to 'peak ages.' I'm suggesting that the symptom under investigation flourishes during a two-year time period and dominates the other five symptoms during that peak age.

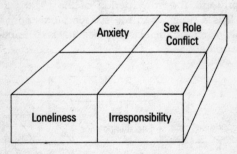

The best way to study the Peter Pan Syndrome is to visualize a three-dimensional construction of seven blocks. First, imagine that you place four blocks together on a table to form a square. Each of these blocks represents one of four fundamental symptoms of the PPS—four cornerstones, if you will. This is the foundation upon which the PPS is built.

The key to the foundation is the sex role conflict. Once it is firmly in place, a continuation of the affliction is assured.

Now, imagine that you set two blocks on top of the four cornerstones. These blocks represent two more symptoms of the PPS and are to be considered 'intermediaries' between the cornerstones and the final crisis period. These intermediate symptoms flow from the foundation and, in turn, form the basis for the final stage in the development of the PPS.

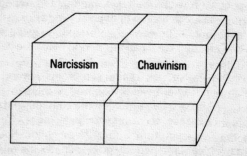

Finally, place one block on top of the two intermediaries. This represents the crisis period of the Peter Pan Syndrome. It is a time when the six symptoms converge to cause the victim the social impotence that is so damaging to future happiness.

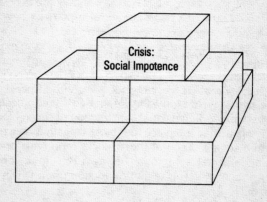

This approach might give you the idea that each of these symptoms develops in a predictable fashion; however, this is not the case. Though you can expect the four corner-stones to surface during ages 11 through 18, they may develop in different children at different times. They may even flourish in a sequence different from the one I outline.

You might also get the idea that all four symptoms must be present before the intermediate symptoms can develop. This is also untrue. My experience suggests that narcissism and chauvinism can develop in the absence of one or two of the cornerstones. If this occurs, the devastation embodied in the crisis period is substantially less, and remediation of the social impotence more likely.

The crisis period of the Peter Pan Syndrome reflects different degrees of incapacity. Some young men might simply wander into a marriage or career that promises years of nagging but manageable frustration. Other victims suffer such overwhelming impotence that satisfactory work adjustment and a fulfilling love relationship are beyond their capabilities. The degree of incapacity is directly related to the quantity and quality of the six symptoms contained in the block construction.

In Chapter 10 I will personalize the crisis stage of the PPS by spotlighting the story of Randy, a twenty-three-year-old young man whose life painfully demonstrates the conver-gence of all six symptoms. You will see how the Peter Pan Syndrome results in a pervasive social impotence, severely curtailing the quality of the young man's life.

The last chapter of this section takes a look at men who have never grown up. You'll see how the sex role conflict has invaded every significant aspect of their lives. You'll see what happens when the crisis subsides and despondency becomes the very texture of life itself.

4   Irresponsibility

PETER: 'I'm youth, I'm joy, I'm a little bird that has broken out of the egg.'

WENDY: 'Ran away, why?'

PETER: 'Because I heard Father and Mother talking of what I was to be when I became a man. I want always to be a little boy and have fun.'

Could manhood be that bad? Whatever Peter heard his parents say must have frightened him badly. I can just imagine him creeping down the stairs to get a glass of milk and accidentally hearing his parents talking of his future.

'Poor Peter,' Father might say. 'He'll have to work crazy hours, put up with the hassles of corporate insensitivities, worry about job security, hold his temper when he sees what taxes do to his paycheck, and then submit to the legal thievery that comes with paying utility bills. I sure don't envy him growing up.'

'And I worry about his family,' Mother chimes in. 'Peter is the kind of boy who'll worry sick about his wife and kids. And the way the economy is going, I imagine his wife will have to work. Then his children will grow up without any parents around. Oh, it's a shame. Poor boy!'

Put yourself in Peter's shoes. If you heard a horror story about growing up, wouldn't you consider staying right where you were? All you'd have to do is concentrate on being a child. That wouldn't be so difficult.

You'd have to play all the time, have fun no matter what happened, and pretend that reality was a joke. Most of all,

46

you'd have to work really hard day-by-day, year-by-year, to become as irresponsible as possible.

It makes sense, doesn't it? Irresponsibility is a key to staying young. The script sounds simple enough: be a total, complete, irresponsible goof-off; do everything in your power to resist such civilized habits as picking up your clothes, feeding the dog, getting good grades, and helping around the house.

To maximize your irresponsibility, you'd have to develop disruptive habits: leave the bathroom a mess; create a war zone in your bedroom; scatter empty milk glasses, decaying pizza cartons, and dirty socks around the family room; and by all means be abrupt and indifferent when adults come to visit. And under no circumstances should you say 'Please' or 'Thank you' to your mom for giving you and your friends a ride to the video arcade.

Once you thought you'd achieved some degree of irresponsibility, you'd want to compare notes with your contemporaries. How big are the dust bunnies under your buddies' beds? How long since the kid down the block brushed his teeth? What's the record for consecutive days of eating only junk food?

The antics of your peers set the pace. With a little study and even less effort, you could become the best at goofing off. Then you'd have a legitimate right to stake a claim on being a kid who won't grow up.

Once you'd gotten a foothold on irresponsibility, you could employ laziness to forestall the development of any significant maturity. Heaven knows you don't want your mom saying to your friend's mom, 'Gosh, my Pete is becoming so responsible. He does what I tell him and never gives me a moment of trouble.' If this happens, your program is shot. You're growing up.

Your friends can help you maintain your irresponsibility. From a classmate you learn the art and science of procrastination. 'In a minute' and 'At the next commercial' are mainstays. From the boy next door you learn how to forget. 'Wow, Mom, I forgot' or 'You can't expect me to remember *all* my chores, can you?' And when these fail, you can

47

always learn new techniques of arguing or complaining. 'It isn't fair,' 'You're always picking on me,' and 'Nobody else I know has to do all this' are excellent maneuvers.

You don't have to be Peter Pan to resist adulthood. Irresponsibility isn't automatically a sign of future maladjustment. It's natural for children to rebel against maturation. Growing up is scary, more so now than ever before. Just thinking about the realities of adulthood is enough to send you into a state of regression in which you curl up with your thumb and your blanket, wishing for a time when the toughest decision was which toy to take into your sandbox.

We all had times of irresponsibility. That's part of being a child. But most of us outgrew immaturity, and now our responsibility is so habitual that we must even schedule our goof-off time. We reach a point where we can't escape responsibility.

Victims of the Peter Pan Syndrome have the opposite problem. *They can't escape irresponsibility*. This trap begins as innocent, typical rebellion, but mushrooms into an adult lifestyle. A fundamental piece of the puzzle of the Peter Pan Syndrome is gross irresponsibility that spawns ineptness in basic self-care skills.

IRRESPONSIBILITY'S PEAK AGE: 11 TO 12

When you're three years old and stick mashed potatoes up your nose, that's expected. When you're six and make your bed but it looks like you're still in it, you deserve some credit for trying. When you're nine and prepare the family meal but the casserole looks worse than the kitchen, you should be applauded for your effort. But somewhere along the line, some responsible adult should say, 'You're too old for this nonsense.'

PPS victims never hear this message. Or, if they do, it never sinks in. They enter their late teens and early twenties with solid habits of irresponsibility. Even though they are ten or fifteen years older, most of them still have sloppy eating habits, can't make their bed, and think preparing a great meal is opening a can of Spaghetti-Os.

Irresponsibility is one of the six cornerstones of the Peter Pan Syndrome. It gains its strongest foothold during the age period 11 to 12; the sudden release of hormones into the child's body seems to stimulate the persistence of the trait.

I am about to spotlight four types of pubescent irresponsiblity. You'll appreciate the divergence of emphasis while recognizing how each style, if left unattended, can eventually destroy adult responsibility.

'Angel baby' This child can appear innocent upon a moment's notice. The angelic role seems to appear whenever the evidence of wrongdoing is the greatest. The child can become instantly teary-eyed as he protests, 'Would I even think of doing something like that?' The silence and sadness of his solemn face and quivering lips capture your heart and you forget to answer 'Yes.'

'Snotty' This child believes that the best defense is a good offense. He uses complaints to get parents off balance. He complains loudly about the inequities of parent power. And he employs all possible snotty attitudes that usually cause parents to give up and simply do the job themselves.

'Deaf, dumb, and blind' If parents didn't know better, they would believe that this style of irresponsibility involved some degree of brain damage. But a large group of perfectly healthy kids use a 'deaf, dumb, and blind' strategy to avoid responsibility. You can recognize their one-liners. Deaf: 'I didn't hear you tell me that.' Dumb: 'I don't remember that,' or 'I forgot.' Blind: 'Gee, I didn't even see the note on the counter.' Each in his own way, these kids believe they can avoid responsibility if nothing above their shoulders seems to work right.

'Good-natured Sam' How do you get angry at an irresponsible child who has the disposition of a gentle puppy? Many parents face this challenge unsuccessfully. 'Good-natured Sam' is quick to do anything you tell him to and smiles no matter how bad he feels. The problem is that he never does his jobs unless you remind him several times. This kind of irresponsibility is most dangerous because parents tend to avoid stern measures to teach the child accountability for his actions.

Let's take a brief look at the stories of four children, each at the peak age of irresponsibility, 11 to 12.

Rickey

Their family doctor said he was an energetic kid who ate too much junk food. The pediatrician suggested that eleven-year-old Rickey Sharp might be hyperactive. The school social worker said that since he was facing puberty, Rickey needed understanding and patience. Grandma said that her pride and joy was simply going through a stage and would grow out of it. In one way or another, they were all right. But Ruth Sharp didn't care any more. She just wanted her son to shape up.

Rickey was a typical 'angel baby.' He had big blue eyes that hadn't changed in clarity or intensity since he was born. His blond rumpled hair would look unkempt on any other kid, but on Rickey it was cute. His voice was as diminutive as his body. He squeaked when he spoke and he could barely reach the urinal in the church rest room.

Rickey had mastered the angelic look and used it with perfect timing. When confronted about irresponsibility, Rickey fixed his baby blues on his accuser and protested his innocence. He raised his eyebrows, wrinkled his forehead, and dropped his jaw in feigned surprise. He persisted in this struggle of wills until the battle was over. If he won, he would bounce happily away; if he lost, he would continue to punish the victor with the moans and murmurations of a deeply wounded but gallant warrior. He rarely lost a battle.

There was another side of Rickey's angelicism. He had unwittingly discovered the hidden powers of innocence. He used these to attack authority, make life go his way, and further his cause of avoiding responsibility. In carrying his angelic qualities to an extreme, Rickey had stumbled upon the alter ego of any angel—the devil.

His shenanigans were most perplexing. He experimented with his mother's flowers by pouring hot grease on them: he'd heard that plants liked carbohydrates. He wanted to see if dogs landed on their feet like cats, so he tossed Bowser off the garage. He idolized Tarzan reruns on Saturday morning television and acted out his hero's role by jumping out of a tree one afternoon. Unfortunately, he landed on Mrs. Wilson, the bent-kneed octogenarian who lived down the street.

How can anyone stay angry at a kid who wants to make the jungle safe for humanity and ensure that plants have a balanced diet? Mrs. Sharp, that's who! She wasn't particularly upset about the limping dog or irate Mrs. Wilson. She was, however, reaching the end of her rope with Rickey's day-to-day irresponsibility.

I unlocked the secret of the angel baby routine during a brief visit with Rickey in my office.

After ten or fifteen minutes of happy talk, I grinned broadly and leaned forward. 'You're really quite a kid, aren't you, Rickey?'

He was bubbling. 'Whaddaya mean?'

'Well, you do some pretty weird things, you know. Like jumping on top of Mrs. Wilson.'

'Oh, that was nothin'.' Rickey was in total control. 'She could have dodged me. Anyhow, I just barely touched her.'

I decided to challenge his recollection. 'Barely?'

'Yeah.'

'Really?' I leaned a little closer. 'Your mom said that Mrs. Wilson has a bruised leg. She's really hurt.'

'I didn't mean to.' Rickey started to squirm. 'What else did my mom say?'

'Well, she told me that you make a lot of messes, that you're pretty lazy, and that you know how to get away with doing bad stuff.'

'Huh?'

51

'You know. When she catches you doing something wrong, you just look at her—you widen your eyes and pretend to be real innocent.' I demonstrated the angel baby routine.

Seeing an adult reflect his own image caught Rickey off guard. He evidently sensed the same kind of attack that occurred when his mom or dad confronted him about misbehavior. Within seconds of finishing my comment, I realized that I was being held captive by Rickey's eyes.

I was the target of an eleven-year-old's sophisticated whammy. It seemed an eternity before I realized what was happening. Rickey was doing to me what he did to other adults who confronted him. He was unleashing his devilish powers.

When I regained my balance, I did the only thing I could. I continued to mirror his behavior. 'Boy, you're really good at it.'

Rickey didn't move. He continued to stare. I think I saw a small tear forming in his eye.

If I was to help him, I couldn't let his silent whammy work. So I pressed on, but gently. 'It won't work with me, Rickey. I know you've learned that staring at adults like this makes them leave you alone. But that's not right. And it's not going to work now. I'm not going to leave you alone. You need my help. You need to learn another way to handle this.'

I knew that Rickey would not want to lose face, so I gave him an easy out. 'Tell you what. I'm going to get a drink of water and when I come back, we'll talk about it.'

I was gone about a minute. When I returned, Rickey was sitting quietly in his chair with his head down. I reinitiated the confrontation but aimed it in a different direction. With a wide smile and excitement in my voice, I said, 'Boy, you are really good at it. You even had old Dr. Dan on the ropes for a few seconds. I bet you can really destroy Mom, can't you?'

His head moved up and down as his eyes remained glued to the floor.

'It's kind of fun, isn't it? You really drive them bonkers,

don't you?' I was enticing him to tell me his secrets.

His eyes came off the floor and he gave me that what-makes-you-tick look.

I continued with zeal. 'Well, you do, don't you?'

He tried to sound tough. 'Don't I what?'

'Don't you drive your parents bonkers with that look of yours?'

'What's "bonkers"?'

'Aw, c'mon," I said. 'You know what I mean. You do something wrong, you get caught, your parents try to punish you, and *whammo*, you whip the old evil eye on them, and—presto!—no more trouble. That drives parents bonkers. Right?'

Rickey wasn't sure what to do with me. His old trick hadn't worked. So, like most kids who try an ambush and fail, Rickey did the only other thing he knew. He told me the truth. 'It works real good.'

'And you're real proud of it, right?'

Now it was his turn to grin. 'Yeah.'

It was my turn to get serious again. 'But it doesn't always feel good, does it?'

'Whaddaya mean?'

'Well, doesn't it scare you a little bit to keep doing dumb things?'

'Yeah.'

'And don't you sometimes wish that your parents would make you pay for your mistakes?'

'Yeah.'

'But you're sure not going to tell them, are you?'

Rickey brightened up. 'Nope.'

I continued to lead him in what I considered to be a positive direction. 'Well, guess who has to do it?'

We both looked at each other. I nodded my head and gave him that sorry-about-that look. 'I have to.'

He didn't give up immediately. 'You don't *have* to.'

'I do if I want to help you grow up to take more responsibility.'

Rickey was feeling more secure as his devilishness returned. He gave me a half-baked whammy look and said,

'I don't have to like it, do I?'

There was no way Rickey was going to like learning responsibility. As I sat down with his parents, I knew that sooner or later he would join voices with other kids who've been frustrated and bellowed, 'It's a wonder somebody doesn't kill Dr. Dan!'

Steven

Steven Jolly was anything but jolly. He was nasty and rude, with a sarcastic tongue and a hair-trigger temper. He was a kid who had dived into the terrible twos and stayed there for ten years. There surely are children snottier than Steven, but I can't remember one. I tell Steven's story so that you'll understand the developmental history of the rage that is often a part of the Peter Pan Syndrome.

It must have taken Steven's parents many years to grow accustomed to their son's snottiness. There was no other explanation for the fact that they tolerated so much emotional abuse.

Sharon and Joe Jolly brought Steven to me because of a deterioration in his school performance. His adjustment at home had always been very poor, a fact his parents had learned to overlook. However, when the teachers expressed grave concern, his parents knew it was time to do more than ignore Steven's problems. It was Mrs. Jolly who had overcome her concern about what the neighbors would say and admitted that her son was beyond control.

Steven was flunking in all of his subjects except physical education. He was regularly sent out of the classroom for offenses ranging from sassing the teacher to hitting other children. When the teacher tried to punish Steven, he would challenge her: 'I don't have to do what you say, you're not my mother.' Confrontations with the principal ended up in the same vein: 'My father won't like you threatening me.'

It took me a while before I figured out why the educators hadn't stepped forward sooner. They were afraid. Steven's attitude had backed them into a corner. Their reasoning went like this: 'If Steven is such a terror at school, his parents *must* know it. Yet they aren't doing anything to stop him. If we raise a fuss, they may take their wrath out on us.'

Given the bureaucrats' fear of the 'get tough' approach to education, it made sense that the principal and the teacher weren't about to jeopardize their jobs by going to bat for a kid they didn't like anyway.

When the school officials stepped forward, it gave Mrs. Jolly courage to do the same. She found it difficult to give me specific instances of Steven's gross disrespect and irresponsibility. Her mind seemed to go blank when I asked her to recount exact details. I learned that Steven's antics had created so much pain that she had erected a protective barrier around her feelings. The barrier saved her from feelings of failure but also made her more insensitive to the necessity for change.

As Mrs. Jolly struggled to recall painful memories, Mr. Jolly remained aloof. As his wife fought to face the truth, Steven's father persisted in denial. In speech as well tailored as his clothes, Mr. Jolly said, 'Steven's been real bad only the past few months.'

Mrs. Jolly tried to mask her hostility and disappointment. 'Joe, honey, I don't think you've really noticed how bad things have been. Steven has been going steadily downhill for several years. Remember how concerned his second-grade teacher was?'

Joe raised his eyebrows, pursed his lips, and sighed. 'Oh.' My third ear heard the unspoken comment: 'What ever you say, dear.'

I resisted the temptation to launch into marriage counseling, knowing it would be futile. Mr. Jolly would continue to deny any significant problems, while his wife was too absorbed in trying to help her son. But there was a silver lining to the tense interchange. Mrs. Jolly remembered a typical example of Steven's snottiness.

The previous Sunday, the three Jollys had had an afterchurch brunch at a local restaurant. After considerable badgering from him, Mrs. Jolly had agreed that

Steven could have a treat when they stopped at the grocery store on their way home.

As they walked into the grocery store, Steven abrasively announced, 'I'm going to get a sack of candy and I'll meet you at the check-out lane.'

His mother protested slightly, saying, 'I think you should have an apple instead of candy this time, Steven.'

Steven's snotty attitude took command. 'You said I could have a treat and I want candy. I don't want an apple. That's stupid. I'm going to get candy.'

Mrs. Jolly tried to exercise authority. 'Steven, I said no candy this time. Get yourself a big juicy apple.'

As always, a no brought out the worst in Steven. 'That's really dumb. I'm old enough to pick out my own treat and I said I want candy.' His voice had reached a screaming level and all the other customers were watching the mother being devastated by a belligerent child. Sharon Jolly was reeling from her son's disrespect and the embarrassment from the public confrontation.

Steven didn't let up. 'If you're going to be so dumb, then I'm just going to walk home.' He started for the door.

Mrs. Jolly succumbed to the pressure. 'You can't walk home, it's snowing and very cold. You'll catch cold and be sick for school tomorrow.'

Steven's last shot is probably the nastiest one I've ever heard from a child so young. 'Don't pretend to be nice to me, Mom. You won't let me have candy and if I catch cold, it'll be your fault anyway.'

Mrs. Jolly chased after her son and caught up with him just outside the door. She was panic-stricken. She begged him to be nice and come back inside. Before he complied, he demanded that she capitulate to his request for candy. She did, and the incident ended as abruptly as it had begun.

Lest you think that a child can be nasty to the bone, you should know that, deep inside, Steven was suffering immeasurably. Two or three times a week he woke, screaming, after a ghoulish nightmare. As best he could remember, ugly monsters relentlessly chased him, trying to devour him.

It didn't take lengthy dream analysis to tentatively conclude that Steven was being victimized by his own snottiness. He avoided responsibility by attacking authority figures with monstrous behavior. As his irresponsibility grew, so did the monster. Without a feeling of responsibility, Steven suffered low self-esteem and poor self-confidence. This left him vulnerable to attacks by the monster he had created. And now the monster was turning against its master.

Steven Jolly's snottiness promoted his irresponsibility. He was fast becoming a master of emotional blackmail, falsely perceiving that duty could be dismissed by hostility. He was developing a trait that often occurs in victims of the Peter Pan Syndrome; that is, they are hard to love and easy to dislike.

There is an ironic twist to Steven's story. When he was seven, his mother had taken him to see a child psychiatrist because she was concerned about his attitude. The psychiatrist had said, 'Don't discipline Steven, because you risk building a backlog of anger and hostility.' Mrs. Jolly followed the psychiatrist's advice. Five years later, she was confronted with a child who had built a tremendous backlog of anger and hostility.

Billy

Few parents are confronted with the loathsome snottiness displayed by Steven Jolly. In most kids snottiness takes the form of back talk or argumentativeness. Whatever the degree, some aggressiveness is to be expected as the boy struggles to become a man. Rickey used an aggressive angelic countenance, and Steven was just plain.aggressive.

Billy Winters used a marvelous technique that is as old as children's rebellion. He did nothing. He just stood there, using one of three stock responses to answer questions about his poor performance. 'I didn't hear . . .,' 'I forgot . . .,' and 'I didn't see . . .' were the key to Billy's ability to avoid responsibility. He pretended to be deaf, dumb, and blind.

By the time I saw the family, eleven-year-old Billy's excuses were so habitual that he was becoming impaired. He often failed to hear classroom instructions, he would rush headlong into traffic while playing catch, and he lost personal items (a hat, gloves, a tennis racket) through sheer forgetfulness.

Mom and Dad Winters were exasperated with their son's deaf-dumb-and-blind routine. They had tried every way they could think of to break Billy of his bad habits. They even went to dangerous extremes in their efforts to get his attention. But nothing worked. My view of the reason for their failure is that they tried to *talk* Billy into being responsible.

Peg and John Winters were educated, reasonable people who loved their only child a great deal. Peg read child-rearing material with a passion and shared the highlights with her husband. John wasn't impressed with the emphasis upon permissiveness and nurturance, preferring the hard-line approach of his father and grandfather. It was with Mom's talk-at-any-price and Dad's do-it-or-else that Billy's parents attempted to cope with their son's stoic indifference.

Billy received three messages when pulling his deaf-dumb-and-blind stunts. When Mom was present, he heard, 'I make Mom sad.' When Dad confronted him, he got the notion, 'I make Dad mad.' When both parents were involved, he got the idea, 'I make Dad and Mom fight.'

Here are three brief excerpts from typical confrontations:

Mrs. Winters would sit Billy at the kitchen table and begin her communication session by saying, 'You know you have chores to do after school, don't you, Billy?'

'Uh-huh,' he would answer.

'And you know that I leave you notes telling you what special things I need done, right?'

'Uh-huh.'

'Then why, Billy, don't you do them?' Peg would feel guilty about getting angry at her son. 'You know how it hurts me when you don't try to help out around the house.'

Billy would put his best excuse forward. 'I don't always see the notes.'

Peg was careful not to explode. 'That's what you say every time. But that doesn't make me feel better. Please tell me what's going on inside. Please.'

Billy's response completed the circularity of their 'discussion': 'I don't know.'

As you might guess, this conversation went nowhere, despite its daily repetition. And Dad's hard-line approach didn't work either.

Billy's propensity to lose things got Dad's goat. 'You must think money grows on trees. Or maybe you just don't think. What the hell is the matter with you, Billy?'

Immediately cowed, Billy would whimper, 'I don't know. I just forgot.'

'Forgot, hell! You lose every nice thing I buy for you.'

When blasted by Dad, Billy typically hung his head and said nothing.

'Answer me, son. I want to know why you like to make me mad.'

'I don't know.'

Dad's excessive force and hostility were just as ineffective as Mom's overbearing nurturance. In both cases Billy felt backed into a corner and uttered the standard phrase 'I don't know.' When both parents were involved in the confrontation, sparks flew in every direction.

Dad usually started the tiff by flying off the handle. 'Damn it, Billy, this is the third time this month you've lost your homework. I just won't accept that excuse any more. If you don't shape up I'll just have to start spanking you as if you were a baby.'

Billy would remain motionless and silent while Mom attempted to soften Dad's blow. 'Billy, explain to us why you're having trouble remembering. Tell us what's bothering you.'

Billy didn't have to answer this entreaty. Dad did. 'Aw,

c'mon, Peg. There's nothing wrong with Billy that a couple of pops on the backside won't correct.'

'John,' Peg would say in exasperation, 'Billy will never tell us what's bothering him if you keep belittling him.'

With this comment, the attention would inevitably turn away from Billy, and Peg and John would engage in a lengthy argument. It was always the same. Dad would espouse harshness while Peg advanced the idea that Billy was irresponsible because he suffered some type of mental anguish. Meanwhile, Billy would be out of it, left to believe he was the cause of his parents' fighting. At no time was Billy held accountable for his deaf-dumb-and-blind routine.

There was every reason to believe that while Billy was earning how to avoid responsibility, he was getting the notion that he was a negative influence in the family. Not only was he deaf, dumb, and blind, but he also thought of himself as a bad kid for upsetting his parents so much. Mom and Dad's extreme measures were backfiring.

Sam

Everybody loved Sam. Good-natured Sam. The neighbors could count on him to capture a runaway pet. The church ladies professed that he was the politest boy in the entire congregation. The park leader lauded Sam for his leadership, kindness, and patience in dealing with the younger boys. Even the principal praised the twelve-year-old's pleasing personality, though he complained that Sam was a bit rowdy from time to time.

There was, however, one major problem. Sam's mother, hard worker both inside and outside the home, didn't know who these people were talking about. 'It couldn't be my Sam,' she would muse privately. 'Sure he's a sweet, good-natured boy, but I can't get him to do even the simplest of chores unless I beg him on bended knee.'

The story of good-natured Sam is typical of that of many PPS victims. They aren't snotty, stoic, or angelic. They aren't particularly nasty or manipulative. In fact, they have public relations skills beyond their years. They are the first to offer aid to anyone needing it. They'll even risk personal safety to help somebody. However, unless hounded to death, they won't turn a finger to help around the house.

How can a kid so willing to help others be so irresponsible at home? The best way for me to make sense out of this inconsistency is to summarize the psychological study I completed on twelve-year-old Sam Koler. Sam's style of irresponsibility is the most dangerous of all because it's so easy for kids to fall into and, without help, it becomes an immutable cornerstone of the Peter Pan Syndrome.

Sam was the oldest of three boys, ages 12, 9, 7 respectively. He attended sixth grade at a public elementary school where he maintained a B average without working very hard. The teacher reported that Sam was very likable but occasionally acted the class clown. Once, when she sent Sam to in-school suspension for acting up, she overheard him call her a bitch as he walked out the door. She was shocked to hear such language from Sam. It seemed so out of character for good-natured Sam. Actually, it wasn't. Sam was an angry young man.

Sam's anger flowed from many sources. His body was changing and making new demands on his childish outlook. He was discovering independence but living in a dependent situation. He wanted to move away from his over-protective mother, a natural occurrence that nonetheless stimulated some guilt. These feelings are typical of early adolescence and would pass. But there was one source of anger that was not harmless and could cause Sam long-term trouble. He felt unloved by his father.

Sam's father was a workaholic. He had little time for his wife and even less time for Sam. In an attempt to win his father's love, Sam threw himself into a grown-up role with all the fervor of an older man and all the efficiency of a toddler. Sam desperately needed love from his father but never got it. He took his search into the grown-up world where he hoped that his actions would cause people to tell his dad how great his oldest son was.

Sam figured that when the grown-ups told his father how great Sam was (which they did), his father would reach out and embrace his son (which he did not). Faced with failure, Sam concluded that he had to try harder. Thus, the more his father ignored him, the more Sam tried to win his love by pleasing other people.

Sam was under tremendous pressure to perform. This made him tense. He constantly worried about being seen as bad by his father. This made him nervous and fearful. He was consumed by shoulds, oughts, have-tos, and musts. This made him angry.

Sam's only relief from this merry-go-round was to rebel at home. Since he felt sure of his mother's love, she became the logical target of his rebellion. If Sam could have verbalized this stance, he might have said, 'Mom will still love me even though I treat her bad.'

Another part of his justification for militant irresponsibility was that he was following in his father's footsteps. 'Be like Dad and Dad will like me' was his thought. Unfortunately, Dad held fast to the chauvinistic notion that housework was woman's work. Sam never said it but he behaved as if he believed it.

Lest we forget, another part of good-natured Sam's reason for being irresponsible was that he was a kid. He was twelve years old and, like any other normal pre-teenager, he was doing everything he could not to grow up. But this part of the normal course of events was out of balance. It gave me the first clue that something was wrong with good-natured Sam.

Sam was too good for his own good. He tried too hard to please. This led me to investigate the cloud behind the silver lining. I found that Sam's behavior was misleading. Despite appearances, Sam was not learning responsibility. Gross feelings of insecurity motivated his 'responsible' conduct. He got temporary relief from these feelings through his glorification in the eyes of others.

Needless to say, there was an emotional buildup throughout this vicious circle. Sam felt estranged from his father and was compelled to perform for social approval that he hoped would solve his problem. But it only deepened it. He worked harder, all the time acquiring a nasty aversion to responsibility. He was developing the idea that responsibility was a sham—something done by people only to gain approval. Consequently he never internalized a sense of responsibility.

When I saw Sam and his family, one cornerstone of the Peter Pan Syndrome was firmly in place. Reversing the trend was a family problem. I'll discuss my approach to the problem of good-natured Sam as well as those of the three other boys in Chapter 12.

5 Anxiety

JOHN: '[Peter] is not really our father. He did not even know how to be a father till I showed him.'

PETER: 'Wendy, you are wrong about mothers. I thought like you about the window [that it would remain open], so I stayed away for moons and moons, and then I flew back, but the window was barred, for my mother had forgotten all about me and there was another little boy sleeping in my bed.'

Peter was a nervous wreck. His anxiety ricocheted around Never Never Land, infecting everybody with an instant case of the jitters. You've all seen such a person. His emotions are so tightly strung that he fills the air with psychic electricity. When you ask him if he's okay, he chops you off in mid-thought. 'Me? Okay? I'm fine! Great! Nothing wrong with me! Anything wrong with you?'

If you take a moment to look beyond his gaiety, Peter's anxiety sticks out like a sore thumb. And it doesn't take a clinical psychologist to see it. Forget about the ink smudges and hours of psychological diagnostics. Just take a quick glance at his daily behavior.

The most reliable evidence of Peter's anxiety is that his sense of urgency was out of balance. For example, he calmly played his pipes as Captain Hook ignited the fuse on a bomb. He was thrilled at the prospect of drowning because dying sounded like a great way to spend the afternoon. It doesn't take a hysteric to get upset about these two calamities. Peter, however, didn't even break into a sweat.

64

Peter did become extremely agitated at the loss of his shadow. He had a temper fit when his loyal followers wouldn't play-act the way he wanted. And he was very jumpy at the possibility of being touched by another person. All in all, Peter's priorities were definitely skewed.

If you believe, as I do, that Peter was not mentally ill, then you have to conclude that something was bugging him. He didn't understand it but felt the negative effects nonetheless. He sensed it but couldn't say it.

Like any anxious person, Peter tried to cover his worry, but his cover belied the cause. That is, as Peter defended against feeling nervous, he dropped clues as to the cause of his anxiety. The two quotes at the beginning of this chapter represent those clues: that Peter was estranged from his father and deeply troubled by what he interpreted as his mother's rejection. The combination caused him immeasurable anxiety. He had no one to turn to whom he could trust. He needed help.

If I had been around to help Peter with his anxiety, I would have focused my attention on his parents, treating Peter's nervousness as an indicator of family trouble. Something was wrong with his parents' marriage. Was Mr. Pan a workaholic who felt sorry for himself? Was he the product of a generation in which boys didn't cry? Was Mrs. Pan content with the traditional role of housewife and mother? Did the Pans give in to peer pressure in raising Peter? Was Mr. Pan a chauvinist? If so, did Mrs. Pan play the 'chauvinette' role? Did the Pans work at their marriage, or just go along out of a sense of habit?

The answers to these and similar questions would shed light on the atmosphere in which Peter was being raised — one of tension and anxiety. Somehow Mr. and Mrs. Pan were giving their son the idea that he should avoid getting too close to his father and worry whether his mother loved him.

The anxiety that is a cornerstone of the Peter Pan Syndrome is born of and bred by marital problems. To one degree or another, the parents are out of touch with each other. They usually don't experience gross disharmony, and consequently see no reason for marriage counseling. Though it sounds a bit trite, their problem centers on a failure to communicate.

The parents of PPS victims believe that they share common values. In truth, time and maturation lead them to the realization that in some respects their values clash. However, they become accustomed to each other and assume that because they are still married, their marriage is de facto productive. This magical belief prohibits them from communicating effectively. They are aware of feeling a bland misery, but they dismiss it as a necessary burden of married life.

It may be dismissed, but it's not forgotten. When parents fail to communicate and resolve their differences, they too will experience anxiety. The frustration of living with someone you don't feel close to will eventually encompass others within the family unit, including the children.

PPS victims are typically very sensitive children. They listen to their parents and try to do as told. They may not always show it (see Chapter 4, 'Irresponsibility'), but they have a strong sense of right and wrong. While counseling older victims, I've often wished they were less reactive to their parents. If they had been more resistant to parental influence, they might not have gotten themselves into such a deep rut. It's ironic that kids who start out so receptive to their parents' messages become so unsettled toward the very people whom they deeply care for.

I've uncovered eight messages that promote the Peter Pan Syndrome. I call them *covert messages*, because they are damaging ideas parents communicate without being aware of what they're doing. It will quickly become apparent how these messages flow from marital discord and foster anxiety. These messages take their toll as parents cover their own anxiety by talking to their kids instead of each other.

I label four of the covert messages mom/son messages, because they are given to the son by the mother. They are:

Don't bother your father;

You're acting just like your father;

Your father doesn't understand feelings;

It's too bad your father's work is more important than his family.

The other four messages are dad/son messages because they are given to the son by his father. They are:

Keep your mother off my back;

Don't hurt your mother;

Your mom doesn't understand men;

Take it easy, you know how women are.

Before exploring these messages, I will explain why they are most damaging during the early years of adolescence.

ANXIETY'S PEAK AGE: 13 TO 14

It's a bit artificial to select a peak age for this anxiety. Marital discord has a continuously negative effect on children as soon as they are old enough to feel the atmosphere of the home. Developmental specialists tell us that this emotional sensitivity is operating even before the child is born. Thus, a potential PPS victim is affected by his parents' lack of communication and the resultant tension just as soon as it develops. Despite this fact, I do have some support for designating 13 to 14 as the peak age of anxiety.

Early adolescents are exceptionally aware of boy-girl relationships. It's no great surprise that the first relationship they will study is that of their parents. If they haven't been aware of marital discord before adolescence, they certainly will be at or about the age of thirteen. And, once aware, they will be highly receptive to any messages coming to them from their parents.

The thirteen- to fourteen-year-old is also ripe for a knight-in-shining-armor routine. He will be intrigued by the covert nature of the messages and appoint himself investigative detective in decoding the hidden meaning. It doesn't take much deduction before he concludes that his parents are in trouble. Being a brave knight, he will hop on his white charger and dash off to rescue them. Being an inexperienced child in mad pursuit of gallantry, he falsely concludes that *he* is the problem. It scares him, but he knows he must save his parents from his wickedness.

COVERT MESSAGES

Covert messages are very dangerous slips of the tongue that cause anxiety to skyrocket. They're unintentional; parents are horrified when they learn what the child heard them say. They're off-the-cuff; parents are embarrassed when they recognize the hidden meaning. They're exceptionally damaging; parents are deeply remorseful when time teaches them that their kids tried to do as Mom and Dad had said.

The covert messages I'm concerned about are the ones by which a parent dumps marital frustration on a child. Rather than clearing the air with private conversations about disappointments, parents keep their frustrations bottled up inside. Eventually the frustration reaches the point where it leaks out. When the spillage places a child in the middle of marital discord, a debilitating anxiety begins to grow.

In examining the family structure of PPS victims, I have found that covert messages cluster around two themes, one given by the mother to the son, the other coming from the father. The mother/son theme is: *Don't be close to your father*. The father/son theme is: *Your mother is a weakling and you're hurting her*.

In order to see how these themes do their dirty work, let's visit a family in which a young PPS victim is about to be given a powerful dose of anxiety.

Mom arrives home from her job just in time to answer a phone call from one of her son's friends. No, she doesn't know where he is, he never bothers to tell her. She then discovers that this same wandering thirteen-year-old forgot to thaw out the meat as her note on the counter had instructed. She's expected to dish up a savory meal in thirty minutes and the main course is frozen solid. All in all, she'd like to take a bath, relax for a few minutes, and then wring her son's neck, not necessarily in that order. The hinge of a kitchen cabinet screams in pain as it once again becomes Mom's emotional scapegoat.

Dad mopes in from work, looking for compassion, pity, and the evening newspaper. He tries to be nice but he's never been very good at it. Several months ago, when his wife started back to work, she asked him to be more helpful around the house. The next night he picked up the paper and took out the garbage. That was the beginning and the end of his participation in housework. His wife should have confronted him; instead, she regularly shoots little bursts of sarcasm at him which he publicly ignores but privately uses to justify his decision to play more golf.

Mom suppresses continual twinges of anger and resentment. Her husband's concern for her stress level is almost nonexistent. She can't even get a hug unless she asks for it. She feels surrounded by an irresponsible teenager, an impossible work schedule, and an insensitive husband. Ironically, her husband feels the same way, except that he laughingly labels his wife a bitch as he's drowning his anger with gin and tonic at the nineteenth hole.

As Mom and Dad pretend that the tension doesn't exist, their only child blows into the kitchen demanding to know how much time he has before dinner. Without waiting for an answer, he plows into the family room and asks Dad for money for the video arcade. Dad mumbles something about his son taking money for granted as he hands the boy five dollars. The hair trigger is tripped and the hammer falls. The covert messages carrying the seeds of gruesome anxiety begin.

'Leave your father alone,' Mom yells at her son. 'He's had a hard day and he needs some rest. Anyhow, you shouldn't have any money after disappearing all day and forgetting to do your chores.'

'What chores?' comes the defiant response.

'I don't know how many times I have to remind you.' Mom's voice belies her overreaction. 'I'm absolutely disgusted with you. Your father and I work ourselves to death for you and you don't even appreciate it enough to do a couple of little chores.'

The boy tries to fight back. 'I don't remember you telling me to do any chores. I don't know what you're yelling at me for.'

His son's backtalk stimulates Dad's first covert message. 'Don't be nasty to your mother, son. She's trying to fix dinner and you're only hurting her. Now stop it!'

Mom damns a recalcitrant can of green beans. She slams the half-opened can onto the counter and stomps off to change her clothes. She glares at her son with a hate she'll regret as soon as she gets halfway upstairs. She's not really disgusted at his irresponsiblity and she knows it. She hurts because she lives with a man who's nicer to strangers than he is to her.

Dad calls to his son to come into the family room. With a gentleness that seems to ease the tension, he says, 'Son, you have to learn to understand women. Your mom can't take working all day and then having you be mean to her.'

There's no way this thirteen-year-old will hear the hidden meaning in Dad's advice. He simply takes it for granted. 'I wasn't mean, Dad.'

Dad isn't interested in communicating with his son. He sticks his nose back into the newspaper and tosses his son one last quickie, 'You gotta remember that your mom doesn't understand boys. So watch it.'

Having been dismissed in this peremptory fashion, the son wanders upstairs to his bedroom. Little does he realize that he is about to get clobbered with a contradictory set of covert messages.

Mom hears her son making a half-hearted attempt to wash his hands and face. The guilt of her kitchen rampage haunts her and she knocks quietly at the bathroom door. She knows that she will be invited in, but her knock signals the beginning of her supplication.

The softness in her voice would seduce any child. 'Can I talk to you for a moment?' Without waiting for an answer, Mom explains her behavior in such gentle words that no one could accuse her of being covert.

70

'I know I really got upset with you and I shouldn't have. It's just that when I see you acting like your father, I really get scared. Daddy is very busy with his work and doesn't have time to help. I don't want you to be like that. You're not like your father; you have tender feelings. I want you to show them and not be so cruel. Right now, Dad's work is more important than his family. You just have to accept that. Someday he'll care about us. But until then, I need you to help me.'

The son stares at the wall over his mom's shoulder, shaking his head up and down. His mom is so consumed with her anger at her husband she doesn't see the well of tears that is rising inside her pride and joy. She pats him on the head and goes downstairs to finish preparing dinner.

Dad's preoccupation with the evening news is interrupted by his wife's banging around the kitchen. He makes a feeble attempt to mend fences by offering to help. This only opens him to attack. His wife still isn't candid and straightforward about her feelings, but the harsh tone of her criticism isn't to be mistaken.

'Why do you give him money as if it grew on trees? You know he spends too much time with those computer games as it is.' Without giving him much chance to respond, she continues, 'If you spent a little more time with your son, maybe you'd know what he's feeling. Maybe you'd know what he needs. He doesn't need you to throw money at him. He needs you to love him, understand the tough times he's going through. Maybe you ought to quit playing so much golf and take time to help your son.'

Dad's protestations fall on deaf ears. Somehow Dad knows that his wife isn't waiting for an answer. Her goal was to make him feel guilty. It works, to a point; the point being that Dad is getting so accustomed to marital tension that he doesn't pay much attention to his wife's complaints. He's refining his skills of emotional numbness.

The turbulent mood carries over into dinner. The son is treated like a shuttlecock, whipped back and forth between two fierce competitors who flagrantly violate basic rules governing decency and discipline.

The son's table manners are atrocious. Instead of issuing a stern warning, Mom picks on him as if he were a meatless chicken bone. He complains about the food. Rather than engaging him in pleasant conversation, Dad makes a paltry effort to placate his wife by belittling his son's taste buds. The son sulks, giving both parents an opportunity to berate him in unison about the fact that no one wants a sulker for a friend. It won't be long before the son will desperately try to prove them wrong.

Since this scene occurs on a fairly regular basis, the son is getting used to it. He's not nearly so upset as you might expect. So it's not amazing to see him clear the table and hear him hum what sounds like a Top Forty song. He's still not numb, but he's beginning to learn the benefits of anesthetizing his feelings.

After an hour and a half of emotional flogging, the son is in remarkably good shape. He had better be. He must endure one last verbal arrow, unleashed from his dad's quiver. In some ways, it cuts deeper than the rest.

The wound comes at a time when the dad and son could share a peaceful moment. Although Dad's tone embodies warmth and sincerity, the son winces when he sees his dad approach. History has taught him that quiet moments with Dad end up being painful. 'Try to shape up, Son, and keep your mother off my back,' Dad says. 'I can't take much more of her bitching at me about you.'

Hearing this cheap shot, you probably want to jump up and confront Dad. But it wouldn't do any good. Not only would he deny any hidden meaning, but he would also be insulted at the slightest suggestion that anything he said could possibly have hurt his son. After all, he would protest, no father in his right mind would ever say or do anything to harm his child.

If you've listened carefully, you'll realize that no amount of emotional Novocain could protect this kid from feeling worthless. It would do no good for him to complain. Like Mom, Dad doesn't realize what he's doing. The only good news about his evening of shrouded verbal daggers is that it is over.

As you walk away from the house, look up to the son's bedroom and tune into the voices inside his head.

I hurt my mom because I'm like my dad, who can't stand to have me hurt Mom. Dad doesn't love us like his work because he doesn't have feelings. Mom can't understand me, and I make her pick on Dad. I'm supposed to protect her, but that means I have to use my feelings to do what Dad doesn't do. To protect my dad, I have to shape up and not be like him.

The covert messages do most of their damage as the boy tries to make sense out of the senseless. Imagine the pain and turmoil that assault this boy's mind. The knot in his gut condemns him as the culprit; the scream in his head points the finger of blame solely at him. Must he not illogically reason that he is the originator of the pain in the people he loves most? By the time he's ready to fall asleep, whatever self-esteem he managed to accrue that day is most assuredly destroyed.

Can't you just see what this boy would do if Peter Pan flew up to his window and asked him to join him in Never Never Land? He'd grab that magical dust so fast it would make your head spin. He would cover his body with sparkles of everlasting gaiety, convinced that in Never Never Land he would be free from everything that had to do with growing up.

This is a grim scene. While a child usually isn't blasted with all these messages in one evening, the PPS victim will hear them over the course of a week or two. But hearing the covert messages is actually the lesser of two evils. Much worse is the fact that *he won't hear a refutation*. Neither Mom nor Dad will come to him later on and say, 'Sorry about the pressure, Son. I was wrong. It's not your problem. So you take care to behave yourself and Mom [Dad] and I will solve our problems.'

Except for magical incantations, there's no relief from a sense of doom. The son knows that something is drastically wrong. His tiny voice of common sense suggests that his parents might be wrong, but his loyalty and naturally self-centered attitude combine to point the finger of blame at himself. He's forced to conclude that he is wrong.

With this *I'm not OK* attitude, several developments occur in the boy's mind. As his self-blaming goes up, his self-confidence goes down. A nagging sensation of sadness creeps into silences, and he avoids being alone. He makes illogical conclusions about his ability to hurt and/or protect his parents. This becomes part of an irrational power trip wherein the boy believes he has the power to save his parents from emotional grief. He condemns himself when he fails to do so.

These mental events mushroom into a cloud of despair. He makes a very damaging generality about the nature of his soul. While he recognizes that his parents love him, he postulates that he is unable to love them in return. Somewhere inside of him he sees a demon that makes him an unloving person.

This negative self-image becomes a self-fulfilling prophecy. Because he views himself as unloving, he doesn't expect himself to be polite and considerate. His inner voice says, 'It won't do me any good to try to behave myself, because I'm not a nice person.'

It will be years before the PPS victim is capable of realizing the vicious circle created by his negative self-image. At the mid-teen stage of the affliction, the boy is only aware of the need to escape from the emotional pain. It is within the context of avoidance that the mother and father hang-up takes shape.

The victim's relationship with his parents never matures beyond this point. His flight to Never Never Land results in a stagnation of emotional maturity. Many victims spend the rest of their lives trying to get close to Dad without feeling panic, to pull away from Mom without feeling guilty. At every turn they are haunted by their belief that they have the power to save their parents from pain. This power simply does not exist.

The PPS victim eventually has trouble with male authority figures. He places impossible demands on male teachers, employers, professors, and coaches, among others.

He pushes himself beyond all reasonable limits in an effort to please these people. In return, he expects them to grant him a special status, which he interprets as a symbolic kinship with his dad. In the process, he hopes to garner absolution for his failure to please his father. This father hang-up contaminates the victim's relationships with male authority figures and, in most cases, causes even more distance to develop.

The victim's mother hang-up will eventually express itself when he gets close to a woman. His way of loving a woman is to make her a mommy surrogate. He will require that the woman in his life behave in a certain pattern. If she deviates from his expectations (the biggest one being that she must always approve of what he says and does), he will have a temper tantrum or, worse, engage in some type of abusiveness. By absolutely pleasing this mommy surrogate, the victim hopes that he will finally learn how to be a loving person.

Because of his resilience and the fluidity of his teenage life, much of this inner turmoil won't surface for several years. The deterioration and stagnation are developing without the young man being aware of it. There are, however, two major indicators of this crushing anxiety and negative self-image.

One thing you might see a mid-teen PPS victim do is pick on someone who is close to him. If there is a younger sister in the family, she will take the brunt of his emotional nastiness. Once upon a time, the boy idolized her. He fed her when she was a baby and wanted to look at her all the time. Now he picks on her mercilessly. He teases her. His envy and jealousy lead to vicious remarks. This is not a normal brother-sister rivalry. Rather, the criticism is unrelenting, often driving the sister to tears. She will say to her mom, 'Do something about him. I don't like to hate my brother.'

You might also see this mid-teen anxiety manifest itself in a sudden drop in grades. Somewhere at the end of junior high or the beginning of high school, the boy's school performance falls apart. Teachers say he is bright but doesn't do the work. They call him lazy. Evaluations label him as an underachiever. His concentration slips. In some cases he takes on the role of the class clown. No amount of studying, pushing, disciplining, or threatening seems to make a difference. The boy truly doesn't care.

IRRESPONSIBILITY + ANXIETY

The 'I don't care' attitude is an outgrowth of the negative self-image. When combined with the gross irresponsibility reviewed in the last chapter, one of the major traits of the PPS victim's psychological profile emerges: procrastination.

The PPS victim's procrastination is much more devastating than the kind you and I occasionally indulge in. We put things off for a day or two because we are tired, our mental energy is sapped, or we just can't find the time. But *we will get it done*.

The PPS victim most likely will *not* get it done. He puts things off because he has little if any reason to invest himself in tomorrow. He figures that any energy spent will only result in more failure. This fatalism turns ordinary procrastination into disaster. Things are *always* put off until tomorrow. Obviously, they never get done.

The cumulative effect of irresponsibility plus anxiety is fatalistic procrastination. This severely hampers the midteen's ability to overcome his emotional stagnation. Not only does he have ingrained habits of goofing off, but now he also feels no *hope* for change. He is lost. His defiance teams with depression to yield a formidable obstacle to growth. His energies are diverted into a frantic desire to belong. In the next chapter we'll see how peer pressure becomes the sociological cement that unifies the plight of the legion of lost boys, captained by Peter Pan.

MODERN-DAY DARLINGS

At the beginning and the end of the story of Peter Pan, the author acquaints us with the family dynamics of one household, that of the Darlings. George and Mary. They had three children: Wendy, Michael, and John. As the story unfolds, Peter recruits Wendy to be his surrogate mother, and Michael and John to be members of his legion of lost boys.

There is ample evidence that the Peter Pan Syndrome was already flourishing in the Darling household. Mr. Darling was chauvinistic and self-pitying, a child in a man's body. Mrs. Darling was long-suffering, mothered her husband, and was sacrificial toward her children. We are not privy to the Darling parents' personal problems, but we do hear many covert messages flying about the house. George and Mary suffered marital discord and their children were caught in the middle. Once you read the first few pages of the story, you'll understand why Peter was drawn to the Darling children's bedroom window.

There are countless modern-day Darling families who unwittingly put out the welcome mat for Peter and his legion. Here's the story of two of them.

The Pilsens

Mary was deeply embarrassed and angered by her impoverished childhood. The railroad track that halved her tiny hometown formed a double-edged boundary in her mind. The south rail was the outer limit of a pristine corral in which kids frolicked who were blessed with acceptance and approval. The north rail could have been made of barbed wire given the way she felt scratched and torn every time she tried to cross it. Although the north side never left her hungry, she never forgave her father for being happy working for the same railroad that held her prisoner.

As she matured into a beautiful young woman, Mary relentlessly pursued two goals: to buy clothes that would tell everyone she was truly an acceptable girl; and to continually achieve honor-roll status, which she could cash into a scholarship to a fine university that would open the door to marriage, forever removing the shadow of her past.

Meanwhile, Barry Pilsen was consumed with one

objective: to compensate his mother for the rough life she had supposedly endured. Barry's father died when Barry was four. He left his wife with enough money for their son's education, but not enough for day-to-day expenses. Hardly a day went by that Barry's mother didn't remind her son of the sacrifice she was making for him. On more than one occasion she told him that all her pain would be forgotten if only he married the right woman and protected her. The bondage implied in this emotional contract caused most of Barry Pilsen's problems.

Mary and Barry were instantly attracted to each other during the first mixer of their respective sorority and fraternity. Mary immediately fixed her hopes and dreams on Barry's propriety and sobriety. Barry saw in Mary the woman who could become his ticket to fulfilling the contract with his mother.

The subject of marriage arose before the end of their freshman year. Mary and Barry took it so much for granted that they never bothered to get to know each other. In fact, Barry never formally asked Mary to marry him. She did, of course, on the day after graduation.

Barry's willingness to quietly sacrifice himself for others made him a perfect corporate man. His meteoric rise in business was matched step for step by Mary's social climbing. Her membership in social clubs was complemented by her husband's invitation to join a prestigious country club. Barry's promotion to sales manager was equaled by the selection of his wife to be president of the hospital auxiliary and adviser to the local beauty pageant. At some parties, Barry was chided about being Mr. Mary Pilsen.

The shadow of Mary's past was nearly gone. She lied so regularly about her childhood that she almost believed she was an orphan who had been raised by an elderly aunt and uncle in North Dakota. She chose that state because everyone in her social circle seemed to think North Dakota didn't exist. The chance of anyone's uncovering her fabrication was practically nonexistent.

Barry's mother was delighted with Mary. She never failed to express her satisfaction with her son's selection of a mate.

Nor did she fail to ask him to do countless little things for her. Because they lived a hundred miles apart, Barry spent hours on the phone, talking to attorneys, bankers, bookkeepers, and even plumbers, all in an effort to keep his mother happy. Barry didn't like his mother's overdependence, but even the slightest complaint left him with mountains of guilt.

Barry and Mary lived out their storyland script by having three children, two boys and a girl. The children brought a gradual deterioration of the Pilsens' fragile arrangement. The emotional needs of the children forced Mary to look at her plasticity. She had marvelous outward credentials, but she felt empty on the inside. Barry was on the road most of the week and the solitude made her resolve to seek a better life. She wanted to change the rules of her marriage.

Barry didn't understand most of what his wife said about sharing, emotional growth, and increasing communication. He chalked up her unrest as an early mid-life crisis. He advised her to get a job and play more tennis. Secretly, he panicked at the thought of having two women making unrealistic demands upon him. He coped with his own unrest by playing more racquetball and increasing his alcohol consumption. He wanted to have an affair but was too frightened to pursue it.

Colin Pilsen entered his teenage years in a home filled with unspoken resentments. He didn't possess the maturity to unmask his parents' marital discord, but then, Colin was oblivious to most everything around him, including his responsibilities. Mary was angered by her smartmouthed, lazy son who had once been very sensitive but now treated people like chattel. Instead of implementing rational disciplinary procedures, Mary yelled and screamed at her irresponsible fourteen-year-old. This only made him more insensitive to his mother's guidance.

Psychotherapy would have taught Mary Pilsen that much of her frustration with Colin was actually displaced anger toward her husband. She would also have learned that she secretly condemned herself for actively denying her own upbringing, which was infinitely better than that provided

79

by her and her husband. She made an appointment with a therapist but backed out at the last moment. The possible tarnish on her social image was too great a risk.

As far as I know, this story has a sad ending. Mary and Barry are still married and spend most of their energies avoiding one another. Mary is chairperson of several committees, most of which are designed to help wayward children. Barry is in line for a corporate presidency and now has a young girlfriend whom he loves deeply. Because of the importance of a positive social image and the specter of financial disaster, divorce is out of the question.

Colin is twenty-four and still trying to finish college. He is an incipient alcoholic, has never held a summer or part-time job longer than a month or two, and is beginning to suffer periods of depression during which he entertains the notion of suicide.

Colin's younger brother and sister seem to have escaped the major turmoil of the Pilsen household. As they usually do, the covert messages hit the older son the hardest. He is the one who searches for an answer and finds it in Never Never Land.

The Tolsons

Jim Tolson's father was never a father. He remained an enigma until the day he died. Jim was afraid of his dad but didn't respect him, a combination that often results in rebellion. And it did. Jim was a hell raiser. 'All boy,' he would later say. In fact, on several occasions his rebelliousness almost landed him in jail.

Jim was raised on a farm and worked as soon as he learned to walk. Hard work was both a boon and a bane to him. He believed it kept him from becoming a juvenile delinquent, but it also became his taskmaster. By the time he was a young man, Jim couldn't let himself relax unless he had sweated and strained over a laborious job. He hoped he would receive his dad's approval; all he achieved was the legacy of a workaholic. Jim entered his adult life with an unfaltering resolution to improve his lot in life and a burning desire to learn how to be a loving father to a son of his own.

Edna, Jim's wife, was the daughter of an adoring father and a disturbed mother. Edna figured that her father stayed with her mother because he felt sorry for her. That, combined with his guilt over excessive drinking, kept him in bondage to a wife who had four nervous breakdowns, all of which she blamed on her husband.

Edna's home was filled with emotional explosions. Her mother regularly accused her father of everything from burning the toast to sleeping with the neighbor's wife. Dad didn't usually say much until he was drunk. Then he became abusive in both words and actions. Edna forgave him; his wife didn't.

Edna became phobic about her parents' fighting. She would do anything to avoid it. She exchanged her own desires for the role of peacemaker. She refrained from dating in order not to have her parents disagree over her style of dress. She abandoned her plans for a college education because she couldn't tolerate complaints about financial matters. She didn't realize it at the time, but she was beginning to blame *all women* for the fact that she couldn't become a person. She was bitterly resentful toward her mother, worshipped her father, and was sorely disappointed that she had been born a female.

After completing a secretarial course, Edna left home. She went to work for a construction company with a million-dollar business and a bright young foreman named Jim Tolson. Edna's shyness camouflaged her lack of social skills. Jim found her modesty appealing. Soon they were making plans for marriage.

Their first child was conceived during a sexually disastrous honeymoon. Neither confided his or her disappointment, which was just fine with both of them because Jim was more interested in a good mother for his children than in a wife for himself, and Edna was looking for a surrogate father who would protect her from life's emotional pain. As so often happens in the PPS victim's family, Jim and Edna fit together perfectly—for all the wrong reasons.

By the time he was thirty-three years old, Jim was a

81

junior partner in the construction firm and had two young sons whom he adored. Between working eighty hours a week and spending every spare minute with his kids, Jim had little time for Edna. He would have been perplexed to learn that his wife felt like the fourth wheel on a smooth-running troika.

Edna was angry at being taken for granted. She suppressed her disillusionment in favor of counting the blessings of a family atmosphere free of emotional distress. She had attained the antiseptic environment that she craved. But she was flabbergasted at the price she had to pay for her Garden of Eden.

Edna's self-loathing reached a crisis stage when Jim's desire to start his own business forced her to go back to work. She hated herself for hating her husband. As her emotions turned explosive, visions of her childhood besieged her. Her older son, a spoiled and lazy teenager, became the target of her unrest.

'Leave your father alone,' was the covert message Edna used to express her resentment. Persistent variations on this theme ultimately resulted in Jim's telling his son, 'Take it easy on your mother, she doesn't understand boys.' Jim, Jr., was caught between a father who was blind to all wishes save his own and a mother who was sick and tired of living her life intimidated by the slightest hint of emotional unrest.

Finally, their respective jobs caused the turning point in their marriage.

Edna's new boss was kind and complimentary—a welcome tonic for her ailing ego. They lunched together, took long walks, and shared their dissatisfaction with married life. Their friendship blossomed into a passionate sexual affair. Edna's feeling of self-acceptance was electric. It also was painful. She was torn between the excitement of being *in love* with a man and the comfort of still loving her husband.

One evening as she was about to leave the house for a rendezvous with her lover, Edna received a call from her husband's construction site. Jim had been badly injured in a fall and was in critical condition. She rushed to the hospital, never thinking of cancelling her date. Emotions bombarded her, but Edna found a bewildering solace in a quiet realization: Whatever the outcome, her life would never again be as it was.

Edna quit her job to dedicate herself to Jim's convalescence. She was tolerant, patient, and loving, while she recognized that Jim was exceptionally demanding and insensitive. In the past she would have blamed herself. Not this time. The experience of loving a man as well as herself gave her the courage to confront her unproductive marriage.

The climax came one evening when Jim was sulking his way around the house, well enough to return to work but not yet released by his physician. He was being particularly obstreperous and obnoxious. Edna did something she had never thought possible. She started a fight with her husband.

Edna cleansed herself of years of suppressed frustration. Much of her catharsis took the form of exaggerated accusations. She was furious and didn't care if she hurt Jim's feelings. Good thing. If she had been any less forceful, Jim would have remained indifferent. Instead, he was shocked. All he could say was, 'Wow, I never knew you felt this way.' Edna was shocked, too. Instead of fear, she experienced relief. It was all out in the open and nothing horrible had happened. She had conquered her phobia.

Jim and Edna Tolson began marriage counseling the next week. They had many bad habits to overcome. But they attacked their problems with delight. They seemed to be talking constantly, making discoveries about each other that proved endlessly stimulating. Their arousal carried over into the bedroom, where they discovered that they were terrific lovers. In a few months they found that not only did they love one another, but they were also in love.

Along with working on their marriage, Jim and Edna completely revitalized their child-rearing procedures. Jim, Jr., joined them in family counseling, as did their younger son. As a 'fearsome foursome' they struggled to reshape the way each contributed to the family unit. Jim became a man who could see beyond his own needs. Edna became a woman who was willing to fight for love. And, most important, Jim, Jr., dropped out of the legion of lost boys and put the Peter Pan Syndrome behind him.

Jim and Edna Tolson gave their boys the courage and skills they needed to become men. But to do so, Mom and Dad had had to grow up first. And they had. Late, but not too late.

'IT MUST BE ME'

The Pilsens and the Tolsons fostered a sense of uneasiness in their children. They didn't do it on purpose. In fact, they never even heard themselves do it. Like all hidden communication, their covert messages led to motive guessing and mind reading.

Parents from diversified backgrounds use an assortment of words at various times in a variety of situations to send covert messages to their kids. Within this heterogeneity, one thing remains constant for the PPS victims. They all conclude the same thing: 'Something is wrong here and *it must be me.*'

Self-blaming becomes a knee-jerk reaction in young PPS victims; the camouflage of denial quickly follows. In deciphering their parents' covert messages, they are thrust into a vicious cycle. They falsely conclude that their very existence causes them to hurt people. They avoid the resulting despair by denying all responsibility for their actions and replacing it with the pretense that they never do anything wrong. They go from one extreme to the other. People who care about them see only the denial, which they interpret as insensitivity. It's an amazing irony that the kids who start out being most sensitive to other people's feelings are the ones who end up behaving so callously.

As time brings him closer to a wide range of adult relationships, the victim is plagued by childhood conditioning that stimulates self-blaming whenever anything goes wrong. Denial protects what little integrity he has. Faced with irrational guilt and shame, the victim absolves himself by pretending never to be at fault. 'I'm sorry' is not part of his vocabulary, because he can't say it without feeling worthless.

The two stories also teach us that parents of the PPS victim have problems of their own. Remnants of childhood insecurities infiltrate their daily life, causing them to live with one foot in the present, the other in the past. They marry without knowing one another and lack effective communication skills with which to remedy the deficit. In most cases, family life plays second fiddle to an excessive preoccupation with money and status. They avoid rational confrontation because they are afraid to hurt their partner. Instead of being honest, they retreat into the pretense of wedded bliss. The presence of covert messages is symptomatic of the fact that these parents often haven't grown up either.

OLDEST CHILD

In the general psychological profile (see Chapter 1), I suggested that the PPS victim is probably the oldest child in the family. Though there are of course exceptions, it is important to note that out of all the cases I've recorded, the PPS victim was the oldest child 82 percent of the time.

It makes sense. The oldest is typically the 'experimental child' and usually the center of concern and controversy. He will most likely face the highest and most unrealistic expectations. His misbehavior stimulates excessive disapproval both from himself and his parents, and he becomes the primary target of covert messages.

The textbook definition of anxiety says that a person is anxious when he faces a situation in which he must do something but the alternatives appear fruitless. The victims of the Peter Pan Syndrome are tormented by this kind of anxiety. They decode the covert messages flowing from their parents' marital discord in such a way as to conclude that something is wrong and 'It must be me.' To solve the problem they must find a way to save their parents from themselves.

If they wish to stay alive (which most of them do), there is no logical way out of this trap. The side effects of prolonged anxiety are incredible. A general feeling of rejection becomes a constant companion, as do anger and guilt toward Mom and estrangement from Dad. An irrational power trip and magical thinking take shape. Thoughts dominate emotions as the child realizes that his head can be used to anesthetize the pain in his heart. Emotional paralysis becomes a respite from the storm. His self-concept and self-esteem suffer severe damage, but he survives as best he can.

Here's how one mother of a twenty-two-year-old PPS victim summed up her explanation of why her son developed the affliction. Let your eyes do the reading but listen to her covert message with your third ear.

His introduction to parental authority was tempered with his exceptional niceness disguised as need. The situation was exacerbated by apparent parental harassment (which was myth, not reality). This all occurred within the context of a boy who idolized his parents while at the same time knowing he was somehow involved in making life very painful for them.

Some distortion of his psyche may have taken place at the hands of a rejective first-grade teacher with a forbidding manner. His disrespect was often so thorough that infrequent but well-deserved parental vacations had to be aborted.

His manner during his teenage years was both cocky and self-preoccupied. His mother had neither the inspiration nor the good health to tolerate his insinuations. She is an easy-to-idolize mother of really charming children and should not have been burdened with such disgrace.

His remarks concerning girls are to be clearly understood as indiscreet, disloyal remarks about social transactions and must definitely not be taken as references to any physical exploitation.

These cold and contemptuous remarks came from a well-educated woman whose son was in serious emotional trouble. Her lack of empathy was astounding. Her reference to his first-grade teacher was a perfect description of her own parenting style. It's little wonder that this youngster was consumed with anxiety and feelings of rejection. You can imagine how lonely he must have felt. He joined Peter's legion without a second thought. At this writing the boy is coming back from Never Never Land, but he certainly isn't getting any help from his mother.

6 Loneliness

WENDY: 'Where do you live now?'
PETER: 'With the lost boys.'
WENDY: 'Who are they?'
PETER: 'They are the children who fall out of their prams
when the nurse is looking the other way. If they are not
claimed in seven days they are sent far away to the
Never Never Land. I'm captain.'
WENDY: 'What fun it must be.'
PETER: 'Yes, but we are rather lonely.'

TOOTLES: (*One of the lost boys*) 'As I can't be anything
important would any of you like to see me do a trick?'

Talk about rejection! The scope of it boggles the mind. Can
you imagine anything worse? You're just an infant and you
fall out of your carriage. To add insult to injury, you have a
private-duty nurse who, after seven days, doesn't realize
you're gone. Once your spirit is shattered, the zephyrs of
loneliness whisk the pieces away and scatter them in Never
Never Land like so much chaff sifted from the grain. If not
for the resilience of youth, you'd suffer a complete mental
breakdown.

Peter Pan was a survivor. When he woke up in Never
Never Land consumed with loneliness, he didn't panic. He
looked around, saw others suffering an identical fate, and
turned potential disaster into victory. He united all the lost
boys into a legion, bonded together by their heartfelt
commonality—they had all been rejected in the worst way.
He sealed the unity by declaring himself captain. And indeed

he was. Only a natural-born leader would have the skill and cunning to convert feelings of rejection into a *raison d'être*.

In spite of their comradeship and group identity, Peter and his legion of lost boys were plagued by loneliness. To cope with it, they had to find ways to turn the nightmare into sport. Since children are the consummate game players, it's no surprise that they camouflaged their loneliness with gaiety and trickery. Tootles reflects this gamesmanship with his compensatory attitude. Most of you should recognize this attitude from your school days. It's the motivating force behind the class clown.

Through his narrative comments, Barrie informs his audience that loneliness takes a severe toll on Peter's character. We learn that the Pan is very shallow. Time and again we hear how he is quick to switch allegiance and entertain magical visions of himself. We are shocked to see how this young boy of happiness reacts to others' care and concern by using pity to manipulate and indifference to intimidate. Try as he might to escape, Peter is held hostage by loneliness.

We all experience loneliness. It manifests itself differently in each of us. It may feel like a gray, cloudy day that never ends. Some people experience a vast emptiness that reaches to the pit of their stomach. Others get outside their bodies and see themselves as minuscule pieces of dust being blown about by the storms of insignificance. Still others crave human contact so badly that they subject themselves to great inconvenience just so they can be near another person.

This last is the type of loneliness that affects teenagers. Most youngsters don't have the experience or the perspective to be poetic about their loneliness. They are only aware of their need for human contact. When they don't get it, they go after it, whatever the possible cost.

Loneliness becomes a cornerstone of the Peter Pan Syndrome when a child feels unwanted in his own home. From the preceding two chapters you can see how a child who is burdened with irresponsibility and anxiety could feel lonely in his own house. Given the estrangement from Dad, the guilt and anger toward Mom, and a low self-image, it's a short step to the sinking sensation of not belonging to your own family.

What makes loneliness worse for these kids is their parents' attempt to compensate for the lack of love by giving them money and material possessions. When this occurs, affluence acts as a catalyst, accelerating the child's movement toward the PPS crisis. The money-buys-love myth gives the child a false sense of security and further undermines his already deteriorating ego. The child is led to believe, 'If I have money and things, I don't need people.' This lie seduces him into pursuing a solution to loneliness that only causes more trouble.

Young PPS victims are torn by loneliness and affluence. They believe that belonging is a commodity, something that can be bartered or bought. So they try to win admiration by acting out phony roles (like Tootles); or they attempt to acquire recognition by purchasing the correct clothing; many skip the middle step and simply try to buy friends.

Belonging is the result of caring; kids who are heading for the PPS lifestyle don't understand that. They are so busy trying to purchase love that they never learn the joys of caring. And because their parents are locked in the vicious cycle of money-buys-happiness, there is no one to teach the children how to find belonging by caring for others.

The PPS victims' search for relief from loneliness slowly becomes more desperate. The worse they feel, the more they surround themselves with an increasing number of other kids. As the herd grows in size, so does the frenzy of gamesmanship, the pursuit of fads, and the pressure to conform. The result is the hysteria of peer pressure that suffocates caring and exacerbates loneliness.

Peer pressure takes its lifeblood from the threat of rejection: 'Do what everybody else is doing or you will be rejected and no one will care about you.' To a kid who feels rejected at home, this becomes a constant reminder that his only chance for human contact is to belong to the group. He will risk anything and everything not to lose that chance.

When peer pressure becomes this strong, the PPS victim

is in serious trouble. His friends become infinitely more important than his family. The morality of the group easily outweighs the values of his parents. Their authority evaporates in the face of group conformity. Their behavior patterns become a classic example of the blind leading the blind.

PEAK AGE: 15 TO 16

Loneliness hits us all, but it's devastating to the child in his mid-teens. I've focused on 15 to 16 as the peak age for loneliness, because it is during this period that kids get into social habit patterns. If the fifteen-year-old learns to cope with loneliness by blindly following the nearest group, his strength to resist the next three stages of the PPS is severely drained.

IRRESPONSIBILITY + ANXIETY + LONELINESS

You'll see it after school when five or six kids roam past your house on their way to nowhere. You'll hear it in a movie theater during the opening credits. You'll feel it late at night when youthful voices create a din as everyone talks and nobody listens. It sounds forceful, daring, and contemptible. You get angry at ill-mannered adolescents. But the rudeness is not what makes you shudder.

It's something more rudimentary, something frightening. The kids sound excited and pleased. Yet their gaiety is artificial, their laughter hysterical. Their happiness is eerie and ominous.

You may not be able to label it, but you are sensing panic. It's a panic that's all-encompassing. Not even the kids realize that they are frightened. Their panic creates a need for oneupmanship. In their race for recognition they'll do practically anything to gain the group's favor. The goal is to belong, or, more exactly, to escape loneliness.

Concern about approval from peers is a part of everyone's life; it's a *major* part of an adolescent's life. But when a child is willing to throw away his morality in order to gain recognition, he has lost whatever balance he managed to gain in his young life. His actions are driven by impulses of panic.

The PPS victim experiences this type of panic. His years of irresponsibility have robbed him of honest pride. Unrelenting anxiety around the home results in feelings of rejection, stripping him of hope for a better tomorrow. Unmet needs of affiliation force him to find belonging outside his family; he takes to the streets, where he eventually finds other kids like himself. A few kids, unable to fit in anywhere, take to the streets as loners.

PPS IN SUBURBIA

The irony of the PPS victim's panicky search for group recognition is that, try as he may, he never quite achieves it. He may participate in many group activities, but he is rarely considered an inside member of any group.

The 'rowdies' leave him behind because he's too compassionate to fit in with their destructive tendencies. The 'jocks' reject him because of his relative softness; they call him a 'fag,' a 'queer,' or make other reference to alleged homosexuality. The 'cuties' push him away because he doesn't reflect their glamorous world. The 'achievers' ignore him because he has nothing in common with them. The 'druggies' include him in their parties, but they don't trust him.

The victim's panic deprives him of any true friendship. He's so worried about rejection that he is forever saying or doing the wrong thing at the wrong time. His laughter is prolonged and silly. His vulgarities are forced and inept. He goes to extremes in word and deed, all for the sake of approval. But his efforts backfire. His panic combines with poor social skills to result in rejection and an increase in loneliness.

The PPS victim pretends that he has friends. Yet these so-called friends rarely call him (he has to call them), and they purposely avoid telling him about an activity, because they don't want him there. Perhaps worst of all, he doesn't understand what is happening. The only lasting relationship he has is with two or three other kids like himself—outcasts who form their own group whose identity is based on the fact that no one wants anything to do with them.

It's amazing that this sad chain of events is centered in middle- and upper-class suburbia, the purported center of socialization and neighborhood solidarity. However, it has been my observation that in many suburban areas, people become so addicted to the pursuit of the 'good life' that they forget what makes life good. They have dollars in their pockets but loneliness in their hearts. This imbalance opens the floodgates to influence peddlers who blitz these families with an endless variety of one message: If you buy this, you will belong!

The parents accept this message; their children follow suit. Belonging becomes the number one item on the family's shopping list. In a state of deprivation, the family members are an easy mark for the ruse that dollars can be converted into feelings of belonging. The icon may be a car, a house, a vacation, a fur coat, a video recorder, or any other adult toy. To the kids, the icon of belonging becomes a new stereo, attending a rock concert, name-brand jeans, or throwing a party for friends.

The icon is quickly shattered. It takes only an instant of loneliness for the purchaser to realize that he or she didn't buy the right thing. Absent is the realization that belonging can't be purchased. In fact, once a person puts a price tag on belonging, he has ensured that he won't get it. Trying to buy belonging only increases loneliness.

Psychologist Abraham Maslow warned us about this inevitability many years ago. He suggested that a simple way to view human behavior is to focus on our needs and how we work to satisfy them. He proposed a five-step hierarchy of needs: shelter, safety, belonging, self-esteem, and self-actualization. Maslow's theory says that once we feel secure that one need will be met, we turn our attention to the next, higher need.

After working with families from all socioeconomic levels of our society, I'm convinced that Maslow's theory explains why the Peter Pan Syndrome is basically a middle- or upper-class affliction. The suburbanite has sufficient affluence and social status that he need not be overly concerned about shelter and safety. He and his wife and children turn their attention to meeting the needs of belonging. Since their affluence was responsible for procuring the first two needs, they falsely assume that it can be used to achieve the third in the hierarchy of human needs. It can't. Worse yet, they don't realize that they are trapped in a fruitless search.

In families where permissiveness and marital discord have kept pace with the rise in income, the children, especially the oldest, fall victim to low self-confidence and feelings of rejection. The kids experience a double dose of loneliness. Their search for friendship becomes frantic; hence the panic I described above. The parents often sense this panic and do the one thing they should never do—they give the kids more money and material things instead of time and loving attention. It doesn't take much for the spirit of Peter Pan to slip into their bedroom and steal their heart.

ON THE OUTSIDE LOOKING IN

It's extremely difficult to identify the PPS victim when you have a casual encounter with a group of teenagers who are trying to find themselves. Adolescent irresponsiblity is a common occurrence and, in itself, doesn't tell you much. Anxiety and loneliness are occasional companions in everyone's life and, in moderation, pose no serious threat. But when the combination of irresponsibility, anxiety, and loneliness consume a young person's life, he can find himself on the outside looking in.

From time to time, all children are on the outskirts of a significant group's activity—it's part of the normal roller coaster called adolescence. However, here are stories of two young men who never found anywhere to belong. If you think your son might be on the outside looking in, take a look at these two teenagers. If you find a pattern that looks familiar, you might conclude that your son is flirting with an escape to Never Never Land. However, you can also conclude that he will survive his temporary bout with magic dust if he belongs to the one group that can bring him permanence—his family.

Tom

Sixteen-year-old Tom hung out with older guys in their late teens and early twenties. He said they were more mature and had outgrown the antics of stupid kids. As part of this group, he was regularly exposed to beer and dope parties, girls whose silly affection made him feel like a man, and attitudes that renounced education, work, and adult authority.

The immediate result of his affiliation was a dramatic deterioration in his academic performance. When he didn't skip classes, he often slept through them. He complained endlessly about boring, inept teachers and classes that were 'gay.' He told his parents to 'stay out of my life' when they complained about his performance. The only reason Tom didn't become a dropout was that he had developed excellent educational attitudes in his earlier years. He had been an A student in elémentary school and junior high and talked of going to college to study math and science. Yet within a year or two those values became the 'stupidity of being a kid.'

Tom's parents blamed his friends for their son's attitude. Dad called them bums and losers. Mom begged Tom to find friends his own age. Tom rejected his parents' complaints without ever hearing them. What his parents never realized was that Tom *knew* these guys were bums and losers; that's why he liked them. He thought he had a lot in common with them.

Tom was being used by these older guys. He probably

understood and accepted that fact of life. He received $25 a week in allowance, most of which went to buy beer and marijuana for his friends. Tom was their ticket to a good time. In addition, they found it an interesting diversion to see how far they could push a dippy sixteen-year-old kid. Tom capitulated to this patronizing attitude in exchange for feelings, however shallow, of belonging.

Tom had the opportunity to associate with nice boys his own age. Church and neighborhood activity brought him invitations to normal teenage gatherings. He rejected these outright. He called the kids 'dumb,' 'airheads,' and other derogatory names and refused to get involved. There was no doubt that these boys had their faults; after all, they were still kids. However, Tom focused on the tiniest of short-comings and magnified them until even his parents had to agree with some of his criticisms. Then he turned right around and pledged undying allegiance to other kids whose faults were so overwhelming that his parents were dumfounded.

The disruptive, pessimistic lifestyle of these older kids gave Tom something in common with them. He belonged to them; they were losers. He had had an excellent moral upbringing and knew that his friends were on the wrong path; that's why he chose them. The anxiety and rejection he felt at home convinced him that he too was on the wrong path.

It took several hours of hard-nosed confrontation for Tom's parents to see what Tom was doing. They had sought help for Tom never dreaming that they would have to confront their own marital discord. They responded quickly to my confrontation, because they didn't want to see the erosion of their family continue. Within a few weeks they were prepared to admit their mistakes to their son and to demand that he follow suit.

Tom fought them. He complained, threatened, and pushed his parents' endurance to the limit. When he saw that his parents would not submit to blackmail, he started to come around. He never admitted his errors, but his improved behavior spoke of renewed hope for the future.

Because Tom had such a poor reputation at school and such bad socialization patterns, the family decided to send him away to a boarding school. We talked at length about the problems of finding a new family solidarity when Tom was absent most of the time. The parents decided that a clean and total break from the past was Tom's only chance to start fresh. He probably couldn't live at home and overcome many bad habits. I reluctantly agreed.

Tom enrolled in a private school several hundred miles away. It was a financial sacrifice for his parents and exceptionally difficult for Tom, who lacked many of the refined social skills of his contemporaries. The school officials gave Tom extra tutoring in academic and social areas. At last report, Tom is moving toward academic honors and has become an outstanding member of the school's hockey team. The parents have undergone a complete renewal of their marriage and are delighted to discover that family life can be beautiful and serene. Tom has had several excellent visits during vacations and is proving to be a splendid example for his younger brothers and sister to follow.

The family is now talking about Tom returning home for his senior year in high school. They are weighing all sides of the issue. But mostly they are listening to what Tom wants. And they should; he's not a loser anymore.

Toby

From outward appearances, fifteen-year-old Toby didn't fit the mold of the PPS victim. He was the second son, he and his father spent a lot of time together, and he was the leader of a group of neighborhood boys. In most cases, these attributes speak of a dropout from the legion of lost boys. However, in Toby's case, the first impression was deceptive.

Toby was not the older male child, but he was the recipient of excessive permissiveness. His parents had been strict with Toby's brother, who was five years older than Toby. His brother had done so well that his parents had relaxed their standards of child-rearing. They believed that since they had been successful with one child, they didn't have to work hard with the next one. Thus, while his brother had been expected to earn his way, gaining a source of honest pride, Toby got everything he wanted without lifting a finger. His irresponsibility left him vulnerable to his father's personal difficulties.

Toby's dad was a frustrated man. He had not achieved the education and life position that he craved and he felt cheated by his impoverished upbringing. He had a hair-trigger temper and tended to blame his problems on everybody else. In short, Dad was an angry man. Because he felt insecure and desirous of his father's approval, Toby tried his best to follow in his dad's footsteps. As a result of being exposed to an aggressive role model, Toby became a fighter. The time that he and his father spent together backfired on Toby.

Even his group identity wasn't what it appeared to be. Toby was indeed seen as a leader. But the neighborhood boys followed Toby out of fear for their physical safety, not because they respected him. His status was upheld by the fact that he could become aggressive at a moment's notice. In other words, Toby was a bully.

Toby was under strict instructions from his father never to start a fight; likewise, he was told never to walk away from one. Rather than channeling his brightness into academic work, Toby devised subtle ways of provoking fights. He was particularly adept at using noxious verbalizations to agitate other kids. He found that references to purported homosexual activity usually led to fisticuffs. He dressed in a disheveled manner with vulgar sayings on his T-shirts, all in an effort to turn a verbal confrontation into a physical one. He assigned himself the role of defender of the little guy, not out of a sense of fair play but because it afforded him ample opportunity to beat up on other kids.

Toby didn't lose many fights. He was over six feet tall and was a muscular 170 pounds. Whenever his parents received phone calls about Toby's aggressiveness, his father demanded details of the physical encounter, supposedly trying to determine whether or not to discipline

Toby. In truth, his father took secret delight in seeing his son express the anger that he himself held inside.

Toby's mom sensed this imbalance and tried her best to stop it. Rather than confronting her husband, she inadvertently gave her son the covert message that he was disappointing his father. In reaction, Toby tried harder for approval by becoming more aggressive.

The good news in this vicious cycle was that Toby didn't like the role of bully. He was not a mean kid. In fact, he was essentially a nonviolent child. He knew deep in his heart that other kids didn't really like him; the loneliness only created more panic and more aggression.

When I saw Toby, he was trapped by his own reputation as well as by his anxiety, irresponsibility, and loneliness. He understood that if he changed his behavior, not only would he lose a lot of friends, but there would also be a lot of kids waiting to get even with him. He was afraid that in order to quit fighting, he would be subjected to more fights. He really needed his father's help.

To my surprise, his father gave him that help. Toby's dad was somewhat honest about his own frustrations and genuinely shocked to learn how they affected Toby. I acted as an intermediary in several father-son discussions during which Toby was relieved of the burden of acting out his father's frustration. Once Toby understood that his father's weakness was not his problem, he was free to change his methods of socialization.

Toby didn't even complain (too loudly) when his parents instituted some stricter disciplinary measures. His curfew was tightened and his school performance closely scrutinized. He was expected to be mannerly around the house and to maintain a high standard of cleanliness and a proper dress code. These rules forced Toby away from the bully role and rewarded him for being a kind and compassionate teenager. Toby confided that they also helped him gain new friends and feel confident about being an excellent student. But the most telling insight was provided by Toby with this off-handed comment: 'I guess my parents now care as much about me as they did about my brother.'

ONE OUTCOME: ROLE INFLEXIBILITY

Toby and Tom had many things in common. One was the outcome of their struggle with loneliness. I call it role inflexibility. They become masters at explaining away failure and refusing to try anything new. They found a way to cope with loneliness and they *would* not and eventually *could* not risk rejection by experimenting with new, more appropriate behaviors. Their socialization pattern was set in stone. Their lack of flexibility made them an easy target of the sex role conflict, the fourth and most pronounced cornerstone of the Peter Pan Syndrome.

It is the role inflexibility that locks the PPS victim into a highly restricted view of himself as a male. In the next chapter we'll see how this inflexibility combines with irresponsibility, anxiety, and loneliness to produce the sexist trait of the PPS.

7 Sex Role Conflict

WENDY: 'What are your exact feelings for me, Peter?'
PETER: 'Those of a devoted son, Wendy.'
WENDY (*turning away*): 'I thought so.'
PETER: 'You are puzzling. Tiger Lily is just the same; there is something or other she wants to be to me, but she says it is not my mother.'
WENDY (*with spirit*): 'No, indeed it isn't.'
PETER: 'Then what is it?'
WENDY: 'It isn't for a lady to tell.'
PETER (*badgered*): 'I suppose she means that she wants to be my mother.'
TINKERBELL (*flashing sparkles of coded light*): 'You silly ass.'

For a survivor, Peter was certainly naive. He didn't understand that he had a mother fixation, nor did he hear Wendy's frustration with his obsession. He missed the sexual signals coming from Tiger Lily, a co-inhabitant of Never Never Land, and never appreciated the common-sense reaction offered by his fairy companion, Tinkerbell.

Peter wanted girls to act as his mother. He was preoccupied with maternal acceptance and approval. His infantile dependency needs inhibited the development of mature relationships. Peter had a one-track mind, and if girls couldn't get on that track, he didn't want anything to do with them.

Wendy tries her best to meet Peter's needs. Although her disappointment is apparent, she continually tries to make Peter feel like a cherished son. But she isn't happy about it.

On one occasion, she pushes Peter into the role of father and husband. This upsets him and he quickly reverts to the role of son rather than lover. Wendy indulges his every whim.

Tinkerbell also wants to be Peter's girlfriend. However, you can tell from her caustic response to Peter's naivete that she won't tolerate magical nonsense coming from the one she loves. Although not human, Tinkerbell experiences a wide range of human emotions, including jealousy and caring. But Peter spurns her, time and again. He simply doesn't like her behaving like a woman rather than a surrogate mother.

Wendy's relationship with Peter is distant and properly controlled. She behaves as she knows Peter wants her to, and is quick to alter her thoughts and actions in keeping with Peter's demands, however juvenile. She cares for Peter, but expresses that care through indulgence and pampering. It confuses her, but she complies with Peter's demand that she not touch him.

Tinkerbell, on the other hand, is made out of vibrant, living stuff. Her reactions are more what you'd expect Wendy's to be. Yet Tink is more human than Wendy, even though she is nothing more than a quantum of light energy. She yearns for a spontaneous, growing, mutually enveloping relationship with Peter, an idea that he rejects without understanding it. The irony of an electrically charged spirit being capable of penetrating human emotions is intensified when we learn that Tinkerbell is allowed to touch Peter.

The story of Wendy and Tinkerbell vying for Peter's affection is a compelling and instructive sidebar to Peter's refusal to grow up. As destiny predicates, one of the girls must win. At story's end, we find that flesh-and-blood propriety triumphs over electrical reality. Peter maintains a highly structured, cold, and distant relationship with Wendy. She wins an ongoing affiliation with Peter, but the hope of a productive relationship dims as her maturity carries her away from Never Never Land. As for Tinkerbell, we learn the fate of that gutsy little ball of light in this cryptic yet instructive exchange:

WENDY: 'I haven't seen Tink this time.'
PETER: 'Who?'
WENDY: 'Oh dear! I suppose it is because you have so many adventures.'

What was it about Peter Pan to make two dissimilar women want him so badly? He doesn't sound as if he considered himself a ladies' man. He didn't have a very good job (you might say he was a military man with an overseas assignment). No one could accuse Peter of being a blueblood, given the fact that he fell out of his cradle and his mother simply ordered another son. And whatever his financial backing, living in a tree stump certainly doesn't indicate a firm grasp on the easy life.

Peter's dedication to eternal youth was both his boon and his bane. It created perpendicular reactions in Wendy and Tinkerbell. Wendy loved Peter for what he was—a little child who needed to be protected. Tinkerbell loved him for what she thought he could become—a young man with the spirit of youthful energy. The fact that Peter chose to stay with Wendy provides the insight into the last of the four cornerstones of the Peter Pan Syndrome, the sex role conflict.

SEX ROLE CONFLICT

If we could hear the 'voice' of the sex role conflict that exists inside the PPS victim's head, it might sound like this:

> There's an emptiness inside of me; a hollow spot in my soul. It haunts me and scares me, but I don't know its name. Sometimes, when I'm with my friends, I think it's gone. But it always comes back, quietly screaming, 'Watch out! Be careful! Something terrible is going to happen.' But nothing ever happens, except that I feel lonely.
>
> Whenever I feel this way, I just want to talk to my mom. When I hear her voice, I'm not afraid. I feel silly always needing my mom, but it frightens me to think about not talking to her.

The emptiness is worst when I'm around a girl. I want to touch her but I don't want to make a mistake when I do it. It bothers me to be afraid of girls. I almost wish I didn't have sex feelings. But I do.

Why is it so hard to talk to girls you like? Why do I get so nervous when a girl excites me? And most of all, why do I get mad at girls who turn me on?

Yeah, I get mad at the girls I like most. I envy them. They've got it knocked. They're free to be tough or sexy, passive or assertive, feminine or masculine. It's not fair that guys want girls more than girls want guys.

I can't talk about all this. My friends think I'm a 'real stud.' Boy, would they freak out if they knew what I'm really thinking. I'd like to be tender, to talk about my feelings, even to cry. But I'm not supposed to. Anyhow, if I tried that crap around my friends they'd just laugh at me and call me names. Then where would I be? I'll tell you—worse off than I am now!

The inner voice of conflict speaks of impotence. It's an impotence resulting from being pulled in opposite directions at the same time. The kid's sex drive pulls him toward exploration of new ways of relating to girls. His insecurity pulls him toward a childish retreat under Mommy's skirts. The sex role conflict handcuffs male children into a do-nothing pattern of behavior. They don't handle sexuality in a particularly positive or negative fashion. They just fail to handle it.

The sex role conflict signals a major decline in the maturation process of the PPS victim. He faces an immense hurdle in his coming of age and falls flat on his face. As reality beckons him to join others in the risky business of sexual exploration, the magic dust of Never Never Land narcotizes his biological urges. His sexual growth is arrested and his impotence masked by an intensification of pretense and false gaiety.

All youngsters have trouble finding out what it means to

be a sexual creature. It's a scary, albeit exciting adventure. However, the frequency and intensity of conflict have sky-rocketed in the past twenty or twenty-five years. While girls experience considerable turmoil, it is the boys who are immobilized by the damned-if-I-do, damned-if-I-don't conflict.

In the late fifties and early sixties, there were clear lines of demarcation that served to protect young people from immobilization as they experimented with their sex role identity. Kids had a clearly defined game plan to follow in discovering their sexuality.

I can look back to 1960 and remember the spirit of Peter Pan hanging around the drive-in looking for recruits for his legion. But even the guys who suffered rejection at home and loneliness on the streets had an equalizer. They could minimize Peter's influence by following the traditional rules for relating to girls: guys were macho; girls knew their place.

The socio-political events of the past two decades have changed the traditional rules. The girls have been given a new script; unfortunately, the boys are left with the old one. For those guys who are secure enough to take a risk, the new game is like riding a roller coaster: you never know when the next thrill is coming. But for those boys who are beset with anxiety and loneliness, the new rules only mean more threat of rejection.

To see how the Peter Pan Syndrome has become an even more threatening sexual affliction, let's compare the PPS victim of today with the one of twenty-five years ago.

Both can be cruel but are sensitive underneath. Both have role inflexibility and poor risk-taking ability. Both are afraid of rejection, especially from women. However, the modern-day victim has less self-confidence because he has experienced more laziness, permissiveness, and affluence.

The scripts may have changed, but the scene is the same—the teenage get-together. In fifties' language, it's a 'sock hop.' All the kids said they wanted to go to the sock hop to hear the music and to dance. Yet it was no secret that their real purpose was to learn how to deal with the opposite sex. Chaperones, usually in the form of teachers, were there to monitor the great discovery and to enforce the traditional rules of the game.

There they stood, boys on one side, girls on the other. The guys stood around bragging about what great lovers they were, not sure what the term meant. They had their hands in their pockets, their hearts on their sleeves, and their stomachs in their mouths. They acted tough and cool, pretending not to notice the girls. Peter was in their midst as they covered fear with jokes about the teacher and guffaws about the latest prank pulled by the class clown.

Meanwhile, the girls giggled up a storm. Each pretended she couldn't be bothered with the obviously immature young men on the other side of the room. Yet they couldn't resist whispering about which boy was the cutest, or who talked with whom on the phone. The brave ones made verbal wagers on which boys would dance with them first.

As the two groups milled around, they were careful not to get too close to each other. The ritual climaxed when the teacher pushed the boys to dance with the girls. The way the boys protested, you'd think they'd been told to commit suicide. Yet one brave soul would cross the imaginary line in the middle of the gym. His buddies held their breath. Soon two or three more would cross the line and the tension would be released. The magic dust of pretense was shed in favor of learning about the strange new powers that made boys and girls blush with excitement. Realizing that there were no recruits to be had, Peter flew away.

In this traditional scene, the boys were expected to be aggressive and the females to be dependent and compliant. The boy was expected to venture forth with reckless abandon and the girl was to protect both herself and the boy from going too far. As they met in the middle of the gym, both played out their respective roles successfully.

The PPS victim, suffering from loneliness and fear of rejection, could recover some self-confidence in this scene. His success gave him the chance to grow beyond his irresponsibility and inflexibility.

The sad part of this scene is that many of these guys and gals never outgrew the limitations of these sexual stereotypes. The boys felt comfortable in the chauvinistic role and the girls adjusted themselves to being second-class citizens. The girls thought of themselves as weak and defenseless, yet they had to be strong enough to endure the immaturities of a self-centered boyfriend.

Many of these kids married one another. They settled into a daily grind associated with the restricted roles of 'breadwinner' and 'housewife.' The excitement in their relationship never got much better than that experienced at the high school dance. Many of these sock hop enthusiasts are now parents of PPS victims.

The liberation movement, spearheaded by the sock hop rebels, has rewritten the script. And it's about time. The hard, cold line that ran across the gym floor may have helped kids safely explore their sexuality, but it locked them into a behavior pattern that took away their opportunity for spontaneous growth as human beings.

However, when we update the sock hop scene, I find that the new script contains just as many flaws as the old one. Let's take a look at the modern teen dance, now called simply a 'party,' and see how the new rules operate.

By all definitions, it's still a party. The setting has probably changed. The high school gym is too drab for today's teenagers; Mom and Dad's spacious suburban rec room offers a cozier setting. The chaperones—if present—walk on eggs because they are afraid of becoming unpopular because of setting limits on having fun.

There are no imaginary lines in the rec room. In fact, there is little if any organization to the party. For those kids who already have some degree of proficiency in social skills, the pandemonium is tolerable. They make their own ground rules. But for a majority of the kids there are no rules guiding sexual exploration. Many of them settle the butterflies in the stomach by drinking a beer or two before the party, or by smoking a marijuana joint early in the evening. The noise level blasts away any remnants of fear that did not succumb to drugs.

Most of the guys are standing around with their hands in

their pockets. The same old topics will be on the lips of those still sober enough to think straight. Those with some social skills will pair up with a girl as soon as possible. Many others will rely upon the old macho script to cover their fear of rejection. The PPS victims sooner or later (usually sooner) end up outside smoking more dope or guzzling more beer. The loners feel miserable and go home early.

The girls, on the other hand, are acting out their new role by being aggressive and noncompliant. Some attempt to outdo one another by telling crude jokes, identifying the sexiest hunk in the group, and bragging about what they might do with the guy when they get him alone. Many feel pressure to be a superwoman, always in control of her every thought and feeling. They often freeze inside, not knowing what to do.

The new script tells girls that they must never be submissive to a male, *even if they want to*. They are to be assertive to the point of aggression, indifferent to the point of sarcasm, and demanding to the point of insensitivity. Those who can't follow this script feel ostracized. Those who don't *want* to follow this script will probably stay home feeling that *they* are wrong.

One fifteen-year-old confided to me that she had had two beers and let her aggressions go. She walked up to a guy, put her hand on his crotch, and said, 'If you're man enough, let's go and get it on!' She admitted that she was trying to mimic the new role model that she thought would bring her acceptance.

Very few guys have the maturity or self-control to cope with this kind of assault. There's certainly no chaperone to tell them that it's perfectly okay to giggle, turn red, and run to the bathroom. As the girls cross the line into traditional masculine traits of assertion (the above vignette is certainly the exception, not the rule), most guys try their hand at the tough macho role and fail miserably.

You can see why the PPS victim, fearful of rejection and too sensitive to enact a successful macho role, will leave the party and team up with others like himself. They go off in a car and drink themselves silly, complaining about uppity women and faggy guys. Far be it from them to admit that they would like to share their fears. Instead, they get angry and stroke their wounded ego with 'rape talk.'

Why is this happening? What's going on inside the kids' heads to make the sex role conflict so devastating? My clinical research suggests that while girls are given a script that permits them to cross into traditional masculine territory, boys are not afforded a guideline for crossing into traditional feminine territory. Hence, it's perfectly okay for girls to become assertive and independent, but it's *not* okay for boys to be passive and dependent. This imbalance creates the sex role conflict in certain boys and makes them prime candidates for pledging allegiance to Peter Pan and his legion of lost boys.

Where are they learning this self-defeating script? My experience suggests that they are *not* learning it from their parents. In fact, their parents are providing them with no guidance for sexual exploration. In a state of ignorance, they turn to the modern-day chaperone for guidance: television.

Let's see what television is telling our kids to do when they are faced with sexual exploration.

The Girls' Script

Most of you will remember the television commercial that says it all.

A gorgeous and seductive woman slinks onto the screen exuding sexual competence and self-confidence. Any red-blooded young man will have to notice; so will any red-blooded young woman. The woman is singing a song and sending a message that is every bit as precise as that espoused by the dance chaperone of twenty-five years ago:

I can bring home the bacon, fry it up in a pan,
And never, never let you forget you're a man. . . .

Wow! The girls have to buy the product immediately. Then they too can send the message to all men. In effect, they say, 'I can get a job and make equal money for equal

109

work. Then I can assume the traditional role of housewife by making you dinner. To top that, I will aggressively seduce you and meet your every sexual need. I'm a total woman and I can do everything well.'

The Boys' Script

As the girls are plotting how to act out this superwoman role, the boys are trembling in their shoes, looking for a way to handle this competence. Within moments the number-one sitcom will give them one answer.

They will see a gentle guy who has feelings and isn't afraid to express them openly. Not bad, eh? But just as the boys are personalizing this script, a new dimension is added. The guy is a fool and a boob. He falls into things, sticks his foot in his mouth, and is treated like a child. If that's not bad enough, he's a liar. He supposedly lives with two girls and enjoys the opposite sex. But in order to assume this modern arrangement, he pretends to be a homosexual. The message: 'If you're going to be sensitive and gentle, you will act like a clown and others will see you as less than a man.' Any kid who wants to be a heterosexual will reject this role immediately.

But all hope is not lost. In the next hour, the boys will see a private detective who's handsome and always socially competent. He doesn't do anything that is foolish; his peers think he is the greatest thing that ever lived. When this hero wants a girl, he doesn't have to say a word. He lets his muscles, hair, and natural aura of strength talk for him.

This guy doesn't lose. No matter what the situation, he comes out on top. Not only that, but he doesn't let anybody see his problems. He never has to admit that he can't handle being afraid or lonely.

Some kids are confused. They realize that they have feelings and want to share them. Yet if they do, they run the risk of being seen as a fool with no backbone. However, if they follow the smooth-talking hero, there is no room for being weak.

As they are sorting out their confusion, they catch a short

glimpse of a sit-com that enjoys marginal success. They see an older guy, a fatherly type. He is gentle, expressive, loves to cook, care for children, and admit his weaknesses. He cries, gets frightened, and isn't afraid to feel. Ah-haa. Maybe this is the answer. Just as the boys are considering the benefits of this script, they find out that this guy is homosexual. They are terrified. 'Maybe this could be me,' they say to themselves.

If this select group of kids, many of whom are PPS victims, pursue this latter script, there's a good chance they will hear about or otherwise come in contact with the gay community. Homosexuality appears to offer them a solution to their internal turmoil. However, most homosexuals have just as much trouble with the sex role conflict as straights do (maybe more). They may have actualized the feminine side of their personality, but they are left with grave doubts about their *masculine* identity. In an attempt to cope with loneliness, they have simply switched the gender of their pretense, but still live in Never Never Land. (It's an interesting sidebar of this conflict to note that Peter Pan is usually played by a female in theatrical productions of the play.)

The sex role conflict incapacitates PPS victims. They are unable to enjoy the fluid, dynamic nature of a mature relationship. Their inflexibility frustrates experimentation and locks them into restrictive roles. Their fear of failure and rejection crushes their risk-taking ability, prohibiting them from investing their heart and soul in a relationship. In effect, they see themselves as incapable of loving. If they accept this falsehood, it can become their reality, leading them to a blinding narcissism. To cope with this falsehood, they are left with three alternatives: find a woman who will mother them and protect them from growing up; run away from the sexual conflict by pretending that gay life is not lonely; or seek help in confronting their loneliness and gaining control of their lives.

PEAK AGE: 17 TO 18

I have three reasons for selecting 17 to 18 as the period during which the sex role conflict peaks:

First, it is during these two years that a young man's sexuality matures to the point that sexual attitudes and preferences start to become ingrained. Whatever attitudes have developed tend to be resistant to change.

Second, the emergence of the sex role conflict is dependent upon the inflexibility that results from coping with loneliness at this age. The rigidity creates a tunnel vision within the young man, making him unable to experiment with different ways of relating to the opposite sex. As a result, the sexual attitudes that develop are often devoid of warmth and limited to the pursuit of biological satisfaction.

Third, it is at this age that the emergence of the sex role conflict opens the door to a labyrinth of other conflicts. They may not surface for several years, but once the victim reaches the stage where confusion regarding his sex role crystallizes, other conflicts take shape. The constraints of socially acceptable behavior are dimmed in favor of a lifestyle in which one extreme act follows another. Whether the PPS victim is your eighteen-year-old son or your forty-year-old husband, the extremes to which he goes may have you wondering, Who is this guy? What is he thinking about?

WHAT IS HE THINKING ABOUT?

Peter chose to stay with Wendy because she protected him from his inner conflicts. She indulged his every whim and pitied him for his emotional weakness. Although she expressed moderate disappointment in his immaturity, she cautiously avoided confronting him about his mercurial sense of loyalty. In response, he exhibited a dual personality. He bounced back and forth between a real world where he experienced rejection and despair and a fantasy world where he pretended he could be a carefree child forever.

Wendy, Tinkerbell, or any other woman who tries to love

or understand one of the lost boys will recognize the Jekyll/Hyde duality in the PPS victim. There are moments when you bask in the gentleness of a warm and caring person, only to be clobbered by cold indifference an hour or two later. There are many areas of his life in which the PPS victim feels one way on the inside but acts another on the outside. The extremes of thought, word, and deed suggest a split personality. Yet you know the guy isn't crazy. You're right. He hasn't lost touch with reality; he knows that he feels rotten. He just isn't strong enough to stop it.

The contradictory behavior patterns that get their start with the sex role conflict of late adolescence can surface in varying sequences. They can even lie dormant until the victim has settled into a routine of job, marriage, and children. Likewise, it's rare that you will observe all the possible conflicts over a short period of time. Whatever the sequence or frequency, the conflicts represent a blessing in disguise. On the surface they confound and confuse, prohibiting a loved one from making sense out of extremes in behavior or mood. But if you take one step back and see what the two extremes have in common, you can answer the question, What is he thinking about?

Hopeful vs. Depressive

There's a cyclic nature to the PPS victim's outlook on life. He vacillates between a manic excitement about the arrival of spring and a depressive despondency that seems to ruin much of his Christmas holidays. Sometimes this cycle is so pronounced that you are concerned about his potential for suicide.

You're apt to say to yourself or a close friend, 'I'm so worried about him. One day he can be so up about life, and then he turns around and sees nothing to live for.'

You've described the seed of doubt that lies deep within this bright, sensitive man. In short, it's the existential question that plagues us all: 'Why am I here?'

When the PPS victim sees a reason for his being, his excitement is infectious. When life holds no purpose, his

113

depression is funereal. As someone who loves him, you feel like a Yo-Yo. One day you're up, the next day you're down. You long for stability.

The victim's lack of tranquillity is tied to the storm in his soul. He doesn't feel authentic just because he is alive. He feels that he must daily prove himself to be a good and *worthy* of being alive. When people like him (espe his mommy), he feels good about himself and feels ho even mania. When he faces failure or disapproval, falsely concludes that he is *not* good and *not* worthy of being alive. That's when he's consumed by depression.

His lack of feelings of authenticity should help you understand why he surrounds himself with buddies, pushes himself to ridiculous extremes to be liked, takes the woman in his life for granted, rejects negative feelings about others, and flies into a rage when faced with criticism. Worst of all, he's never free just to be himself. The pretense and false gaiety of Never Never Land provide his only respite.

Devotion vs. Despisal

In their early years, PPS victims have an undying respect for the females in their lives. Extending kindness, demonstrating gracious manners, and offering a helping hand are common practices flowing from this respect. This respect endears victims to neighbors, teachers, clergy, and parents. Retrospectively, one might argue that this respect is insincere and manipulative. It is not. It is deeply felt and honestly expressed.

As conflicts begin to sap the victim's ego, the fear of rejection deepens and this respect is adulterated by excessive devotion. The resultant idolatry traps the victim into feelings of servitude. Anger is inevitable; so is rebellion. To shed himself of this contrived subservience to females, the victim adopts an attitude of despisal toward the opposite sex, blaming them for his feelings of powerlessness. The despisal is as convoluted and distorted in one extreme as the devotion was in the other.

Men caught up in this conflict will exhibit exaggerated

respect when face to face with women, yet heap criticism and derision upon all females when talking with their buddies. This braggadocio will often include their superhuman ability to put women in their place. When fear and anger speak as one, this boastful ego-stroking will have strong overtones of sexual dominance through physical force—what I call 'rape talk.'

You may suspect that your man vacillates between devotion and despisal. Chances are that you will never hear the 'rape talk,' since in most cases it's said only in front of other men. You can, however, detect the paradoxical nature of the respect this man shows to women. My favorite example is the guy who has a mouth like a sewer yet is deeply offended if any vulgarities are expressed in front of a lady. He puts a woman on a pedestal, only to turn around and make fun of her when she's not there.

Gregarious vs. Lonely

The PPS victim loves people; at least he acts as if he does. He surrounds himself with countless 'friends' and is miffed if he thinks he's missed any fun. He'll remain at a party, overstaying his welcome, just so that he doesn't miss a laugh. You've sat there on the other side of the room thinking, 'I don't see anything funny in that. Why is he laughing so loud?'

The answer is that through his uproarious laughter, he is attempting to drown out the voices of loneliness. For all his gregariousness, friends, and addiction to parties, the PPS victim feels very lonely, even in a crowd.

There is a substantial psychological distance between the victim and other people. Even if he is rubbing elbows with a buddy, he feels a million miles away. In most cases he becomes accustomed to this estrangement and sees it as normal.

The loneliness-in-a-crowd attribute makes a lover or wife feel sorry for the victim. One woman asked herself aloud, 'Why is he trying so hard? Why can't he just relax? Doesn't he know that other people will like him just the way he is?'

The answer to this last question is no.

Sensitivity vs. Aloofness

PPS victims start out as exceptionally empathic and sensitive children. Their mothers nurture in them a sense of emotional validity that permits them to feel comfortable in expressing their feelings openly. However, given the lack of self-discipline that accompanies laziness and irresponsibility, the kids are unable to learn how to control their emotions. They do not know the basics of protecting themselves from life's inevitable disappointments. As a result, their feelings get hurt easily.

Shortly after puberty, they face peer rejection and their inability to handle it. They begin to withdraw. They don't know how to protect themselves from the hurt, so they resort to avoidance of feelings. Hence, whenever they feel most vulnerable, they are apt to retreat to aloofness and indifference. This helps explain why the PPS victim adopts an 'I don't care' attitude just about the time he begins to feel sad or remorseful about something. In later years, this aloofness takes the form of the victim protesting that he is above silly emotionalism.

Kindness vs. Cruelty

This is probably the most painful conflict for a loved one to handle. The PPS victim may leave you in the morning with a warm kiss or hug of kindness only to hit you with cruel sneers in the evening. He expects that his lover, his wife, or possibly his mother will endure his immaturities and nastiness because *that's her job!* Your destiny is to put up with his cruelty, excuse his insults, and love him no matter what he does. He never understands your rebellion or expects to apologize. He believes, 'You'll always love me no matter what I do.'

The PPS victim takes his wife or lover for granted. He equates a mate's love with a mother's love. Adult love is distorted to the point that a wife or lover is never supposed to expect more of the victim than what he chooses to give at the time he chooses to give it. He doesn't understand that adult love is conditional—it involves give and take. Rather, he is the taker and his wife or his lover is the giver. If a woman challenges this inequity, she is seen as a bitch who doesn't know how good she has it.

Needless to say, if this conflict remains unresolved, there is no hope for the development of a mature, loving relationship.

Victim vs. Rescuer

The PPS victim knows a thousand ways to feel sorry for himself. He mumbles when confronted about his cruelty, turns to ice when encountering an angry wife, and sucks his psychological thumb when his overbearing mother tries to run his life. If he had lived in Old Testament days, he might have been first in line to make a sacrifice of his own self-esteem to appease the gods.

Yet this same willing martyr takes it upon himself to save you from the world. He has secret ideas about how you're supposed to behave, and he'll run out to do a good deed for others while you don't even know where he is or what he's doing. He seems to rescue everybody else but just stands motionless when you need help.

To understand this conflict you must remember that Peter Pan refused to see females as anything but mother figures (reread the dialogue at the beginning of this chapter). Once you realize that the PPS victim sees you as a projection of some ideal mommy, you can imagine how he reacts when he hears that mommy needs his help.

First of all, he doesn't understand how a perfect mommy can be improved upon. He makes you as perfect as he wants you to be and is dumfounded when you don't conform.

Second, he is afraid to offer help to you because, with his low self-esteem, he is sure he will make a mistake. His biggest mistake is not even trying to help. The easiest way for him to cope is to withdraw from the situation or deny (sometimes vehemently) that you have any shortcomings.

If you understand these two reactions, then I expect you will protest, 'But I don't want to be his mommy!' Fine. But be sure to consult Chapter 13 to make certain you aren't *acting* like his mommy.

Faithful vs. Flirtatious

You think you know him, but you don't know him at all. Does this sound familiar? When it comes to your man's fidelity, it should. You believe him when he says that he's always faithful, yet at parties or neighborhood gatherings he does little to hide his flirtatiousness. He gets so carried away with trying to impress other women that he ends up looking like a fool.

The PPS victim will tell his girlfriend, his lover, or his wife that she is the center of his world. And, in a distorted sort of way, he means it. Yet he has a roving eye for other women that is more than just a passing fancy. He seems drawn to making overtures, however immature, to women who are nothing more than casual acquaintances. And he's not very discreet about his flirting. It's not unusual for the PPS victim to want to tell you about his sexual desires for other women as if he had little or no awareness of your jealousy. He wants to share it with you as if you were his big sister (or, not so surprisingly, his mother).

To understand this flirtatious attitude you must comprehend the victim's narcissism. He is so desperate for recognition that he distorts reality by concluding that he clearly outranks all other men in desirability, and to deprive other women of the greatest man in the world is to run the risk of hurting them. I know this sounds unbelievable, but it's quite often true. The next chapter will give you ample opportunity to understand the complexity of this narcissistic fantasy.

8 Narcissism

PETER: 'Wendy, don't withdraw. I can't help crowing, Wendy, when I'm pleased with myself.'

WENDY (to Peter): 'It is so queer that the stories you like best should be the ones about yourself.'

Imagine yourself walking into a room filled with mirrors. Every place you look, you see your reflection. At first you can't help smiling, pleased with endless visages of yourself. You make some funny faces, if for no other reason than to see how much versatility you bring to the world.

Being quite alone, you forgo embarrassment and say to yourself, 'Am I cute?' 'Does my nose look too big?' 'Is my body sticking out where it shouldn't?' These mildly self-critical questions seem natural and harmless. You can't resist the temptation to find out how other people see you. You want others to like you; it makes life easier and more enjoyable.

After a few minutes in the room, you become uneasy. The mirrors turn on you. They pick on you. No, you're not cute. Yes, your nose is too big. Ha! Your body sticks out everywhere it shouldn't. After a while the tiniest wrinkle in your face looks like something out of a monster movie. There is an entity in the room and it is attacking you.

The mirrors appear to have taken on a personality all their own—a hostile personality. You find yourself talking back to it, defending your integrity. You are too busy answering the criticisms to realize that this personality is just another dimension of yourself. The mirrors become a focal

119

point around which your insecurities gather. The more accustomed you are to lying to yourself about your weaknesses, the more hostile and unrelenting the mirrors become.

After several minutes of doing battle with your insecurities, the flaws in your character become as clear as the flaws in your body. Your poor self-assertion is just as noticeable as your flabby thighs. Your sexual hang-ups are as pronounced as the unsightly crow's feet around your eyes. You think back to your last social encounter, convinced that the other people saw what you now see. You are terribly self-conscious about your transparency.

Can you imagine what would happen if you were trapped in that mirrored room for days, weeks, or even years? First, you would shut your eyes, cutting off the vision of your faults, which now have become grotesque. You would try to block out the world in which every one of your faults is magnified a thousand times. With your eyelids pushed tightly together you would burst into song in an attempt to drown out the voices of disapproval and reaffirm your presence.

Eventually your denial falters. You are battered and bruised and must find a way to cope with the hostile personality. You yearn for a friend, someone to tell you that you are okay, despite all your faults. But there's no one. There's only one thing left for you to do. You must defend yourself.

You open your eyes. But this time, instead of waiting for the hostile personality to attack, you attack first. You use the material in your memory to construct fantasies that contradict the indictments you have endured. You take charge of the battle by projecting these fantasies onto the mirror. It's like sitting in a theater, forced to view a bad movie. You use your brain to edit the movie to your satisfaction and then project the more acceptable version onto the screen.

You overwhelm your insecurities. You now have the best possible nose. Your cuteness is staggering. Your body is better than any 8-by-10 glossy you've ever imagined. You feel renewed by the fact that you don't need anybody to make you feel better. All you need to guide your fanciful projections and thereby guard against any future hostile attacks is perfection. Everything that come out of your mind's eye and is projected onto the mirrors must be perfect. There's only one problem. When the doors are open, you can't leave the mirrored room. You are a prisoner of perfection.

THE PURSUIT OF PERFECTION

Peter wanted to hear stories about himself to reinforce his projections of perfection. He ignored the fact that Wendy helped him with a problem, because he was so delighted with himself. Peter pursued perfection with undaunted zeal. But he *had* to. His only alternative was to confront his massive insecurities. His narcissism protected him from loneliness and fear. He wouldn't let go of it.

The victim of the Peter Pan Syndrome is obsessed with the pursuit of perfection. The greater his insecurities, the more vivid the critical reflections and the stronger the need to project perfection. The attack of the projected insecurities is exacerbated by the absence of close friends and confidants. Years of anxiety and loneliness have cut him off from seeking refuge in people who really care about him. He sacrifices love for the safety of perfection.

The victim pursues perfection with a compulsive fervor. But, because he is woefully inept in many survival skills, he is unable to achieve perfection in any socially acceptable manner. He compensates for his gross imperfections by remaining in his mirrored room, seeing what he wants to. A pattern of narcissistic traits unfolds. The traits form interconnecting hallways in the mirrored room, each starting out as a defense against imperfection and leading the victim around reality and back to where he feels most comfortable—surrounded by images of perfection.

Here are the predominant traits of narcissism as they are manifested in the victim of the Peter Pan Syndrome:

Exploitation. The PPS victim will readily exploit friends and acquaintances in order to promote his perfection. He will even shift values in order to enhance himself. To the mother of a desired girl he will make a convincing argument for premarital celibacy. An hour later he will bewitch the girl with his theory that the young should rebel against the oppressive sexual mores of parents. The PPS victim has few if any feelings of loyalty.

Rage. When the victim is unable to make reality disappear, the supremacy of his perfection is threatened. That's when his sweet disposition can turn into rage in an instant. If exploitation fails, he will call upon rage to intimidate whoever is pushing reality upon him. The rage is so acute and sudden that one feels assaulted. It's like having someone shoot emotional bullets at you. Most people back off, letting the victim have his way. Bullies and other narcissistic individuals do not. This is why PPS victims sometimes get into fights. They usually lose but you'll never hear them admit it.

Rage keeps people away from the victim's fragile self-esteem. Unfortunately, it also keeps love, concern, and warmth away. Rage is the wall that keeps the PPS victim isolated from close contact with others.

Blamelessness. The PPS victim is never to blame. No matter how disruptive his behavior or malignant his intentions, he can always point the finger of responsibility at something or somebody over which he had no control. He is late getting home because he had to take several friends home. He is caught with marijuana because he was holding it for a friend. He left the house in a mess because he was trying to see about a job (which he didn't get). His girlfriend dumped him because someone told her a lie about him. To admit blame would be to admit imperfection—something he simply must not do.

Recklessness. Because he doesn't take responsibility for his own actions, the PPS victim has a remarkable ability to be associated with accidents. Broken household items, lost books, stalled cars, and forgotten appointments follow him around like a dark cloud hanging over his head. What's even more frustrating is that the victim doesn't learn from one mistake. He keeps repeating the same ones. Because he won't permit mistakes to be his fault, it never dawns on him that he could do something to avoid his recklessness.

Drug abuse. The PPS victim is usually associated with drug abuse. Despite his pursuit of perfection, he is plagued with a nagging sense of worthlessness. This stimulates the need for relief. Since so many of his friends are engaged in drug abuse, it is easy for the victim to capitalize on the expanded consciousness that is typically associated with drug use. Excessive consumption of beer and marijuana becomes a regular habit. In more severe cases, cocaine becomes the one-way ticket to inviolate feelings of perfection.

Sexual promiscuity. Nothing feeds the fragile ego of the PPS victim like the oohs and aahs of girls whom he has sexually seduced. The more girls he can add to his sexual scorecard, the more perfect he becomes. As he is with other people, the victim is most comfortable if the girl remains emotionally distant. He is not disappointed if the girl feigns excitement and satisfaction; in fact, his exploitative attitude usually prohibits him from hearing the pretense.

CRACKS IN THE MIRRORS

I've tried to give you a *textbook* definition of narcissism. Mental health professionals rarely see this classic case. They just don't occur that often. A person who suffers from the degree of narcissism I've just outlined is in bad shape; there is little hope for such a severe case.

PPS victims experience a narcissism that is much less lethal. The traits don't fit together into such a destructive whole. The victims may be reckless, but they secretly blame themselves for many of their failures. They may flash into a rage, but their sense of propriety moves them to apologize. They may exploit others, but they do have a close friend or two. They are occasionally struck with the fact that their thinking is magical and they are not nearly as perfect as they pretend. And those who are sexually active usually encounter a woman who truly loves them. The warmth touches their heart and can often be the stimulus needed to

123

help them risk their imperfections and walk out of their mirrored prison.

Thus, in order to better understand how narcissism fits into the developmental picture of the Peter Pan Syndrome, you must imagine that the mirrors in the room in which the PPS victim is trapped are cracked. Reality seeps through, giving him a better than even chance to escape.

PEAK AGE: 19 TO 20

As you already realize, the symptoms that comprise the PPS do not start at preselected age periods, as if cued by some biological or psychological clock. They are mixed together, each feeding off the others. Narcissism is one of two intermediate symptoms (chauvinism being the other) that are an outgrowth of the interaction of more fundamental problems (see the diagram on page 44). Although the seeds of narcissism are sown early, they take time to grow. Since narcissism is so dependent upon other factors, there is much hope that its growth can be frustrated.

The seeds of narcissism take life when the demanding two-year-old always gets his way. If parents submit to the terrible twos, their indulgent posture denies the child his need to learn about his imperfections in a safe and secure environment. If the child reaches puberty with the promote-myself-at-any-cost attitude and the four cornerstones of the PPS—irresponsibility, anxiety, loneliness, and sex role conflict—continue to function, narcissism will eventually flower.

If the growing conditions remain unchallenged or unchanged, narcissism will reach its peak at age 19 to 20. This is the time when the transition from adolescence to adulthood causes the young man to be keenly aware of his imperfections. If he takes control of his life, accepts his limitations, and learns from his mistakes, he will overcome the Peter Pan Syndrome and get on with the business of growing up. If he denies his limitations and pursues perfection, he takes a giant step toward living his life in a prison, barred from reality by his own insecurities.

TWO NARCISSISTS

Narcissism is not a harmless flirtation with magic dust. In the Peter Pan Syndrome it represents a dangerous diversion from reality. Rational thought, reasonable judgment, and common sense take a back seat to illogical and even bizarre thought processes.

The PPS victim uses his intelligence to devise a system of thoughts and opinions that are impervious to criticism. No matter what background, training, or credentials, you cannot successfully argue a point with such a narcissist. He operates with prejudicial premises that you'll never understand. And if you do uncover and challenge his first premise, he will simply change it in mid-thought. If you catch him in this sleight-of-hand maneuver, he will subdue you with the imminent threat of rage.

Here are stories of three PPS victims who were engaged in the pursuit of perfection. The emotional panic and role inflexibility explained in previous chapters were covered with a narcissism that was characterized by one central distorted thought. However hopeless these young men may appear, it is heartening to remember that there were cracks in their mirrors. Otherwise, they never would have been sitting in my office.

Denny

'The Lord is my shepherd.'

Even if you are a deeply religious person, you must admit that the opening line from the Twenty-third Psalm is a bizarre response to the question 'What brings you to see me today?'

I really didn't expect such an off-the-wall response from this particular young man. I knew his parents; they were good people and had done their best with three sons. The young fellow sitting across from me, refusing to relax even though he was half buried in my overstuffed chair, was the oldest of the three. His name was Denny.

Denny was a tall, good-looking young man with dark, curly hair, generous mannerisms, and a smile that said, 'I like you.' He was nineteen and soon to be a college sophomore in a major state university, where he had already received rave reviews for his dramatic talent. His parents reported that he had had a difficult adjustment to college but had made average grades, and he was reportedly looking forward to returning.

So why the biblical quote in response to a standard question? It had an ominous ring to it. It was both defensive and hostile; that is, unless he was insane, which I knew he wasn't. I tentatively concluded that he was frightened and angry and, in effect, telling me that he wasn't going to communicate with me.

I ignored the opening comment, figuring it wouldn't lead me anywhere anyway. I proceeded to try to gather information.

Denny had come to see me because his mom thought it might help.

'Why might it help?' He didn't know. Probably had something to do with the changes he had made in the past year.

'What changes?' He had found God and the saving grace of Jesus Christ, but his parents would never understand.

What did he mean, 'found'? This question created an instant of hate, but he used his plastic grin to give me that you-poor-misguided-soul look as he quickly suppressed his emotions. He couldn't resist pontificating about his newly discovered transcendental awareness. He put bits and pieces of the theology and remote concepts of metaphysics and epistemology together in a container labeled spiritual tranquillity—a cerebral tossed salad that made absolutely no sense.

I stopped him after about five minutes of his disjointed ramblings to bring us back to some semblance of constructive dialogue.

When had he found Jesus? Sometime during the middle

of his freshman year. Again he began to ramble. I interrupted him immediately.

Why did he suppose that God selected that particular time to imbue him with the Holy Spirit? He didn't know, but he had many speculations about how God had finally made him aware that what we take for reality isn't truly real. True reality is represented by an afterlife in Heaven or Hell.

'Hold on,' I said. 'This isn't the real world?' 'Absolutely not,' he replied. 'What we humans are at this point in time is a mirage. This is a testing ground for God and the devil to evaluate us and see who wants whom in the next life.'

'Sounds like God is getting in on the lottery,' I said.

He didn't conceal his anger this time. 'You're like all the rest. Tempters of the faith. You try to confuse the believers, drowning us in your decadence and fleshly evils. Well, you'll never touch my soul. It's tough to tell God from Satan, but I know, I know in my heart who is who.'

He continued to juxtapose one confounded theological thought with another. His verbalizations made no sense. But his nonverbal communication made a lot of sense. As he pounded me with cognitive nonsense, he kept rubbing his face in a circular pattern, round and round, never covering his eyes or nose. Just round and round the rest of his face.

'Why are you rubbing your face?' 'Just a silly habit,' was the answer.

I wouldn't back down. 'What are you hiding from? It looks as if you don't like the face that God gave you in this unreal world?' *Bingo!*

'Would *you?* Would *you* like it? It has bumps all over it. It's ugly!' Tears glazed his eyes. 'People can't possibly realize how ugly it is. But I know. I know how ugly it is.'

'What people?' 'Oh, just people. You know—people.'

'No, I don't know what people. But I can guess. You mean girls, don't you?'

An instant blush. 'Yeah, maybe.'

Did he like girls? More blush. 'Yeah.'

Seeing the cracks in his defenses, I pushed the questioning, focusing on girls. It wasn't long before he trusted me enough to let his pain pour out.

He loved girls and desired sexual gratification but was afraid of rejection. His enriched fantasies and his fear of socializing resulted in what he considered excessive masturbation (an average of twice daily). He had tried to have sexual intercourse with one girl but had had a premature ejaculation before entering her. He condemned himself for trying but simultaneously condemned himself for failing. In fact, he condemned himself for almost everything he did.

He condemned himself for being in college without knowing why, for not studying, for wasting his parents' money, for smoking marijuana, and for being a virgin. To cope with his massive feelings of guilt, he hid inside the mirrored room of narcissism. But the more he looked in the mirrors, the more ugly his visage became. His facial features embodied the ugliness of his soul. Spouting cultist incantations was the charm he used in seeking salvation from relentless self-condemnation.

Denny and I worked through this complicated maze of psychological explanations, putting as much of it into perspective as time would allow. When he left for college, he understood that the fear of rejection was preventing self-understanding and future growth. His goals included accepting the fact that masturbation and virginity were not abnormal, improving his study habits, and asking girls for dates without pushing himself toward sexual intercourse. As we discussed these things, his preoccupation with sin decreased, as did his metaphysical mumbo-jumbo.

When I last heard from Denny he was delighted with his life. He was about to graduate with honors and to work for a master's degree before striking out to seek his fame and fortune. It sounded as if he had ventured outside his oppressive narcissism and at last found his place in the real world.

Jerry

'What's a nice kid like you doing with a record like this?'

Theft, shoplifting, larceny, criminal trespass of property, stealing, and assorted disorderly conduct charges. And that's just the stuff Jerry got arrested for. Heaven knows what else he'd done.

How was this nineteen-year-old dedicated thief a narcissist and a PPS victim? That took a while to find out. Why was he even bothering to talk to a shrink? The answer was simple: his mother had told him to. He still did what his mother told him to; reluctantly, but he did it. After all, she was his ticket out of trouble. She had bailed him out of jail and other kinds of trouble more often than he could remember. The least he could do for her was talk to some guy. He wasn't worried. He wasn't about to tell him anything.

Jerry had been to a lot of shrinks. Psychiatrists, psychologists, social workers, high school counselors, ministers, and an endless number of juvenile workers. He knew all the lingo and was more adept at psychobabble than most people twice his age. But I don't think he was ready for me. I tentatively labeled him a victim of the Peter Pan Syndrome as soon as I sensed his narcissism. With this diagnosis I was a step ahead of him. Forewarned is forearmed, so to speak.

To understand Jerry's narcissism you have to recall the last time you saw a two-year-old child play hide-and-seek. The seeker counts to ten and the diminutive hider runs behind the couch. It takes just a moment to hear the giggle, and a quick glance at his feet sticking out from behind the couch pinpoints his location.

The child is dismayed to be discovered so quickly. He might even accuse you of cheating. 'No fair, you peeked!'

To understand the child's distress is to grasp the nature of Jerry's narcissism. *Because the child couldn't see you, he figured you couldn't see him.* What his eyes saw—the back of the couch—is what he believed you saw—only the couch. It never entered his little mind that there was more to him than met *his* eyes. And in his excitement he didn't hear himself giggle, so he had no reason to expect that you heard any clues to his whereabouts. Thus, his only conclusion is that you cheated by peeking.

I gleaned this interpretation from Jerry's rote review of his history of arrests; he had been caught more often than one would have expected. Also instrumental to my conclusion was the fact that the only real emotion Jerry showed was his anger at getting caught. 'The cops just like to hassle me,' was his explanation for his arrest record.

Jerry did his best to dazzle me with his insights and baffle me with his bull. But I wouldn't play the game.

When he said, 'I need to get a job and pay my mom back for all her trouble,' I simply agreed. When he professed that I was the greatest counselor he had ever talked to (after fifteen minutes), I quietly doubted it. When he got nervous because I wasn't responding the way a shrink was supposed to, I pointed out that he was obviously edgy; that made him even more nervous. When he got mad at me and said I wasn't helping him, I replied, 'Of course I'm not. You don't want help; you're just here because you don't want Mommy to get angry at you.'

Now he did get angry. And in his anger he told me the truth. 'You think I'm just lazy, don't you?' No reaction. 'You think I like to rip people off, huh?' Silence. 'You think I'm just looking for the easy way out, right?' Still nothing. 'Well, why don't you say something? You don't seem like much of a doctor to me.'

Finally I confronted him. 'I'm not a doctor to you. You're just trying to set me up to rip me off as you do everybody else. And I simply won't let you do it. You just told me that you're looking for the easy way out. That simply won't work here.'

He leaned back in the chair, took a deep breath, and, believe it or not, relaxed. 'How did you get so smart in such a short time?'

'You don't give up easily, do you? Now you're playing "Let's tell the doctor how great he is." Is that the only thing you can do—play games?'

'That's all I've ever done. I should be good at it.'

His candidness was also childlike, and refreshing as well. 'Does it really feel that good?' I asked. 'Being able to fool everyone with ghosts and gimmicks?'

'It gets me by until something better comes along.'

'When will that be?'

'When I see something I like better than what I've got.'

I couldn't resist the temptation. Since I didn't think Jerry would make another appointment, I took the risk of telling him what I thought he was hiding from and what he could do to make something better come along. I told him about the life I suspected he lived as a victim of the Peter Pan Syndrome.

I didn't pull any punches. He had come out from behind the couch and I gave him my best shot before he ran and hid somewhere else.

'You're the oldest son and your parents are still married to one another. You tested out to be of above-average intelligence but school was a bore. You really love the girls but you're still a virgin, a fact you're very embarrassed about. You can't hold a job and you'd rather party and drink beer than breathe. You've never been close to your father and you can't stand your mother, but you're scared to death to tell her. You think you have a lot of buddies, but you really know better. You don't have one friend and you spend hours avoiding feelings of loneliness. The only thing you have left to be proud of is your ability to steal; but you're not even good at that. You hide from this whole mess by pretending you don't care. You wish you could be cold and calculating, but you're not. You're a lost little boy wanting somebody to love him.'

He just sat there. I thought perhaps I had been too hard on him. Before I had a chance to feel sorry for him, he blew a sigh of relief. 'Gosh, it feels good to have somebody know the real me. How did you figure all that stuff out?'

I avoided any possible trap by hanging back. 'That's not important. Only the truth is important. With the truth, you can begin to build something better for yourself.'

'Will you help me?' This question sounded legitimate.

'Yes, but only if you demonstrate that you're serious about finding something better.'

'Where do I start?'

'By coming back next week.'

Jerry came back the next week, and the week after that. We discussed his lack of communication skills, as well as his

131

need for help writing a resumé, keeping a job, and saving money. Throughout our talks I kept reminding him that he would have to prove his desire for change by actually *changing*. He agreed.

Jerry quit coming after his fourth visit. He found a job and used that as an excuse for not making any more appointments. I haven't heard from him for some time. His mother and father haven't called, so I assume that at least he hasn't gotten into any trouble recently.

I wish I could say that he has absolutely escaped from Never Never Land. But after years of battling the Peter Pan Syndrome, I'll have to see it to believe it.

9 Chauvinism

PETER: 'Wendy, one girl is worth more than twenty boys.'

PETER: 'No, you must not touch [Wendy]; it wouldn't be
sufficiently respectful.'

WENDY'S MOTHER: 'But, Peter, I shall let [Wendy] go to you
once a year for a week to do your spring cleaning.'

Put her on a pedestal. Deify her humanity; worship her
divinity. But make sure she cleans your house and fixes
your meals. She has a twenty-fold value over men and
there's no way to touch her and respect her at the same
time. However, her life begins and ends with a clean toilet
bowl and non-sticky rice.

This double-dealing nonsense went out with the
women's liberation movement, right? Wrong! Chauvinism
is alive and well. The evidence abounds in our daily life.
The mass media reflect sexist social roles. Unequal pay for
equal work persists. You can hear chauvinistic attitudes
bouncing off the walls in bars, sports clubs, or wherever
three or four men gather to pretend that they don't have
feelings, weaknesses, or doubts about their egos.

I meet chauvinistic attitudes in my office all the time.
They undermine healthy family interaction. They prohibit
growth in a marriage. Worst of all, they set a bad example
for children. And the children do follow the example, especially male children; most especially, male children who are
looking for a way to avoid growing up.

The PPS victim exhibits a variation of the typical chauvinistic theme. It's usually more subtle and sneaky. You don't

always know it's present until you feel its negative effects. I remember one young man who spoke of having a warm, caring, and sharing relationship with his girlfriend. He tried to convince me that he reveled in the tenderness and rationality of equality between the sexes. Being skeptical, I asked him to explain what he meant by human equality. He told me of the wonderful times that he and his woman friend enjoyed together. She cared for him, understood him, and supported him. Conspicuous was the absence of his reciprocation. He had obviously gotten carried away with his own narcissism when he said, 'She doesn't have to tell me what she wants, I always know. Then I give it to her.'

The PPS chauvinism is, in some ways, more lethal than the standard, blatant variety. The braggart doesn't hide the fact that he believes in two sets of rules—one for men, another for women. I have little sympathy for a woman who gets involved with this kind of chauvinist. It's her own fault. He is honest about his sexist attitudes, giving any woman plenty of warning to stay away. Any woman who 'loves' the braggart obviously doesn't have enough pride in herself to demand more from a relationship than being treated like a second-class citizen.

The PPS victim, on the other hand, is a master at deception. He might even say that he believes in an egalitarian relationship between men and women. Worse yet, he might even believe it at that moment. At the outset of a relationship, he might even practice it, by cooking dinner for her, helping her clean up, and running errands for her. In the excitement of new love, many women misread these acts of kindness as evidence of a non-sexist attitude. The real test comes when the woman has a problem or is emotionally upset. That's when the PPS chauvinist reveals his true colors.

If you are involved in a close relationship with a PPS victim, watch for these signs of his chauvinism (obviously, they occur in varying degrees). If you have a problem, he immediately takes it on his shoulders as *his* problem and tells you how to handle it; or, he simply handles it for you.

One example might be at a party when another guy flirts with you. Your PPS victim will 'take *your* problem away from you' and tell the guy to leave you alone. In short, the PPS victim finds it almost impossible to leave his girlfriend/wife alone and help her solve *her* problem herself.

Another indicator of PPS chauvinism occurs when you are emotionally upset. This will create unpredictable, even obtuse reactions in your mate. He will become upset at you for being 'too emotional' and, dismissing your concern as silly, demand that you stop it immediately. Many women suppress their emotions until the guy has left, just to keep peace with him.

Chauvinism is a key ingredient in the PPS victim's 'maturity' for a number of reasons.

It closes the gap between him and his father. He follows in his father's footsteps and feels that now his father will love him. He sees himself as a man's man and believes that Daddy will eventually praise him for it.

It explains away his anger and guilt toward his mother. His chauvinism dismisses Mom's complaining as an unfortunate but natural inclination of women.

Chauvinism answers the nagging self-doubts associated with the man's sexuality. He decides that his sexual inadequacies are actually the girl's fault. *She* has the sexual hang-ups, not him. He concludes that the problem is that women take advantage of his generosity and kindness. This, in turn, increases his callousness.

It cements his relationships with other men as it defines his masculinity. It also gives him the chance to find steady work in a 'man's world' where his problems with women are shared by his boss and co-workers.

Finally, and maybe most important, chauvinism is the PPS victim's way of pretending that he is a grown-up. It gives an overall consistency to his life of pretense and denial. Hand in hand, narcissism and chauvinism give him a self-serving attitude that is rooted in self-deception. His prejudices become wisdom; his rigidity, understanding; and his callousness, worldliness.

It's amazing how a soft, sensitive kid can turn into such a

social monster. In fact, the more sensitive he was as a child, the more entrenched the chauvinism is in the man. This really shouldn't come as a surprise. Once you grasp the emotional insecurity associated with loneliness and sexual conflict, and see how narcissism permits the victim to excuse his shortcomings, the emergence of chauvinism as the final symptom of the PPS makes sense. It's the logical, albeit irrational, outcome of a struggle that has been going on for most of the man's life.

To round out your understanding of the PPS victim's chauvinism, keep in mind that the sexist attitude is not so much an attack on women as it is a defense against rejection. It's another in a long list of lies perpetuated by the victim to make himself feel justified in living the way he does. What you must hope for is that somewhere beneath the denial and the projections is a person who is aware that although his body has arrived at the head of the table, his mind is still in the playpen.

PEAK AGE: 21 TO 22

It takes time for chauvinism to become a part of the victim's daily life. The positive side of this fact is that loved ones have years to identify the sexism and confront it. It doesn't just pop up one day and stay there forever.

Although it is tough to designate a peak age for the overlapping symptoms of irresponsibility, anxiety, and loneliness, it's relatively safe to say that chauvinism usually unfolds in the victim's early twenties. I choose 21 to 22 as the peak age for several reasons.

First, society designates age 21 as the official 'coming of age.' Once a young man reaches it, he is expected to behave like an adult. If he is a PPS victim, he lacks adult skills and needs a method of camouflaging his deficiencies. Chauvinism provides that mask.

Second, the victim has been experiencing a good deal of pain in his life and would like to be rid of it. Chauvinism permits him to explain away his pain by blaming it on other people, especially women.

Finally, the successful establishment of some degree of narcissism in the victim's life a year or two earlier leads him to chauvinism. The two tend to be comfortable bedfellows. Once the young man has projected his insecurities onto other people, an unreasonable devotion to his masculinity is likely to follow.

HE'S NOT THE MAN I MARRIED

Jennifer's whole manner was apologetic and guilt-ridden— eyes downcast, head bowed, voice soft. 'I shouldn't be here,' she said. 'I'm so mad at myself for not being able to handle it. I shouldn't have to talk to someone about this.'

'Why don't you just tell me what's wrong?' I said.

'It's me.' She stared blankly ahead. 'I'm just not adjusting well to married life.'

I remained silent, and she continued.

'I'm bitter and disappointed. Forgive my language, but I'm turning into a bitch.'

'In what way?'

'It seems I'm always either crying or complaining. I accuse Mark—that's my husband—of not loving me, of working to get away from me, of liking his friends more than me. Isn't that terrible?'

'Why is it terrible?'

'I'm ruining our marriage. We've only been married for ten months, and already I'm destroying all my dreams. I don't want to be a divorced woman.'

'What makes you think you're heading for a divorce?' I asked gently.

'Mark doesn't want to be around me anymore, and I can't say I blame him. He works hard and needs time to unwind. But I hardly ever see him. When I tell him how I feel, he just says I'm jealous. I ask him to spend more time with me and he says he has to work to save enough money so we can start a family.

'But I don't want a family just yet. I want to finish my last semester of college, get a better job, and adjust to married life before having children. Mark says I'll be happier when I have children and stay at home. I say I don't want to be a housewife, but he says that no wife of his will work until the kids are out of elementary school. I tell him I don't want to be trapped in the house for the next fifteen years, and he says I'm going back on my commitment to raise a family.'

'He seems to have your life all planned out for you,' I said.

'What do you mean?'

'Well, he tells you what you're going to do, how you're going to do it, and why you'll be happy doing it. And he doesn't listen to what *you* want.'

'He's just trying to be helpful.'

Again I kept silent.

'Mark says I couldn't make it on my own. He says my money doesn't count for much. And I *don't* make as much as he does; that's true. I guess I wish he'd say it in a nicer way. I'm too sensitive.'

'Is that your opinion or his?'

'Well, Mark says . . .'

I couldn't remain silent any longer. 'Don't you get sick and tired of "Mark says"?'

'Hey, Mark's a wonderful guy. And he's smart, too.'

'Okay, I believe you. But doesn't that mean that everything that goes wrong in your marriage is your fault? Mark's the good guy and you're the bad guy, right?'

'Well, it seems that way. He's changed and I complain all the time. So he stays away, which only makes me more unhappy, and so I complain more.'

'So you *caused* his change? You're saying that Mark doesn't have a mind of his own, that he's totally dependent upon your behavior, and that you must protect him as if he were your son instead of your husband.'

'That's awfully harsh, isn't it?' Jennifer asked.

'Perhaps, but you need to hear the truth. Isn't it true that you're trying to protect Mark from you?'

'I guess you could say that.'

'That makes him a weakling. Is he that weak?'

138

'Not at all. When I first met him he was happy-go-lucky and independent. He never worried about work; we played all the time. My folks even thought he would never be a success because of his laziness. But we had fun. He might have been a little immature, but not weak.'

'Or—' I hesitated to make sure she heard me— 'you never saw his problems because you were as immature as he was.'

'Could be,' she admitted.

'And now, you're growing up and he isn't.'

Jennifer seemed frightened by the implications. 'Don't get me wrong. He's a wonderful man. He works hard and gives me everything I want.'

'Everything?'

She reached to the nearby box of facial tissues to wipe away the tears that had come to her eyes. 'Well, not really. But he's so good to me.'

'He is?'

She remained silent. Her crying intensified.

'It sounds as if you're afraid to criticize Mark. Is he some sort of god, a perfect person?'

'No way! Sometimes he's a royal pain in the butt.'

'Tell me about that side of Mark.'

'Well, he's changed. He works like an idiot—eighty or ninety hours a week—and he complains about other guys not working hard enough. This is the same person who dropped out of college because he didn't want to get up for morning classes.

'He spends most of his free time drinking beer with his friends. He never really had any friends before, and now he can't seem to live without them. He always told me that I was his only true friend. And now, when he does take me out, we have to go to the same old dingy bar with his same old loud-mouthed friends. He laughs and drinks with them and ignores me.

'And he's cruel. The things he says about people are just awful. There are these two older women who sort of run the construction company Mark works for; they do the book-keeping, secretarial work, arrange the jobs—stuff like that.

139

And they're kind of set in their ways, if you know what I mean. Well, the other night Mark and his friends were sitting around the bar saying horrible things about these ladies, and Mark yelled, "Hell, there's nothing wrong with those old bitches that a good screw wouldn't fix." I was shocked. Mark has never talked like that before.'

Silence. I let her own words sink in.

'Yeah, he's changed.'

'But you take the blame for it.'

'Well, I've done *some* things wrong—like complaining.'

'Okay. So you've made some mistakes. So you're human. But it seems your biggest mistake is taking responsibility for Mark's problems.'

'Can you help us?' she pleaded. 'I don't want my marriage to go bad. I love him. I really do.'

'I can help you with *you*, but I can't help Mark or your marriage if Mark isn't here.'

'He said that coming here is a waste of time and money.'

'And what do you say?'

'It's not a waste if it helps our marriage.'

'Will he come?'

'I think he will if I pressure him enough. I'll have to nag him about it and then he'll come.'

'Is that how you get him to do things for you?'

'Yes, but it doesn't always work. For instance, I'd been begging him to go away for a long weekend, just the two of us, and last weekend we planned to go. But what did he do? He invited two of his buddies to come along. And he didn't tell me until the last minute. I ended up spending the weekend talking to two other wives while Mark and his friends played and drank. I hated him for that. Hating him scared me. That's why I finally decided to call you. I don't want to hate my husband.'

'Do you think he'll come to see me?'

'Yes, he'll come. Once, anyway. He'll probably tell you that we would have no problems if I'd just stop complaining.'

'Can you stop?'

'Maybe. But I wouldn't get anything I wanted.'

'Do you really enjoy getting what you want this way?'

'I wouldn't be here if I did.'

She had reached her own conclusion.

'So there's nothing to lose except unnecessary turmoil,' I said. 'If you stop complaining, Mark must face his own problems.'

'So what do I do?'

'Well, stop acting like his mother, stop blaming yourself for his problems, and stop being responsive to his macho chauvinism.'

'His *what?*' Jennifer was surprised. 'I never thought of Mark as a chauvinist.'

'Maybe he never showed it before. But what else can you call it? He sets double standards of conduct, complete with insensitivity and cruel sexist remarks. He defines your role, forces himself to become a workaholic in order to demonstrate his superiority, and then confines you to a stay-at-home position while he pledges allegiance to his beer-drinking buddies.'

'God, it sounds terrible when you say it!'

'I can appreciate Mark's fine points even though I don't know him yet. But I don't like chauvinism, and I have an aggressive way of confronting it. If Mark will take a moment to hear me, he'll see his chauvinism and stop it before it gets any worse. And you can help.'

'Me?'

'Yes. Don't be Mark's mommy, or a martyr, or a guilt-ridden, bad little girl. Hold onto your hopes and dreams and refuse to participate in his chauvinism. If you love Mark, don't walk away from him until you've given your marriage the best shot you've got.'

She nodded. 'But what if he doesn't come back to see you again?'

'Yeah, what if?'

'Then I'll just love him more and more. It's only been a few months; there's plenty of time for us to get back to the way we were.'

'I doubt you'll ever be the way you were. The hope is that you'll become more of what you want to be.'

As she walked out of my office Jennifer paused and said, 'Please don't hurt him.'

141

Smiling, I gave her a wink and said, 'Yes, Mother.'

She burst out laughing. 'Oh, damn, I did it again.'

I gave her a gentle pat on the shoulder. 'Don't damn yourself, Jennifer. Just stick with love and go for it. Love can beat chauvinism any day of the week and twice on Sunday.'

10 The Crisis: Social Impotence

WENDY: 'What is wrong, Peter?'
PETER (*scared*): 'It is only pretend, isn't it, that I am their
    father?'
WENDY (*drooping*): 'Oh yes.'

Somewhere in his early or mid-twenties, the PPS victim
begins to realize that he has a problem. He tries to convince
himself that it's only a minor problem, that everyone experiences it. But because he's still in touch with reality, he
knows it's *not* minor. He knows he is paying a price for
his pretense. His desire to change clashes with his over-
worked denial. He enters the crisis stage of the Peter Pan
Syndrome.

It's a nagging sense of surrealism that pushes the young
man into a confrontation with himself. The natural forces of
warmth, logic, and human decency push their way into his
conscious mind. The conflicts demand resolution.

He is forced to see the weakness of his emotional paralysis. Procrastination has left him a legacy of poor survival
skills. His blind pursuit of group identity and the resultant
loneliness take their toll. His belief in mental magic and his
disregard for cognitive law and order are challenged by
common sense. His ambivalence toward his parents and his
inability to love a woman honestly cloud his mind. The
combination thrusts him into a state of gross immobilization. Twenty years of 'growing up' have left him socially
impotent.

During the crisis, the PPS victim wants help. But
his mirage of competency and his lack of courage are

formidable obstacles. Let me take you inside the life of one PPS victim who found the courage to overcome the obstacles and challenge his impotence.

'My mom was right all along, but I was too stupid to see it. And now it's too late to go back and make it right. You can bet she'll never let me forget it.'

Despondence. Regret. Guilt. Twenty-three-year-old Randy was a mess. It sounded as if he was angry at his mom. But beneath the veneer he was thoroughly disgusted with himself. He had finally gotten down off his adolescent high horse and taken a good look at his life. He hated what he saw. It was amazing that a young man so bright and personable had made a shambles out of every significant aspect of his life.

He had been to three colleges in four years and had yet to accumulate one year's credits. He couldn't balance a checkbook, had little or no conception of what constituted a balanced meal, couldn't hold a job longer than a week or two, was living in a two-bit flea trap with five ne'er-do-wells, and was one step ahead of a bevy of bill collectors and an irate landlord. Randy had joined a generation of young men who were so bored with life that even smoking marijuana wasn't any fun. He had given up dope and returned to the old standby, alcohol. Worst of all, Randy's procrastination was all-encompassing. It wasn't the kind in which you put things off until tomorrow, but a fatalistic procrastination that said, 'To hell with tomorrow, I'll just put it off—period!'

A drab gray film of hopelessness shrouded the brightness of Randy's tomorrows. He had persuaded himself to believe that each new day would only bring more failure and disappointment. In effect, he saw the hope of tomorrow as nothing more than a cruel hoax, mocking a yesterday filled with failure. His prophecy was self-fulfilling.

My primary concern was for the intensity of Randy's depression and anger. He obviously had reason to be depressed, and his anger was thinly disguised. If these two powerful emotions were to converge on Randy's life energy, it would not be long before his desire to sustain his

144

own life would deteriorate. Given his degree of despair, Randy could become suicidal.

Yet, during our initial meetings, it became clear that he was not in danger of killing himself. Over a period of several weeks I came to learn that Randy had a very efficient system of denial.

I knew the answers to the first few questions, but it was important that Randy hear himself answer them. 'Why are you here?'

He flashed a sheepish grin as he said, 'My mom said I had to.'

He heard it. He would go on if I waited.

Randy's agitation increased dramatically. 'She said that if I didn't come to see you, she would cut off my money.' He was getting redder by the minute.

'Blackmail.' I was serious.

'You're damn right, blackmail. She has no right to force me. She treats me like a little kid. "Do this, don't do that. Be careful. You'd better see that doctor." ' His voice was mockingly sweet.

I confronted him immediately. 'So why did you come? Do you always give in to blackmail?'

His anger darted out of his eyes. 'What do you think?' His silence punctuated his self-assertion. He caught himself losing control and quickly apologized for his temper. He then told me of his financial plight.

Randy had flunked out of one university and become bored with the 'Mickey Mouse' atmosphere of the local junior college. When he quit and went looking for a job, his mother told him he couldn't live at home without paying rent. He couldn't find a satisfactory job, so he went to another university. He didn't want to be there, but it got his mother off his back.

Mom paid his tuition and gave him $250 a month for room and board. All he had to do was get passing grades. At the time of our talk he was in danger of flunking all his courses. Then he and his mom would have another blowup.

I tried to sound upbeat when I said, 'You seem to have quite a hang-up with your mother.'

'Whaddaya mean?' He seemed genuinely surprised.

I reminded him of his opening remark, indicating that he appeared to blame his mother for his troubles. Then I paralleled that attitude with his dependency upon Mom's money and contrasted those two with his unwillingness or inability to pull away from her apron strings. I thought he would be confused. Wrong again.

'I'm afraid that's a bad habit. As I was growing up, I was always blaming Mom for my problems. I thought I had a good reason. She constantly nagged me, reminding me of all the things I did wrong. It got on my nerves. It was easier to blame my problems on her nagging than to do anything about them. I guess I'm still doing that.'

Now *I* was confused. 'If you have such great insight, why don't you change?'

The answer came quickly and easily. 'I don't know.'

It took a minute before it dawned on me. 'You don't change, because you don't think you can. You figure it's not going to do you any good to care.'

'I don't understand that. Why would I think that way?'

'I don't know. Let's find out.'

I explained to Randy that I didn't consider him mentally ill. Therefore, his pattern of behaviour, however complicated and mysterious, makes sense. It may be irrational, but it is logical. The only problem was to uncover his logic.

We talked about how his life was going steadily downhill. He explained in detail how he consistently mis-managed money. He told me of quitting jobs after having words with the boss, of being fired after blowing up at co-workers. He was perplexed by his rage and confused by his impulsiveness. The more he trusted me, the more he described himself with words like 'failure,' 'a jerk,' and 'dumb.'

It became easier to explain to Randy what seemed to be happening to him. He was suffering substantial psychological pain. He was returning to old methods of coping. It was convenient to find fault with his mother, to blame her for his problems. Randy wanted to believe that blaming his mother would somehow make his current troubles disappear, just as it had when he was a teenager.

This introduced another of Randy's quirks: he believed in mental magic. It had begun early in his life when he was permitted to impose his magical thinking upon reality. 'If I think it, it will be so.' This is frivolous for children, disastrous for adults. It was a trait he should have outgrown but hadn't.

Confronted with the ominous threat of depression and self-destruction, it was little wonder that Randy returned to his old defense mechanisms. It was like the seven-year-old who, faced with the anxiety of the first day of school, returns to the warmth and security of thumb-sucking. Randy was sucking his mental thumb. Only in this case, to find a respite from life's stresses, Randy was feeling sorry for himself because his mother was causing his problems. Once he accepted this reaction to anxiety, we could dig deeper into his personality.

One major problem that Randy couldn't dump on his mother caused constant torment and sadness and gave birth to his first nightmares. It thrust him unceremoniously into one state of rejection after another. When I pushed him about the reality of using his mother as an emotional scapegoat he explained that he had problems with women in general. He said it this way:

'I really want a lasting relationship with a woman. But like I am with everything else, I'm a loser when it comes to love. I seem to mess up a good relationship just about the time things start to feel good. Every time I find myself falling in love, I start looking for the nearest girl and thinking about conquering her. Sexually, if you know what I mean. Needless to say, no decent girl will put up with that, especially when I'm so obvious about what I'm doing.'

What a complicated statement! It expressed Randy's hopes, dreams, fears, sexual frustration, insecurity, mistrust, and insight. With a bit of psychological detective work, it also opened the door to a problem shared to one degree or another by many of Randy's contemporaries. The story behind this statement is the key to Randy's peculiar logic.

During the next few sessions, Randy talked about his sexual experiences. He shared the circumstances of his first date, first kiss, first steady girl, and, with considerable embarrassment, his first act of sexual intercourse. With each story came the notion that Randy was playing a do-or-die game. He viewed every successful sexual encounter as a victory. There was something to be won by having sex with a girl.

Randy wanted to physically possess a girl, but he rejected any attempt at emotional contact. On three separate occasions Randy had shoved a girl away when she tried to get close to him. As he had said, his method was 'obvious.' It was also exceptionally pernicious. It was my view that Randy committed emotional execution on the women who dared to love him.

I suggested that Randy's attitude toward females was distorted, that he appeared to harbor considerable anger and resentment toward the opposite sex. He seemed genuinely shocked.

'I'm not aware of hating girls. I want to love them. I just can't believe that I have such feelings inside me. But something is there, isn't it?'

'Yes, it certainly is.' I took the idea one step further. 'And you know what, it's revenge. That's the number one message I hear as you talk. You're getting even with girls.'

He was truly flabbergasted. 'What? That doesn't make any sense at all. Revenge? Why would I want revenge on girls?'

'That's why you're here. To find out why. So do this for Randy, not Mommy. Together we'll find out why.'

Why indeed? That's an excellent question. Why was Randy so mean to girls? Why the emotional execution? Had he been wronged by a girlfriend? Not that we could discover. Was his mother a spiteful woman, a sadistic schizophrenic? Not at all. Perhaps his father had brainwashed him into hating women; or Randy had latent homosexual tendencies. . . . No on both counts.

To get to the heart of the matter, I asked Randy to focus on a recent sexual experience. I wanted a running account of everything that had happened. He spoke of physical encounters that were highly symbolic. They involved a complex web of infantile fantasies, illicit and sometimes illegal exploitation of young girls, and a smorgasbord of pills and booze. In short, the heart of his story was of sex and drugs.

Randy lived in a mid-America college town where 70 percent of the inhabitants depended upon the university for their living. Many older homes had been converted for student housing. The landlords charged each student a flat rental fee and did as little as possible to keep the property in good condition. Randy had found five students living in a dilapidated old house who were looking for a sixth roommate. Randy paid $80 a month and was responsible for buying his own food. He moved into a small room on the second floor. The room had once been a spacious walk-in closet.

Parties were as necessary to Randy's survival as air and water. He took it for granted that there would be an ample supply of parties with a bunch of 'cool' college students. He wasn't disappointed.

Randy's roommates welcomed him with a little party. Nothing big, just a few cases of beer, some Quaaludes, speed, hashish, marijuana, and a precious line or two of cocaine. By 9 P.M. fifteen or twenty nondescript young people were milling around the downstairs of the old house. The vibrations from the stereo shook the walls. The squeals and screeches of delight signaled the onset of drug-induced sociability. Everyone was talking, sharing his or her newest experiences and the latest college gossip. As usual, no one was listening.

Into this typical party walked three unlikely participants. Their youthfulness said they shouldn't be there, yet they were clearly familiar with the house and the five roommates. They were juniors—in high school—who lived in the area, and this house was their home away from home. They looked as if they had just come from cheerleading practice. Indeed, one of them had.

The three girls were best friends. They had first happened upon the house quite by accident. They were taking a walk, started talking to three of the guys, and were soon spending their afternoons drinking beer and exercising their desire to be seen as sophisticated ladies. The guys gave them all the attention they wanted, all the beer they could drink, and, occasionally, a 'toot' or two of cocaine. The girls' payment was simple: sex.

Randy was immediately introduced to the three girls. They had their lines down pat. They oohed and ahhed at Randy's stories and giggled at his ethnic jokes. They sipped their beer, by now well able not to wince at the sour taste. Randy was instantly accepted as a 'special friend,' a label that was crucially important to the girls, as if with it they could justify their actions.

Within an hour Randy was in bed with the cheerleader. She adhered to the script well. Her praise of his lovemaking parroted the heroine of a historical romance. She even smoked a cigarette after their four-minute love match. She bubbled with commendations of Randy's masculinity, cooing about how great it was to feel so close to a person in such a short time.

Randy felt great. The gratification of his ego matched the satisfaction in his body. He was a championship lover. He was a championship person. As the cheerleader continued her phony praise, Randy experienced an ebb and flow of passion, alternating between peace of mind and sexual arousal. He was pleased with himself. That turned him on more than anything.

He removed the cigarette from the girl's mouth, mumbled something about loving her, and aggressively expressed his renewed passion. A short time later, Randy lay beside this stranger trying to think of something to say. He always hated the time after sex when you were expected to talk.

He broke the silence by uttering words of praise for his young friend's physical endowments. She responded by rubbing his chest with her fingers and massaging his ego with counterfeit endearments. The meaning of 'special' became clearer. His partner was only sixteen years old, but she was a special woman to him. A woman with the ability to make him feel alive. Too bad he couldn't remember her name.

The girl returned to the party despite Randy's protests. He

consoled himself with a joint of marijuana. He smoked it out of habit instead of need; he was already floating as high as he could get. It took only a moment for Randy to realize that he was glad the girl was gone.

Several minutes later, Randy's high was interrupted. The raven-haired friend of the cheerleader hesitated in the doorway and then, without saying a word, exposed her perfectly formed fifteen-year-old body and crawled into bed. She slipped the joint out of Randy's mouth, inhaled deeply, and permitted the bittersweet smoke to dangle around her sensuous lips.

Within moments, Randy and his new friend were making love. Although aroused, Randy started to lose his erection. His heavenly feeling would be crushed if he had to explain his impotence. As he had done before, he faked an orgasm. His partner followed suit. It was all part of the game.

The girl cooed with delight. Randy was offended by her plasticity but reminded himself, 'You've never kicked a chick out of the sack.' Randy didn't like this girl, but he regaled her with his pretense of satisfaction. He even agreed that he was a 'special friend.' He had to. She had asked him as if the answer no would have been unthinkable.

This special friend left after finishing the joint. Randy was a bit confused. There was an unsettling gnaw in his guts. Having sexual intercourse with two strange minors didn't seem right. Neither did his impotence. He dismissed his concern by reminding himself that he had stumbled into a young stud's dream. He couldn't help wondering when he'd get the third teenager into bed.

It was several days later that Randy committed his most pernicious emotional execution. He had made arrangements for his girlfriend from back home to come and visit him in his new home, promising her a weekend she'd never forget. At least he hadn't lied on that point.

It was three o'clock in the afternoon, and he expected his girlfriend at four. At a quarter past three, the third girl of the party trio bounced into the house and grabbed a beer out of the fridge. Randy was alone in the living room, listening to a new album.

The girl plopped down on the sofa next to Randy, letting her long blond hair fall where it might. She explained how she had cut her last class in order to get a head start on the weekend. She giggled at the thought that the other two girls had had to do some extra work and couldn't get there for another hour.

The girl didn't wait for what would have been Randy's clumsy advance. She confided that her two friends had marveled at Randy's warmth and gentleness. She was talking about their sexual encounters but used words that suggested something far deeper. It was ten minutes to four when Randy and his latest 'special friend' slid into bed.

Randy's girlfriend pulled up in front of the house at precisely 4 P.M. One of Randy's roommates arrived home just as she was about to ring the doorbell. He introduced himself and invited her inside. The music was blasting away. The roommate said that Randy must be upstairs getting dressed, and then suggested that his girlfriend sneak up and surprise him. She did.

Randy had had a difficult time achieving an orgasm. He purposely shut out all thoughts extraneous to his imminent achievement. He sensed the moment of inevitability just as his girlfriend walked into his tiny room. For an instant, Randy mistook his girlfriend's screams of distress for his special friend's delight. 'This one is excellent,' was his first thought.

Randy's girlfriend turned and was gone before Randy had realized what had happened. The blond teenager's exclamation of surprise stunned Randy. He jumped out of bed in amazement. It took only seconds to calculate what had just occurred. He stumbled down the stairs and looked out the window just as his girlfriend roared away.

Randy tried repeatedly to call his girl. He wanted desperately to explain. She wouldn't talk to him. In the coming weeks, the incident would haunt him continuously. Each time he attempted to have intercourse with one of the three girls, visions of his own insensitiveness and raging guilt would interfere with his passion. He could not attain an erection.

The word quickly spread among the three teenagers that Randy was not a special friend anymore. Each in turn expressed her disappointment and resentment at his callousness. They bitterly complained that Randy had used them. They seemed especially offended by what he had done to his girlfriend. Soon Randy was ostracized by his roommates. They had had to choose sides between Randy and the three girls. Randy lost. In a state of confused agitation, Randy moved out of the house.

As Randy finished his story, it became apparent that he was still agitated. His recent sexual exploits may have sounded like a lot of fun, but they had caused him unbelievable turmoil. He may have had many 'victories,' but he had lost the game. Worse yet, he didn't understand what had happened.

Randy was out of touch with himself. Most of his life was comprised of self-deception. Even his looks were deceiving. His captivating smile covered self-doubts; his smoky blue eyes were glassy from unspent tears of guilt; his firm handshake belied gut-wrenching embarrassment. He was a bright, alert young man who should have had the world by the tail. Instead, he acted like a vulture, lazily circling about the world, eking out an existence by feeding off young girls who were more immature than he was. No wonder he felt so bad.

I had to take advantage of Randy's pain in order to help him. My next move would be to slowly point out the contradictions in his lifestyle: he talked of being special to people, yet he had no friends, his words of warmth hid actions of cold indifference; and he manipulated others, all the while pretending to experience feelings of closeness. He wanted to love a woman, but if one got too close he would punish her severely.

I started Randy's journey toward self-understanding by reflecting on the heart of the matter. 'You're really terribly lonely, aren't you?'

Tears welled up in his eyes. Though he didn't say a word, he communicated everything.

'How does it feel?'

He seemed to choke. 'Terrible.'

'You can't make it go away right now, can you?'

'No.'

'Well, can you stick with it? Learn from it?'

His furrowed brow told me he was serious. 'I don't know what you mean?'

Teaching anyone to trust his feelings and learn from them is so simple it's almost impossible. Randy was no exception. 'You've always run away from feelings of loneliness, haven't you?'

'I guess you could say that.'

'Well, this time, don't. Don't fight it. Go with it. Let it happen. Let yourself feel lonely. It may be the only real feeling you've had for a long time. You can build upon it.'

He was beginning to follow me. 'What good will that do?'

I began the process of helping him focus on his feelings and regain a grasp on reality. 'Let me show you. Let's take your feeling of loneliness and see where it leads, okay?'

He still wasn't sure where we were going. 'Okay, if you say so. You're the doctor. Where do I start?'

'Right where you are.'

'Huh?'

'You're feeling lonely right now, correct?'

'Yeah.'

'Okay. Feel it. Experience it. You're lonely.' I hesitated while that simple notion sunk in. 'Now, what happens to you when you think about being lonely?'

'I want to stop the feeling. I want to get away from it.'

'You're scared, right?' He nodded and I continued. 'Now, you've got two emotions, you're lonely and scared. How does that make you feel?'

'I want to get out of here—fast.'

'So, when you get lonely, you get scared and you want to run away. Right?'

'If you say so.'

'No! Not if I say so!' My confrontation caught him unaware. He tensed and stared at me intently. '*You* just expressed *your* feelings. *You* have the feelings, not I!'

'Okay. Yeah, I feel a little panicky. Like I was in a fire. I just wanna run.'

'All right. See what's happening? You started with a true feeling, the feeling of being lonely. Then you felt scared and experienced panic. You're moving.'

Randy seemed puzzled. 'Sure, I'm moving. Moving in circles.'

I stuck to my guns. 'Okay. That's your next feeling. Moving in circles. Around and around. Now you're confused. What does confusion do to you?'

'Weird reaction.' He turned red and giggled. 'You won't believe where my head just went.'

'Try me.'

'I just thought of that first night with the cheerleader. God, what a bod!'

I raised my eyebrows and smiled as if to say I'm human too. Then I continued the task, only this time I made him do more of the work. 'Now, you tell me what's going on inside your head.'

'I went from lonely to getting turned on. Told you it was weird.'

'Actually, you went from loneliness, to scared, to panic, to confusion, and then to recalling a *specific* sexual encounter. What did that sexual experience mean? What did you get out of it?'

Randy temporarily lost track. 'Hey, that's really strange. Crazy. I shouldn't think that way.'

It was important to confront the implied irrational idea. 'No, all experiences are good. Whatever you did with your head in having sex with the cheerleader was okay.'

'What? All experiences are good? Loneliness is good? Gimme a break. How can loneliness be good?'

'Because you experience it and *you are good*.'

'That doesn't make any sense.'

'It doesn't make any sense because you believe that if you have a bad feeling, you are bad. And *that* doesn't make any sense.'

Randy just looked at me. I thought I saw a small light of understanding. He had never considered that his self and his feelings could be seen as two different things. I used my confrontation to get us back on track.

'It appears to me that when you get confused, you feel bad yourself. You recall a sexual experience and somehow it makes you feel better. At least for a moment or two.'

'Believe it or not, I'm following you. I mean, following me. I mean—following you and you're following me. Wow, now I *am* confused.'

'No you're not. You're exactly right. You started by feeling lonely and after a few other feelings, you end up in a particular sexual experience. You feel weird about the transition. No problem. Just stick with it. Let's see where it leads.'

'Okay. Guess it can't hurt.'

'Let's go back to your memory of the sexual encounter with the cheerleader. What did it do for you?'

Randy started laughing. So did I, catching the double meaning.

'I know what it did for your body. I meant, what did it do for your head?'

Randy thought for a moment. 'The first word that comes to my head sounds dumb. But it's there.'

'What is it?'

'Victory.'

I let the word do its work. 'Victory.'

'Yeah, victory. I won.'

'Sounds like you were in a game. Or a battle. The girl was trying to win something from you or *at least you thought she was*. But you beat her. What did your victory get you?'

'I don't know.'

'Well, how did the victory feel?'

'Good and bad. One part of me feels great, another part lousy.'

'What does the lousy part feel like?'

'I used the kid. I really hurt her.'

I thought it was time for another piece of reality. It had struck me as soon as he told me about the party. 'Maybe you did. But maybe you're overdoing your power and pride.'

'Whaddaya mean?'

'I know you're dashingly handsome and a great lover. But

your so-called special friend was just doing her imitation of the Welcome Wagon lady. You were just another guy on the scene. What do you think she did with the last new roommate? Or, for that matter, what do she and her pals do after drinking, smoking, and snorting? Screw, that's what! That's the payment. You were just another piece of duty. Sorry to burst your balloon.'

Randy was suddenly sobered. He was hurt. I was surprised as I realized that he hadn't thought of that before. He really had thought of himself as special to the teenage trio. His false pride had gained the upper hand, blinding him to reality. It's never a pretty sight when one shatters the mirrors of narcissism.

I gave him a moment or two to collect his thoughts and then I renewed the effort. 'So you feel that you conquered her. You won. And that relieves your loneliness.'

'Maybe. For a few minutes. And then I get angry. I get angry—at myself, at the situation. I hate being there. I hate myself and I don't know why.'

Randy was getting agitated again. He was clearly angered by his own actions. Frustrated. He was trying to run away again.

'Wait, slow down. You don't have to run away from the anger and frustration. You conquered the lady but you feel lousy, right?'

'Yeah.'

'So you don't really win. You lose. You lose the game. You *think* you win, but you really lose.'

'Huh?'

'Just think about it for a second. You're running away from loneliness because it panics you. You run into the arms of some immature kid in order to score a victory. But she's no match. She's not even in the game. She's just a body that you use to perform interpersonal masturbation. The battle is with *yourself*, Randy. You feel angry and lousy because you're fighting with yourself. There's no way you can win.'

'Why do I do that?'

'I'm not sure. But you use the girls for your own internal

needs, to combat loneliness. And I'm not talking about sexually. I don't mean to offend you, but based on your description, you're not exactly the Don Juan of lovers.'

His sheepish grin told me that he understood my intent.

'You use these girls emotionally. And, with your memory, you *keep* using them. You seduce them—which is no great task—and then, while they're cooing about how great you are, you stroke your ego with internal messages about how great you are. You so badly need their recognition and awe that even when it's phony you gobble it up like a parasite.'

'That's awful.'

'There you go again. We reach a point where I'm able to help you grasp reality and you damn yourself. If you keep that up, you'll never learn from your mistakes.'

'But it's wrong.'

'Well, let's say that it's ineffective. You get a booster shot by emotionally seducing girls. You should give yourself pride and not try to steal it from females. But you don't know how. So you keep engaging yourself in battles you can't win. You probably even keep a mental scorecard.'

'It's not mental.'

Now I was confused. 'Huh?'

'It's not mental; it's written down. I have a list in a sort of diary. It contains the name of every girl I've been to bed with. I write down what her name was, where we were, and anything that was unusual.'

I couldn't resist. 'I'll bet the old scorecard is really hot after the teenage trio.'

Our laughter cleared the air and set the stage for more of Randy's secrets. 'You see, one of my goals—boy, does this sound stupid—I know, I know, don't be so hard on myself. Anyway, one of my goals is to screw enough girls so that my diary will have at least twenty-six names in it—each of the girls' names starting with a different letter of the alphabet. You know, Amy, Barbara, Cindy, Dolores, all the way down to the letter Z. Told you it sounded stupid.'

'It's not stupid when you think about it *inside* your head, is it?'

'No, not really. It turns me on.'

'But what does the coldness of a list and a word game do to you in the long run?'

Randy thought for a moment and then his eyes lit up. 'Gosh, it leads me back to loneliness.'

I looked at him as if to say, 'How does that feel?' Neither of us spoke a word for a minute or two. Randy used the silence very productively.

'Now I have another weird feeling. But it's good. Peaceful, like everything fits. My actions finally make sense.'

'Explain, please.'

'Well, I start out feeling lonely most of the time. I get really scared and run away to my diary. Then, in order to make myself feel better, I look for girls to screw so that I can add names to the scorecard. This feels good for a little while, but then I end up right where I started, feeling lonely. Then the whole damn thing repeats itself.'

'How does—'

Randy interrupted me with a good-natured grin and palms extended outward. 'I know. "How does that feel?" Well, it feels sad. That's it, sad. Sad that I have to be this way.'

'You *have* to be this way?'

'It seems that way. I can't love a woman. Not really. So how else am I supposed to be?'

Now it was my turn to use extended palms. 'Hold on just a sec. "You can't love a woman"? That's an incorrect conclusion. In fact, it's a lie. You *could* love a woman. The problem is that *you won't let a woman love you*. You see yourself as *unlovable*. And you've become very effective at keeping girls from getting too close. You're in a prison of loneliness that is of your own making. And you will certainly never escape that prison if you continue to let the oohs and ahhs of pseudo-sophisticated teeny-boppers massage your wounded ego.'

Randy seemed to relish my hard-line confrontation. Truth is a marvelous therapeutic tool. There was one last silence before the end of a particularly fruitful session.

Randy set the scene for future work by asking, 'How did I get this way?'

How indeed! In the coming weeks we would explore the whys and wherefores of Randy's affliction. We would discuss his laziness, his procrastination, his low self-esteem, and his lack of discipline. We would delve headlong into the estrangement he felt from his father and the mixture of guilt and anger he experienced toward his mother. And his irresponsibility! If Randy had spent half as much time solving his problems as he did trying to avoid them, he would have pulled himself out of his rut in no time at all.

Randy was in the crisis stage of the Peter Pan Syndrome. It is both a time of difficulty and hope. It is difficult because the mirrors of perfection become brittle and the crudeness of chauvinism often brings a sobering rejection. It is a time of hope because, during this crisis, a young man has the opportunity to turn his life around. With help, whether professional and/or friendly, a PPS victim in crisis can take those first few very important steps away from Never Never Land.

11 After Thirty: Despondency

PETER: 'To die will be an awfully big adventure.'

Once the PPS victim begins his fourth decade, his life starts to disintegrate. The promise of endless joy and excitement is still unfulfilled. He finds this difficult to comprehend. After all, he did his best to follow in Peter Pan's footsteps. He avoided responsibility, bowed to group pressure, drove his insecurities away, blamed others for his sexual inadequacies, and resisted acting like a grown-up. Denial was supposed to be the key to eternal youth. Instead, it has led him to despondency. Discouraged and disheartened, he sees death as the only promise of excitement left to him.

The despondency the victim feels inside is compounded by the confusion rendered by his daily lifestyle. He has surrounded himself with the trappings of adulthood—wife, children, house, car, steady job, vacations, and proper friends. These things give him very little comfort. He acquired them simply because he was supposed to. He acted out a socially appropriate script in order to gain approval, but his heart and soul were never in the role. He is awed that others derive satisfaction from such grown-up things.

Although wearing thin, the pretense continues. The reality of others enjoying adulthood challenges his beliefs. He curls up inside himself, sucks his mental thumb, and laments, 'Is this all there is? When do I get to have the fun that I was promised?'

The self-pity does little to repair the cracks in the narcissistic mirrors. They open further as harsh realism displaces illusory fantasies. He was supposed to stay young forever; instead, he dozes on the couch and wakes up with stiff muscles. The meadows of his nightlife were to be alive with everlasting playmates; instead he finds himself waging a solitary war against crabgrass in the front lawn. He was to attain the status of a revered leader with uncompromised greatness; instead he is confronted with relentless financial obligations, a wife who resists his chauvinism, and kids who want to belong to a family that doesn't exist. Under these circumstances, depression is inevitable, despondency unrelenting.

The PPS victim often dismisses his despondency as a normal part of the transition into middle age. And maybe *some* of it is. But there is also a great deal of emotional turmoil that is the result of many years of avoidance and denial. He's been so successful in projecting an image of competence that he can't even take his own pain seriously.

The PPS victim remains alone with his struggle. He would like to seek help but several things stop him. His loneliness and his fear of rejection shield him from risk-taking. His chauvinism makes him too proud to admit his frailties. His long-standing habit of false gaiety is tough to break through. He has become so adept at hiding from himself that even those closest to him don't suspect that anything is really wrong—except his wife or lover.

The woman in the victim's life knows something is wrong. She's known it just about as long as she's known him. And she knows that it's more than just his problem. It's a relationship problem, which means she's involved. She may not comprehend the extent of her personal involvement, but she can't deny the presence of despondency in her own life.

Chances are that the problem has never been discussed—not in a rational way, at least. Instead, hostilities are muted and repressed, confrontations are twisted into useless accusations, and sharing and trust are eroded by the lack of communication. Those not yet married delay the wedding; those who are sometimes wish the wedding hadn't taken place. Two people who were once in love now think they don't even like each other.

162

But, oh, the brave front! 'Nothing wrong here. We're just two happy people churning along life's waterways. Sure, we have our problems, doesn't everyone? But nothing we can't handle.'

In all of this repression and denial, one thing just won't stay hidden. Some consider it the strongest link in the chain that binds people together; others say that it isn't the strongest, just the most noticeable. Whatever the opinion, this link is basic to our nature, and if we try to repress its need or refuse to nurture it, it will snap back at us. This unyielding link in the chain of interpersonal relationships is sex.

PPS victims have sex problems. These problems are carried over into the relationships they form with women. Rare is the case in which the PPS victim has a productive sexual relationship with his wife or lover. If he does, then he must be considered to have only a mild case of the Peter Pan Syndrome.

More often than not, the rampant dissatisfaction with sex is felt privately by both partners, but never shared openly with each other. Embarrassed apologies, caustic indictments, and unchallenged lies, all whispered in a darkened room, are the ways in which the two people cope with the problem. Although they try to put it out of their minds, the sexual appetite demands satisfaction. Sexual disappointment becomes the one characteristic of a disturbed relationship that just won't be silenced.

One can't consider the despondency that builds within the PPS victim without dealing with sexual unrest. Sexual complaints are often the one thing that breaks the bond of silence. At the moment of disclosure, 'bad sex' is usually seen as *the* problem. In truth, it is only a symptom. Only if a couple looks beyond the symptom to the real cause does the relationship have a chance to improve.

LEARNING HOW TO FEEL

Glenn was forty-two, prematurely gray, with a voice that boomed self-confidence. Not only was he highly successful, but he also had a vivacious wife, two beautiful kids, and a spacious home in the suburbs. Many would have said Glenn had found the golden goose.

Shortly after his fortieth birthday, Glenn's golden goose had started to lay rotten eggs. His wife had begun to challenge the restrictive role of wife and mother, his kids stormed into adolescence, he found his work more demanding and less rewarding, and his body was quietly reminding him that alcohol had taken the upper hand. Worst of all, a relentless despondency had crept into Glenn's life, making each day a little darker than the one before.

He denied any deterioration in his life, however, until his wife broached the possibility of a legal separation. Dana had been seeing a psychotherapist for several months and had repeatedly told Glenn to find help for his problems. He went to his physician for a complete physical and was almost disappointed to hear that he was in good shape. He had hoped that his problems were not emotional. Deep inside he knew the truth; he just hadn't admitted it to himself yet.

He came to my office with an abrupt warning: 'Basically I don't like you guys. You seem more screwed up than any of the rest of us. And you never say what's really on your mind. I don't want to sit here, pour out my guts, and then leave wondering what you think about something I've said.'

Boy, had he come to the right place!

'My wife says I need psychotherapy,' he said, and waited.

'Do you?'

'I don't know, you're the doctor.'

He had given me a license to be blunt, so I didn't pull any punches. 'I don't know either, so I guess we're both in trouble.'

'Maybe you could give me your opinion on one thing. How does a man handle it when his wife turns on him and takes away everything he's ever wanted?'

'That doesn't sound like a question. It sounds like you're trying to tell me something. Why don't you just tell me?'

'All the things I've ever wanted are being ripped away from me. And I can't do a damn thing about it. My wife needs to find herself—so she says—but while she's finding whatever the hell she misplaced, I'm losing my family.'

Glenn's despondency was hidden behind anger. I moved slowly. 'How so?'

'Dana decides she wants to finish college, so I have to wade through her English papers in order to find the *TV Guide*. Then she wants to get a part-time job, so I have to come home to a messy house. Then she wants to take an extra night class, so I have to hurry home to replace some dippy little teenage babysitter who's plopped into my chair, is drinking my pop, eating my pretzels, and talking on my phone while my kids, who probably don't need a babysitter anyway, are trying to destroy one another.

'I work hard, I make a lot of money, I have status in the community—and I've earned every damn bit of it. And now, what's my payment? My wife sees some damn shrink, suddenly decides she's unfulfilled, and starts talking about careers and a separation. And then *I'm* supposed to get help. What a rip!'

Since he had declared open season on shrinks, I decided a low profile was the best idea. 'Sounds like you're upset.'

'Damn right I'm upset. A man works to give his family the best, and then what does he get? I'll tell you; he gets dumped on, that's what.'

'Have you talked with your wife about this situation?'

'What do you think?' He glared at me as if I were the one who had smashed his dreams. 'Hell, yes. But every time I try talking, she says *I'm* not listening! I tell her I'd listen if she had anything interesting to say. But no, I just get more of the same old crap. "I need to find myself and you don't understand." ' His falsetto voice was filled with derision and cynicism.

'Do you make fun of your wife to her face?' I asked.

'I'm not making fun of her. I'm just trying to find out why she wants to see me suffer. After all I've done for her, I don't deserve to see my world crumble right before my eyes. Hell, I've had hundreds of opportunities to cheat on Dana, but

I've never done it. I've been true blue, and now I see what it's gotten me.'

I remained silent, purposely skirting the sexual issue, knowing it would come around again.

With a self-righteous smugness, Glenn dared me to engage him in mental gymnastics. 'So what do you think, Doc?'

'What do I think? Well, since you want me to shoot straight with you, here's what I think. You ought to get off your self-pity trip and tell me about your pain, because it's obvious you're hurting like hell.'

He leaned back in his chair, took a deep breath, and loosened his tie. A twinkle of schoolboy charm danced across his face. 'Don't be afraid to say what's on your mind, I can take it,' he joked.

'You said you wanted me to call 'em the way I see 'em. Was I too strong?'

His answer surprised me. 'No. I just thank God you aren't going to let me get away with any of my bullshit. You may not know this, but I can con people very well. I even con myself into thinking I know what's going on. But I don't. My world is coming apart and I don't have the foggiest notion what to do. Sure I need help, but where I come from, a man just doesn't admit that. It's not good for the image, if you know what I mean.'

'You're scared, aren't you?'

'Damn right. Wouldn't you be?'

'Sure.'

'I'm forty-two years old, on my way to being a national sales manager, have a gorgeous wife whom I love dearly, two kids who I think are the greatest things since sliced bread, and my life is disintegrating right before my eyes. And I don't know how to stop it. Yeah, I'm scared. *Panicked* is probably more like it.'

Glenn talked about several major areas of his life during a marathon session that lasted over three hours. He expressed regret that he and his father had never been close. He felt disgusted with his compulsion to please people and the fact that he had no true friends. He was disap-

166

pointed in his selfishness; he heard himself saying 'my' much too often. He experienced gross ambivalence over the way he still seemed attached to his mother's apron-strings.

When we reached the topic of sex, Glenn was guilt-ridden and embarrassed. He started to talk about himself as if he were the world's greatest lover. But with a gentle nudge he reversed his 'macho man' routine, confiding that it was difficult for him to accept his sexuality openly and honestly. He recounted a recent event that he thought proved he was 'coming out of the closet' and accepting the spontaneity of his sexuality.

'I came home early one day last week. Dana was dusting the furniture and looking very sexy in her cut-off jeans. I walked up behind her and grabbed her tits.' Glenn opened his hands and flexed his fingers, recreating the manner in which he had begun his 'foreplay.'

'I pushed her over the dining room table and started unzipping her jeans. She pushed my hands away, saying she didn't want to do it there. The kids were gone for a while, so I knew we had time. I kept undressing her. She told me to stop, but I knew I would make her like it.'

As Glenn continued, his pride was as great as his boastfulness. Our emotions went in opposite directions. He got excited; I was saddened.

'I sort of pinned her on the table and shoved it in. She finally stopped complaining.' He grinned sheepishly. 'It didn't last very long. I don't think I even made it for thirty seconds, but it was good.'

I sat in silence, replaying the essence of what Glenn had just told me. It was evident that he was totally unaware of the nature of his actions. In the softest, most supportive tone I could manage, I hit him with harsh reality. 'You raped your wife, Glenn. Maybe not legally, but physically and emotionally, you raped Dana.'

His face turned ashen, his mouth dropped open, and his eyes, wide with awe, stared off into oblivion. He didn't move; I don't think he could have. Then small droplets of tears formed a glaze over his eyes, and he whispered, 'Oh, my God!'

Thousands of floodlights had been switched on inside his head. Suddenly, hundreds of things he had never realized he knew were visible to his mind's eye. Glenn was in shock. Every four or five seconds he whispered, 'Oh, my God!' Every fifteen or twenty seconds he looked at me, each time more tears forming in his eyes. His incredulity lasted over five minutes, a lifetime in psychotherapy.

Glenn choked over his words. 'Of course—that's exactly what I did. I raped my wife. The only person I truly care about. Damn, I'm a helluva guy, aren't I?' His self-criticism was filled with overwhelming guilt.

More silence.

The shock of his insight pushed Glenn all the way down. 'I've hit bottom. Everything Dana has been saying is true. I've been too damn stupid to see it. She tells me I don't really know how to love her, that I don't respect her. She says I don't know how to express my feelings. She tells me I need to grow up. I listened to all those things, but I never *heard* them.'

He paused, his mind racing. 'How do I ever recover from this? How do I make up for what I did? Where do I start?' He was searching desperately for relief from his guilt.

'There are several things you need to do. First, knock off the guilt. It's useless. Second, dedicate yourself to the process of growing up. Psychotherapy can help you immensely in that area. Third, go home, hug your wife, tell her you love her, and let her know that things are going to change.'

Glenn was dubious. 'Don't we have to talk about what I did?'

'Why? What good is there in singling out one inconsiderate act when it's best forgotten? If Dana is anything like you say she is, she certainly doesn't want to rehash such an event. She may want to talk with you about her sexual needs, but I hope she doesn't want to ruminate on one mistake. Anyway, if you start showing her love instead of focusing on what an ass you are, she'll be more than happy to forget about the past.'

'But I need to tell her I'm sorry.'

'Fine. Tell her. Just don't start pounding her with cries and pleas for mercy.'

'What if she won't forgive me?'

'Then *she* has a problem.'

A week later, I saw Glenn and Dana together. Dana wasn't an unforgiving person, but she did have a problem. She had developed a strategy to protect herself from Glenn's insensitivity. And it was one that she would have to change if the 'new Glenn' was to emerge within their marriage.

I explained it to her this way: 'You haven't been able to retaliate against Glenn physically, so you've done it emotionally. You are in touch with your feelings; Glenn, for the most part, is not. This makes you stronger than he is, at least in this area. So it's understandable that you would try to equalize your footing with him by hitting him where he's the weakest. I hear evidence that you've developed the habit of belittling him for his lack of feeling, ridiculing his emotional blind spots, scoffing at his attempts to be warm. And now, with the advent of change, you may have the unconscious tendency to use this battle tactic when things get strained. But you needn't worry about it. With mutual growth, it will eventually disappear.'

Dana was also dedicated to change. She asked, 'So what do I do about this "battle tactic" when it comes back?'

'You accept it. You don't have to like it, just tell yourself that it's okay. You have to accept the fact that you've both fallen into some bad habits. But together, you can change the way your marriage works.'

With moving tenderness, Glenn leaned toward his wife and said, 'I want to make our marriage better and I'll work my tail off to do it.' He hesitated, then continued with a question he was afraid to ask. 'Do you still want me?'

Dana smiled through her tears. 'Of course I do.'

Glenn turned to me with tears of his own and said, 'God, I just want to hug her.'

With the bluntness Glenn had come to expect from me, I said, 'Well, don't tell me about it, you damn fool, *do it!*'

Glenn almost jumped across the room and grabbed Dana

as if she were about to run away. I excused myself for a timely 'rest break.' When I returned, they were holding hands on the sofa like two kids on their first date.

I gave them one final directive. 'You *will* have problems. The same old stuff may rear its ugly head when you least expect it. But you can handle it easily. To do so I recommend a 'touch-and-hug' program. When things go sour, walk away from each other as soon as possible. Go to opposite ends of the house if you have to. Then, within thirty minutes, seek each other out, and *without talking*, touch and hug each other. *Then* you can discuss what went wrong.'

Their smiles spoke of commitment to this idea. Glenn was bursting with energy; he could hardly contain himself. 'There's so much to say. There are so many feelings inside me. I'm afraid I might lose them if I don't put them into words right now.'

I tried to slow him down. 'I understand your fear. But you won't lose them. Feelings are always there, you just never knew it.'

'But what if they leave me and I can't find them?'

'Don't panic. The touch-and-hug program will bring them right back.'

'But how do I get good at the touch-and-hug program?'

'Like anything else. Practice, practice, practice.'

'But . . .'

'Hey,' I interrupted, 'I have a great suggestion for you. Why don't you quit worrying about feelings for now, take your wife out of here, and continue practicing the touch-and-hug program.'

Glenn and Dana beamed with delight as they walked hand-in-hand out of my office into a blissful spring evening.

Part 3
WORKING FOR
CHANGE

The next four chapters contain specific recommendations—things to think, do, and say in trying to help the PPS victim.

Parents will learn how to prevent their children from falling into the PPS trap, or how to help them return to normal growth and development if their behavior reflects an excessive influence of magical dust.

Chapter 13 challenges female readers to confront their own weaknesses, and suggests that making changes in their daily life-style can have a positive impact on the PPS victim they love. These women should also pay close attention to the first section of Chapter 12, 'For Parents,' even if there are no children in the relationship. If you are in love with a PPS victim, you know how parts of your relationship resemble that of a mother and son. This can be corrected by reestablishing mature lines of communication.

Friends and relatives will discover, in dealing with the PPS victim, that their first instincts are most likely correct. Instead of backing away from their initial thoughts, they should probably follow them.

Victims of the Peter Pan Syndrome will find inspiration in Larry's story (Chapter 15). In fact, all readers will learn, no matter how bleak the outlook, that it's never too late to start working for change.

12   For Parents

Sorrow has taught Mr. Darling that he is the kind of man who whatever he does contritely he must do to excess; otherwise he soon abandons doing it.

Mrs. Darling does not often go out to dinner, preferring when the children are in bed to sit beside them tidying up their minds, just as if they were drawers.

Mr. and Mrs. Darling (Wendy's folks) were the kind of parents who contribute to the development of the Peter Pan Syndrome. Barrie paints a picture of Mr. Darling as a shallow and narcissistic individual. His self-pity and sarcasm are thinly disguised as playfulness. In a complementary vein, Mrs. Darling is seen as overprotective of her children and condescending toward her husband. Time and again we see Mrs. Darling's martyrdom. She suffers in silence at the childish antics of her husband and finds meaning in obsessively protecting her children's fragile minds from what she interprets as a cold, cruel world.

The tension in the Darling household is palpable. Early in the play, Mr. Darling has trouble tying his tie. He complains bitterly about the inequity of being plagued by a recalcitrant piece of clothing. His wife reacts with stiff and pretentious disapproval. Mr. Darling demonstrates the excesses of his narcissism with this response:

I warn you, Mary, that unless this tie is round my neck we don't go out to dinner to-night, and if I don't go out to dinner to-night I never go to the office again, and if I don't go to the office again you and I starve, and our children will be thrown into the streets.

Mrs. Darling gives in to her husband's tantrum and ties his tie. The children watch in horror, believing that if their mom isn't successful, they face homelessness and starvation.

Such crudeness and pettiness are typical of the father of the PPS victim. Also representative is the patronizing reaction of Mrs. Darling. Although overstated in this example, the two reactions combine to create a family atmosphere in which the children must endure endless anxiety. As you learned in the first section of this book, this anxiety is most detrimental to the boys in the family.

If you think your child may be a victim of the Peter Pan Syndrome, you have two decisions to make:

First, you must decide whether to focus your effort on prevention or remediation. I can help you with this decision by suggesting that if your child is under sixteen, you probably ought to work on prevention. If he's over sixteen and you've seen evidence of role inflexibility, narcissism, or chauvinism, I suggest that you concentrate on remedial action.

Your second decision is tougher. This blunt reality might guide your thoughts: You won't be able to help your child unless you are willing to change at least part of your personality and confront whatever marital discord is present. If the child has lived in your house or had a significant relationship with you, you have contributed to his problem. You have made some mistakes. I will help you find them, but it's up to you to rectify them. If you are unwilling to make the second decision, don't bother with the first one.

If you are determined to help your child, use Barrie's dialogue to initiate self-examination.

If you are a father, examine your emotional life. Do you engage in self-pity? Are you afraid of your feelings? Do you even know what you feel? Do you pretend to feel things you don't really feel, while hiding from other feelings? Are you actually confused about your emotions? Do you sublimate your disappointment in your marriage by giving your son

175

covert messages about the weaknesses of your wife (see Chapter 4)?

If you are a mother, evaluate your overprotectiveness and patronizing attitude. Do you tolerate your husband's chauvinism because you are afraid to stand alone? Do you feel sorry for him? Do you avoid confronting him about his childishness? Does your lack of courage cause you to back away from responsible and consistent discipline? Do you sublimate your marital disappointments by telling your son not to be like his father?

These are tough questions to ask as well as to answer. If you have the courage to face personal limitations, you are halfway toward constructive change. You need to follow through on this self-examination by doing something that has probably slipped away from you in the past few years. No matter what your child's age, start talking and *listening* to your marital partner. You need to truly communicate with your spouse. While it may take several months to accomplish this, you can solve one problem as soon as you put this book down.

STOP THE COVERT MESSAGES

You can take immediate action to thwart the development or further progression of the PPS process. Without delay, *cease all covert messages*. Without going into unnecessary details, tell the children that you have been wrong to dump your frustrations on them. Tell them that your disagreement with your spouse is *not* their fault. Then implement rational disciplinary procedures against their misbehavior and hold them accountable for their actions.

It sounds simplistic to say that you can immediately stop all covert messages. But you can. If you're truly motivated to free your children from needless anxiety, you'll listen for covert messages that creep into your conversation. Once you hear them, you will stop, even if you must interrupt yourself in mid-sentence. If you catch yourself conveying a covert message, bring your error out in the open as soon as possible, apologize for it, and use your mistake to demonstrate *your* problem. If you're bold, ask your children to help you identify these messages. You can be sure that they will hear them.

Take the blame off your children's shoulders by explaining how your frustration gets dumped on them. Tell them that you will use rational disciplinary measures to hold them accountable for their behavior rather than picking on them. You can overlook their complaints by concentrating on their behavior. This behaviorial approach eliminates any prejudicial actions on your part.

If your spouse cooperates with you in this remedial process, you will be able to eradicate most of the tension from your home in a relatively short time. If not, then you must proceed alone. If, for example, your husband refuses to admit his part in the covert process, then you must warn him that you will be forced to talk about him behind his back. This is a very undesirable situation, but freeing the children from guilt makes it necessary. If you have the courage to attack this problem by yourself, you may eventually entice your husband to follow suit. Employ this distasteful strategy only *after* you've made *every* reasonable attempt to improve communication with your spouse.

COMMUNICATION

Once you've stopped the spread of covert messages, you and your spouse must eliminate the cause of these messages. You do this by reestablishing lines of effective communication. If you have the courage to face the negative parts of your relationship, you can dramatically alter the atmosphere of your home. The sooner you overcome communication barriers, the quicker you'll reduce pent-up frustration and banish the anxiety that propels youngsters toward the Peter Pan Syndrome.

The first obstacle you'll encounter is your justification for avoiding the truth. I've identified two viewpoints that are equally faulty. One is held by the father, the other by the mother. From the synopsis below, you'll recall the covert messages detailed in Chapter 4 and see how these viewpoints foster the messages. I also offer my standard response to each of these viewpoints. If you accept my logic, you will be encouraged to confront the truth.

First, let's look at the PPS victim's father and understand his reasoning. Then we'll see how the mother complements her husband.

Father / son covert messages:
'Keep your mother off my back.'
'Don't hurt your mother.'
'Your mom doesn't understand men.'
'Take it easy, you know how women are.'

Dad's justification:
'My wife is weak and it's my job to protect her. Her hair-trigger emotions get her into trouble all the time, especially with the kids and most especially with my son. I hate it when she's upset, because then she picks on me. Being a woman, she doesn't understand that boys will be boys. If I can get my son to understand her, maybe we'll both be saved a lot of grief. Anyway, he'll have to find out the truth about women sooner or later.'

An alternative view:
If you protect your wife when she doesn't need it, you are encouraging her to be overly dependent, and *that* will cause ϟou grief. She's certainly not a mental weakling, and I'm sure you can give me many examples of her strength. If you avoid confronting her, you treat her as a child, and she, in turn, will rebel.

Boys may be boys, but does that excuse their disruption and negate your responsibility? If you continue in this viewpoint, you are passing your weaknesses onto your son and he will most likely have the same problems and prejudices with *his* wife.

178

Mother/son covert messages:

'Don't bother your father.'

'You're acting just like your father.'

'Your father doesn't understand feelings.'

'It's too bad your father's work is more important than his family.'

Mom's justification:

'My husband sometimes acts just like another child. He wants his way and sulks when he doesn't get it. He often treats me like a second-class citizen, preferring his work and his buddies to being with me. When my son acts insensitive, he's just following his father's example. If I don't change that, I pity the poor woman who gets stuck as I did.'

An alternative view:

Did you ever think your husband treats you like a second-class citizen because you take it? Do you really have the courage of your convictions? If you do, then you must not accept his prejudices. By accepting the way your husband treats you, you too are demonstrating to your son that women are inferior. It's quite possible that instead of changing your son, you ought to be changing yourself.

These prejudical viewpoints keep the parents apart and put the kids in the middle. They lead to mind reading and motive guessing, two mental activities that spell disaster for a marriage. If you and your spouse have the courage to do some soul-searching, and if you can accept the logic of the alternative viewpoints, then you are ready for a person-to-person confrontation. Clearing the air will be scary. However, the fresh air that will enter your relationship will not only arrest the growth of the PPS but also add new life to your marriage.

If you face up to unspoken complaints and hidden plans, you and your spouse will probably have a fight. You will dump your frustrations on each other, creating momentary tensions that might appear overwhelming. In order to make these fights productive, you need a guide that will reduce the possibilities of making a bad situation worse. I suggest you buy a book written by a doctor who has taught thousands of couples the art and science of 'fair fighting.'

Like all self-help books, *The Intimate Enemy* (see page 259) can be misused. If you fight with your mate without the dedication to marital renewal, it won't work. However, if you strive for constructive change, you will find a gold mine in this book. The authors sensitize the reader to the effect on children of marital discord when they say, 'Children are a favorite target when intimates displace their own fights onto other people. Most parental fights about children, for example, are not about children at all. The disagreement is between the parents; the child is only the battleground.'

If you decide to use this book to help you fight fair, here are a few guidelines that I've gleaned from Dr. Bach's work:

- You have a responsibility to state your concerns or gripes in terms of personal beliefs and feelings. State your position as clearly as you can.
- A 'fair fight' actually takes the form of a serious discussion conducted in an adult manner.
- Do not be afraid to learn how to express disgust and hateful feelings. Loving one another is easy; it's learning how to fight that takes work.
- Compromise is an essential by-product of fair fights.
- 'Hitting below the belt' is disastrous. If you bring up past occurrences only for the reason of hurting your spouse, you've hit below the belt.
- Be careful when introducing complaints about sexual issues into a fight. They are usually brought up in an 'unfair' manner.
- Listening is a critical factor in pursuing a fair fight. 'What are you trying to tell me?' 'What did you mean by that?' and 'Let me tell you what I heard you say,' are three feedback techniques that will aid listening.
- If your fights don't produce results or if you continually hit or get hit below the belt, you should seek a marriage counselor to monitor your fights.

In counseling marriage partners, I've devised several

other guidelines that can be added to those suggested by
Dr. Bach.

- Don't force a resolution of issues involving feelings.
  Some emotions do not lend themselves to change, only
  understanding and acceptance.
- Be very wary of the phrase 'I feel that . . .' This phrase is
  a smokescreen that hides rather than clarifies emotions.
  Simply put, you can't feel 'that'; rather, you *feel* angry,
  sad, disappointed, joyous, confused, etc. When your
  mate introduces his or her feelings by saying, 'I feel that
  . . .,' he or she will then say something that is *not* a
  feeling. Do not be misled by this smokescreen. Confront
  your partner by saying, 'Tell me how you feel, not what
  you think.'
- Listening to your spouse is crucial. But so is listening to
  yourself. One way to check your ability to listen to
  yourself is to ask your spouse, 'What did you hear me
  say?' Another is to practice self-listening when you are
  with a friend who will help you.
- If you get tongue-tied when trying to confront your
  mate, write notes to yourself that will help you state your
  position clearly and unequivocally.
- Avoid mind reading and motive guessing. You can do
  this by sticking with the pronouns 'I' and 'me' rather than
  'you.' Don't tell your mate what he or she is thinking or
  feeling; that's his or her responsibility.
- Here are a few introductory words that will set you on the
  right course:

When introducing a problem, say 'I wish to confront you
about——— .' 'When you do this, I feel——— .' 'My
request is that you ——— .' In responding to such a
confrontation, say: 'When you say that, I feel——— .' 'My
intentions are——— .' 'I (will or will not) comply with your
request.'

- Don't push for a total confrontation within a short period
  of time. Permit your thoughts and feelings to come alive
  as you *want* them to, rather than as they 'should,' 'ought
  to,' or 'have to.'

One more thing I've learned about parents of PPS victims is not very pleasant but it's true nonetheless: *Chances are that the wife will have to be the initiator of any confrontation regarding marital discord.*

Women are usually more in touch with (not necessarily in control of) their emotions. As a female, you have probably been encouraged to learn about your emotional life and actively participate in sharing personal feelings. You may even have gone to the extreme of thinking with your heart. If you are a male, you've probably learned to suppress your emotions to the extent that feelings are instantly converted into cognitions. You feel with your brain.

The imbalance in thought and feeling is never more apparent than when parents are faced with the Peter Pan Syndrome. Dad believes that the problem can only be solved with cold and efficient logic. Mom, on the other hand, is flooded with emotional pain and is so overwrought that any coping strategy is lost in excessive emotionalism. Mom criticizes Dad for being unfeeling; Dad accuses Mom of being hysterical. Both are powerless to solve the problem.

Unfortunately, people must be in considerable emotional pain before they will risk changing the status quo. They know innately that change means things will get worse before they get better. Since the female is more apt to feel the pain of family turmoil, she will most likely be the one to start rocking the boat.

This reality often causes women to express resentment toward their husbands for being 'cold and insensitive.' Not only are they hurt by the stockpiling of bad feelings, but they are also angry because they feel they have been lied to by a person who supposedly loves them. If you feel cheated by your husband's lack of caring, consider this possibility: there are many men who care desperately about their wives and children, but they've lost touch with their emotions. As strange as it may sound, these men truly *don't know what they feel*.

Many fathers of PPS victims suffer the same kind of emotional impotence as their sons do. These men have circled the outskirts of Peter's legion for many years. The only thing that keeps them from falling into the main stream of the legion is their ability to work. While it may lead to the excesses of 'workaholics,' their job does give them something to be sincerely proud of; unfortunately, it's often the only thing in which they take pride.

If this man is the father of your children, you'll want more details about what you can do to reverse the deterioration of your relationship. Since this chapter is dedicated to the parental concerns, I suggest you carefully study the next chapter, in which I turn my attention to recommendations for wives and lovers of PPS victims because, if you are a wife and mother, there's a chance that, at least in the emotional arena, you may be faced with *two* victims of the Peter Pan Syndrome.

HELPING THE PPS VICTIM

Once you've confronted the communication issue in your marriage, concentrate on the children. While this book is dedicated to helping the PPS victim, many of the following recommendations apply to all young people. Keeping that in mind, turn your attention to your oldest son, or to any son who exhibits the behaviors outlined in Chapters 3 through 8. If the boy is under sixteen, focus on preventive efforts; if he's over sixteen, emphasize remedial suggestions.

Why sixteen? Once a PPS victim reaches his sixteenth birthday, he has experienced widespread irresponsibility and several years of pervasive anxiety. He has found respite in belonging to a peer group that probably has more input into his life than you do. The inflexibility associated with an ongoing sex role conflict insulates him from parental influence. Even if you make a major turnaround in your relationship and eliminate tension from the home, it may be too late. It's possible that he's learned to ignore you.

However if the sixteen-year-old is a late bloomer or hasn't developed all the symptoms (for example, he holds a good job), you may still have time to prevent narcissism and chauvinism. You won't know until you try. Thus, if a PPS victim is at or near age sixteen, he's on the edge of becoming trapped in the legion of lost boys. You should try both preventive and remedial measures. You'll have to experiment with all my advice to find the most effective combination for your son.

BACK-TO-BASICS PRINCIPLES

Whatever the age or sex of your children, you'll want to acquaint yourselves with my back-to-basics parenting principles. These ten guidelines give any parent the foundation for preventing trouble or remedying a problem. They lend consistency and respect to the authority of parents, work to offset irresponsibility, and promote security in the home. You'll also find that they provide a common-sense middleground that can stimulate agreement between parents who disagree on child-rearing.

I will introduce each principle and then give you an example of how the guideline could be used to forestall the development of the Peter Pan Syndrome.

1. *Communication may prevent problems; but action solves them.*

In the past twenty or thirty years, child-rearing experts have misled parents into thinking that talking is the best strategy to use when faced with a problem. It isn't. The exchange of ideas and feelings or an explanation of whys and wherefores may help the child learn from a mistake, but only *after* the emotional upheaval of the situation has subsided. Attempts at rational communication in the midst of a problem tend to make matters worse. When parents are faced with a problem, talk is cheap. Action will solve the uproar, teach a meaningful lesson, and pave the way for effective communication.

Whenever I consider this principle, I envision a young mother in a grocery store with a four-year-old who is screaming because Mom said he couldn't have a candy bar.

As the kid stands in the middle of the aisle with a quivering lower lip and a face full of tears, Mom bends over and tries to reason with him. She explains the negative effect of sugar or tells him that other kids will think he's funny (a very dangerous use of peer pressure). Instead of listening to her, he only screams louder. There's no communicating with a child who's upset. Mom's best alternative is to take some action.

Many mothers spank a child in this situation. I don't particularly like that option. I suggest that Mom simply take the child's audience away by walking to another aisle. Whatever she does, Mom ought to suspend communication until her child is calm enough to listen.

2. *Many rules are negotiable; some are not.*

Every household should have some rules that are in keeping with reasonable and rational moral principles. I encourage parents to separate rules into negotiable and non-negotiable. Non-negotiables are absolute and unbending. For example, children will not break the law, disrespect is forbidden, and lying and cheating are wrong. There is never room for granting an exception to a non-negotiable. Violation always results in some disciplinary action.

Negotiable rules are open to discussion, change, and exception. Curfew is often dependent upon the activity; bed-time might be flexible if the child demonstrates self-care; extra privileges can be granted if a child increases school performance. Parents retain veto power in all rules but are encouraged to negotiate as much leeway as the child can handle.

One of the things that impede the development of the PPS is the trait of *positive submission*. We all need to learn to submit to certain realities of life in a positive manner; that is, we accept the limitation but work to see the positive side of it. The distinction between negotiable and non-negotiable rules helps a child learn positive submission.

If your son learns to submit to the absolute nature of

certain rules and is rewarded with increased freedom when he presents a positive negotiation, he will be prepared to deal with boring school subjects, unfair employers, and any magical thinking that may creep into his teenage life. Frustration tolerance and impulse control are two reality-based by-products of the distinction between negotiable and non-negotiable rules.

3. *If children 'take care of business' (curfew, manners, grades, chores, and money), parents should stay out of their business.*

This principle is an adjunct to principle 2. In effect it says that if your child is demonstrating responsible behavior in critical areas of life (my experience suggests that the five areas listed above are the most critical), you should grant exceptions and offer him the opportunity to enjoy increased freedom.

This principle permits you to confront an irresponsible child with his behavior, reminding him that the reason you are intervening in his life is that he failed to 'take care of business.' Likewise, it enables you to tell him that if he improves his performance, you will be only too happy to keep your nose out of his business.

This approach reduces the conflict, arguments, and hostility that often arise when a parent tries to discipline an older child. Experience has taught me that this principle has more impact on irresponsibility than any other single strategy.

4. *A good punishment is over quickly and isn't repeated very often. That is the reward of punishment.*

If you heap punishment upon punishment, or punish a child for an extensive period of time, you run the risk of punishing yourself more than the child and decreasing the overall effectiveness of punishments. You also stimulate unnecessary rebellion and feelings of revenge.

A good example of how this principle can be imple-

186

mented is the following: Say your son comes home late and lies to you about where he's been. Rather than grounding him for two weeks, you impose a penalty that is more intense and of shorter duration. At your earliest convenience you supervise the child while he does one hour of menial labor (scrubbing the pots and pans). In addition, the child is grounded that evening with no phone, music, or television. He must also go to bed an hour earlier. The penalty for curfew violation and loss of reputation (lying) is over in one or two days. Then the child can start a new day fresh and unencumbered.

If such a punishment must be repeated often, then it isn't working. Chances are that something else is happening (anxiety, for example) and you should evaluate the home environment to remedy the causes of the child's disruption.

5. *Children's complaints are often true ('You're not fair. Everybody else gets to do it.'). You can accommodate, not capitulate.*

When you must take an unpopular stance on an issue, you shouldn't expect a bright and self-seeking child to succumb without some complaints. Inequity, conformity, and misunderstanding are just a few of the topics that lend themselves to verbal protests. When you hear a complaint, remind yourself that there is probably a kernel of truth in what the child says. Remain calm and try to use the complaint to start a positive exchange of ideas.

This principle is especially helpful in dealing with a young teenager. For example, 'You're not fair' is a complaint you're bound to hear after making an unpopular decision. Rather than berating the boy for backtalk, listen to his complaint and accept the kernel of truth in it. *From his viewpoint, you are probably being unfair.* You can defuse a potentially nasty situation by admitting that he's right. Then, if he's listening, you can explain how a loving parent must make decisions for the long-range welfare of the child; because he doesn't fully understand this, feelings of inequity are probable and understandable. However, this does *not* change your decision.

6. *Children find confidence and self-esteem through reasonable limits and rational discipline.*

In an attempt to give children a positive self-concept, many parents believe that they must: be a child's best friend, not enforce limits, and make sure that the child is always happy. These goals are unrealistic.

A child needs a parent; he will find his friends elsewhere. Limits teach a child self-control, a trait he needs to achieve self-development and, with it, honest pride. Finally, failure is part of living, as are feelings of sadness. Our children need to learn how to fail and how to feel sad without becoming self-pitying and depressed.

If there is a key to the prevention of the Peter Pan Syndrome, it is expressed in this principle. Teach your toddler that you will be friendly as long as he stays inside the limitations you set. A school-age child can learn the importance of controlling his frustrations by getting all his home-work done before he is allowed to play. And, throughout his life, a child can be helped to tolerate failure and overcome feelings of sadness by receiving warmth and compassion *without pity or special treats* that say, 'You poor baby, I feel so sorry for you.'

7. *Parents reduce peer pressure by deciding with conscience, not conformity.*

If you recall the main message of Chapter 5, you'll realize that reducing the influence of peer pressure is absolutely esential to the prevention of the Peter Pan Syndrome. It's never too early to exercise your informed conscience when making decisions. Unfortunately, it often becomes too late to do so; that is, once your teenager chooses peer group impulses over parental thoughtfulness, your ability to instill a sense of individuality is severely limited.

To reduce peer pressure in your child's life is to control it in yours. Do you refer to other children when trying to influence your child's behavior? Do you criticize your spouse for his or her nonconformity in front of the kids? Do you base your decisions on outside influences (PTA, *The*

New York Times, Good Housekeeping) rather than on what *you* think is right and wrong? Does parental peer pressure stop you from disciplining your children in public?

These questions should open the door to self-examination. If you based your decisions on conformity rather than conscience, then you teach your children to do likewise. The next time you hear, 'But, Mom [Dad], *everybody's* doing it,' renew the spirit of your informed conscience and reply, 'You may be right, but that's not a reason for *you* to do it.'

8. *Children are strong and creative. Parents can find delight in their manipulations.*

Children are much tougher than we give them credit for being. The current generation is better nourished and nurtured than ever before. They are brighter and more creative. Consequently, they will regularly test authority's limits, looking for a solid morality to guide them through a difficult and often dangerous life.

Parents can take delight in childish manipulations. They indicate that your offspring are healthy and conducting a natural search for the boundaries of their ego power. This principle also reminds you to follow through on your moral guidelines, ensuring that your word is your bond.

No matter how old your children, let them know that you believe in their strength and that *they should too*. When you discover a youthful con job, permit some understanding and warmth to fill your heart. You needn't scream or condemn. Your kids are just hunting for someone to teach them self-control. You can be that someone.

9. *Families who work and play together, stay together.*

An atmosphere of tension exists in every family where the PPS flourishes. The tension is rooted in marital discord and branches out into daily outbursts of negativism. If there is tension in your home, then you know that your family can rarely be together wihout someone picking on someone else and everybody getting edgy.

To reverse this negative attitude, the family should

engage in an activity that all members will find enjoyable. Movies, going out to dinner, trips to the library, and sporting events can be the stimulus for a positive family experience.

Even if your spouse won't help you, there is still hope for change. Start by having a family meal on Sunday and *do not tolerate* any nastiness. If one child won't shape up, ask him or her to leave the table and make certain that he or she is grounded for the rest of the day. It may take a time or two, but you can guide the family into thirty or forty minutes of pleasant conversation. During this reversal process, you may not always be successful (especially if you don't have any help) but, at the very least, control any negativism so that a bad situation is not made worse.

10. *Practice it, don't preach; your action, not words, will teach.*

Many parents substitute words for actions, believing that they can talk their children into compliance. These are the same parents who lack self-discipline in their own personal lives. While most don't fit the PPS profile, they too have failed to grow up.

Many of these parents were raised in a no-limits household. Their children represent a second generation of permissiveness. The kids aren't likely to impose inhibitions upon their impulses; sadly, their parents don't know how to do it either. The parents set the tone by talking one way, behaving another. Their children, more often than not, follow their example. The result: the blind leading the blind.

If you have the courage to admit that you don't know the rudiments of self-discipline, then you have some catching up to do. Rather than blame your parents for their failure, turn your attention to the task of growing up. It need not take you very long. If you work diligently, you ought to be able to compensate for several years of arrested maturity in a few months. If you're not sure how to go about catching up, I have a simple suggestion: The same back-to-basics principles that you use to raise your children can be used to raise yourself.

190

UNDER SIXTEEN

You've seen how six chronological symptoms—irresponsibility, anxiety, loneliness, sex role conflict, narcissism, and chauvinism—have resulted in the gradual development of seven observable psychological traits. In giving you specific prevention strategies, I will relate my recommendations to the remission of each of these traits. Since this section deals with the younger victim, my advice will center on counteracting the influence of the four cornerstones of the PPS: irresponsibility, anxiety, loneliness, and sex role conflict.

Unless otherwise designated, each of my recommendations should be employed by Mom and Dad in a like manner. Some suggestions require that Mom and Dad each emphasize a different approach.

Emotional Impotence

Immediately cease all covert messages. Explain to the child that past messages were wrong and that he's not to worry about protecting his mom and dad.

Eliminate the negative attitude of family gatherings, even if you must suspend family activity altogether.

Don't get upset when your son expresses disgust with an unpopular parental decision. As long as he demonstrates some control, ignore his outbursts.

Dad: Do not dismiss your son's feelings with trite phrases. Encourage him to express his emotions honestly and openly. Work with him by expressing your feelings in a mature manner. Show him that it's okay to experience a variety of emotions.

Mom: Refrain from giving your son pity. Likewise, don't give him the notion that he can barter his feelings to obtain special favors.

Procrastination

Assign chores to the child and enforce the rules with

discipline that holds the child accountable for the work (see pages 185-6).

Do not permit yourself to issue a second warning. Once a directive is given, follow through on the 'or else' after one warning.

Do not attempt to force an older child to study. Assign a study time and hold him accountable for grades on a regular basis.

Limit the times you take responsibility off the kid's shoulders by doing something for him because it's too much of a bother to make sure *he* does it. Don't give him an easy way out.

Reduce a child's allowance to an absolute minimum (preferably down to zero) as he approaches teen age. Teach him responsibility by helping him replace the money through a job or special contracts for work around the house.

The *quitter attitude* can be offset with this approach: once a child decides to start a project (music lessons, a sporting activity), he is not permitted to quit until he has successfully begun a complementary project; if he quits anyway, he is restricted in freedom and privileges until he meets that requirement.

Dad: Teach your son how to set goals, and project and evaluate the outcome. Show him your problem-solving method. It gives him a valuable lesson as it reduces any estrangement.

Mom: Curtail any unintentional use of guilt-provoking. 'You like to see me suffer,' 'You never like to help me,' and 'You don't know how much you hurt me' are comments that cause guilt, despair, and an 'I don't care about tomorrow' attitude.

Peer Susceptibility

Do not belittle his friends or compare him to 'good' kids.

If he chooses 'bad companions,' try to understand why he selects this type of friend. There is a reason. If you find out why your son needs a certain type of friend, maybe you can help him overcome any weakness that has caused his choice.

Follow your informed conscience when explaining why you make certain decisions. Be careful not to allow parental peer pressure to influence your conscience (see back-to-basics principle 7).

Make this rule concerning individuality: all school-age children will engage in an extracurricular activity that emphasizes personal achievement (tennis, running, track and field, golf, gymnastics, dance, drama, speech, etc.) Allow the child to choose the activity in keeping with this rule.

Use this guideline in controlling sibling fights: if you're not friendly with your brothers and sisters, you'll not have the privilege to be friendly with your friends. Grounding and suspension of phone privileges until the children do something nice to compensate for their nastiness is advised.

Share with your children your informed opinion regarding social and political issues. Get their thoughts on the issues that interest them. Take action on these matters by getting involved in community affairs. If you face time constraints, the least you can do is to vote in *every* election. If possible, take your children to the polling place and let them watch (quietly) as you exercise your civic duty.

Reduce the emphasis on alcohol consumption. Increase the social aspects of friendship. Your children need to see a clear distinction between 'social' and 'drinking.' The very least you can do is to talk with your guests for a few moments before saying, 'What'll you have to drink?'

Sexual Hang-Up

Make sure your child has accurate sexual information. In addition to your discussions, you may want to use educational books. For younger children a series by Peter Mayle presents solid information in a lively fashion. *Where Did I Come From?* and *What's Happening to Me?* are excellent for younger kids. Teenagers will get a lot of help from *Changing Bodies, Changing Lives* by Ruth Bell, et al.

Let your son know that talking to the opposite sex is more important (and difficult) than touching them.

Know what your son is learning in sex education classes, often called 'Health.' Reviewing his homework will give you a natural situation in which to ask questions and see how much reliable information he has.

Prohibit unchaperoned dating prior to 14 to 15 years of age.

Keep a close eye on the movies and television programs your son watches. If you see unrealistic attitudes being portrayed as normal, challenge them. For example, many shows tell the young man that big breasts are an absolute key to good relationships.

Dad: Don't try to relive your youth by playing the role of a voyeur when asking your son questions about potential girlfriends. Let him see you hug and kiss your wife. Hold hands with your wife during family outings.

Magical Thinking

Teach your children the difference between explanations and excuses. Children explain the circumstances; parents excuse a misbehavior. When children concoct an explanation and automatically think they have an excuse, they begin to believe in mental magic.

Help the kids learn to live with failure. When they face disappointment, give them patience, not pity, and do not exempt them from rules of moral conduct. Keep this statement in mind: 'Have your pain but mind the rules.'

When you exercise your authority, don't talk too much. If you preach, nag, or argue, you teach the kids that they can make rules magically disappear by manipulating words.

Beware of any complaint that begins, 'If it weren't for . . .' This is a magical incantation that is usually followed by placing blame for failure upon some other person. Your best response is to help the child sort out the problem and see what *he* can do to overcome whatever adversity he faces.

Father Hang-Up

Dad: Learn more about the house rules and exercise your authority whenever necessary. Don't try to win a popularity contest by always being seen as the good guy.

Do things with your son that both you and he will enjoy. You don't have to spend a lot of money to be close. The key is to enjoy each other.

Share embarrassing times from your past with your son. Let him see the human side of his dad.

Spare your son from hearing any chauvinistic attitudes that you may still hold.

Mom: Never say, 'Wait till your father gets home!'

In addition to suspending all covert messages, don't share husband-and-wife problems with your son.

Mother Hang-Up

Mom: Protect your son from any stereotyping of a wife's role in the home. Teach him to cook, sew, and do laundry; he'll need those survival skills.

Make sure that you have some life away from the kids. If you don't, you can easily fall into martyrdom and over-protection.

Be especially careful to implement and enforce no-nonsense rules.

Spare your son from hearing any 'chauvinette' attitudes. These are attitudes that are complementary to a chauvinist's viewpoint. 'Your father is the boss' and 'Men shouldn't help with housework' are two examples.

Dad: In addition to suspending all covert messages, don't share husband-and-wife problems with your son.

Help your son explore his feelings and attitudes whenever he experiments with being independent from his mom.

Let your son see your masculinity, but do not be afraid to lean on your wife for support, understanding, and other help.

If you must chase other women, protect your son from

your infidelity (even though he will probably sense that something is wrong).

Mom: Never disclose information, good or bad, about your sexual life to your children.

Retain some modesty in dress.

FOR MOMS WHO STAND ALONE

It has been my experience that the mother of the PPS victim is the first to see that her son is in trouble. However, because her husband habitually ignores her concerns and is estranged from his son, he will often dismiss her diagnosis as overreactive. If Mom can't convince Dad of the need for changes, she stands alone.

If you've failed to get your husband involved in the family's problems, you need not give up. While there are some things you can't do alone, there are other things you can do that will impede the development of the PPS. The following suggestions are for moms who stand alone, whether because of divorce, death, or, in the case of single mothers, because a father figure has never been present.

Find a support group. This might be a discussion group for parents sponsored by the PTA, your church, or a local mental health agency. A more informal group might be formed from concerned neighbors and friends. Don't be bashful about sharing your worries; many other mothers are in the same boat as you. And that's the major goal of a support group—gaining the hope and courage that come from sharing similar experiences.

Get back to the basics. Review my ten principles very carefully. Discuss specific implementation with your support group. Pay close attention to the principles that direct you to set and enforce rules without nagging, arguing, or preaching. If your husband won't cooperate with you, maybe he'll just stay out of the way.

Do something for yourself. Nothing eradicates martyrdom like doing something you enjoy. If you are living with a man who seems like a stranger, you need an outside activity to cope with your loneliness. If you don't know where to start, check out the programs offered by your school district's adult education department, the park district, and the local college. Many mothers who stand alone have found a release in aerobic dance, bridge lessons, tennis and racquetball leagues, or in continuing their formal education.

Seek professional help. You don't have to be maladjusted or crazy to visit a counselor. Nor do you have to be rich. No matter where you live, there is some type of professionally trained counselor available to listen to your story and offer some objective help. Many of the agencies who employ these counselors will charge you a fee dependent upon your financial resources. It certainly wouldn't hurt to try it a couple of times. You might eventually get your husband to go with you.

OVER SIXTEEN

As he reaches mid-adolescence, the PPS victim becomes disdainful of parental authority. As you lose your clout, preventive strategies will probably prove fruitless. The boy will expect you to give him what he wants and then stay out of his way. As you consider my hard-nosed advice, keep in mind what I say to parents who face this 'last ditch' effort (forgive the grammar): 'Don't do nothing no more!'

Admit your mistakes. Don't expect acknowledgement or decency, but apologize nonetheless. You may want to say it this way: 'We have made mistakes in giving you too much money and not enough time. We've let you ride roughshod over us without taking strong action. For these and other things, we are sorry.'

Once you've admitted your mistakes, tell the boy that you love him and will try to help him any way you can. But remind him that his problems are *his* and that you will not take responsibility for them. Use these comments to introduce the actions you are prepared to take to help him stop himself from being trapped in his piratical lifestyle.

Seek professional help. The older PPS victim needs

counseling. He will, however, resist it very strongly, and there's a good chance it won't be successful (see Chapter 2). To maximize any positive outcome, consider these suggestions:

Ask the high school counselor or local probation officer who has a good record for working with teenagers.

Lean toward a male counselor because of the boy's need to be close to a father figure and his ambivalence toward females.

Depending upon how the counselor works, try to see him before your son attends (even if you have to go alone).

With the counselor's guidance, explain to your son that he is talking to a counselor about a *family* problem; you're all in this together.

Be prepared to twist your son's arm a bit in order to make him attend. Involuntary clients don't make for a good prognosis, but at least the counselor will have a chance to help. (More on this arm-twisting below.)

Education/Work. I sincerely believe that the best therapy in the world is a combination of education and work. If the boy is in the advanced stages of the PPS, his educational and vocational track record are probably poor. Little, if anything, gives him honest pride. Do your best to reverse this downward spiral by considering the following suggestions:

Expect the boy to pursue a total, not part-time, work/study program. If he is a full-time student, he must earn his own pleasure money via a part-time job. If he is not in school, he must pay you for living at home (I suggest a minimum of $50 a week).

Do not advance him any money unless he has *clearly and consistently* proven that he repays loans on time.

If he sincerely works at finding a job but is unsuccessful, you may agree to pay him a preselected amount for work around the house. Washing and waxing the car might be worth $5 to $10, for instance.

Eliminate any gratuitous allowances over a period of four weeks by reducing the original amount by one-fourth each week.

Do not argue with him about money. It will only flame the fires of his rage and will solve nothing.

If he has academic or disciplinary problems at school, remain in the background, allowing the boy to bear the major burden of accountability. At this stage of his affliction, you should be happy with C's or better. You can always move your expectations upward after the current semester.

HOUSEHOLD DISRUPTION

Do not get him up in the morning, even if it means he may lose his job.

Expect him to do a chore or two in addition to keeping his room somewhat clean.

Establish a curfew (even if he's twenty-one years of age and paying you rent). You can be very flexible with his curfew if he is performing well in the work/study area.

You must have absolutely *no tolerance for drug abuse*. Do not discuss it beyond saying, 'I know you may party and drink and smoke dope. However, if I see any evidence of it, I will be forced to take action against you. Just because you're older doesn't mean that I quit being your parent when you decide to act irresponsibly.'

Expect him to show respect and consideration for others. Thus, if he won't turn the stereo down after requested to do so, and yells, 'It's *my* stereo,' unplug the machine. If you are concerned about being physically attacked, flip the switch at the power box or pull the fuse that governs his bedroom.

Do not give him uncontrolled access to a car. As long as he lives in your house, you must demonstrate to him that you have some control over his activity, even if he pays for the car.

SHAPE UP OR SHIP OUT

I'm sorry to say that most of the above recommendations will probably *not* work, especially if the boy is eighteen years of age or older. You will therefore have to implement a shape-up-or-ship-out program that puts into action your decision not to just stand by and let him continue to destroy himself while he's living in your house. This is where the arm-twisting comes in.

Move gradually with this program. Remember, you've contributed to his affliction and you should give him time to shape up. It's very convenient to throw all the blame on the kid in one swift get-tough statement. Convenient, but it doesn't work.

Keep your eye on his behavior. If you worry too much about his motives or feelings, you'll be immobilized. Even though you know he feels bad and his motives are skewed this reality must not stand in the way of his shaping up.

Check with your attorney about your rights and your child's responsibilities. If your child is considered a minor in your state, then consider taking him to juvenile court and seeking an alternative placement or having him declared emancipated.

If your son repeatedly and flagrantly defies your guidelines concerning work, study, curfew, chores, money, and the car, you will be forced to take stronger action.

Implement 'passive resistance.' Don't cook for him or do his laundry. Refuse to take phone messages or give him any money under any circumstances. Tell him, 'I won't do anything for you if you don't shape up.'

If this doesn't work, then you must turn his bedroom into a sewing room or den. Make him sleep in the basement.

If this doesn't get his attention, lock him out of the house. If he breaks in, have him arrested.

Once you've reached this stage, you are at the make-it-or-break-it point. You must be prepared to go all the way to the end to back up your statement that you won't take it any longer.

You may elect (if the counselor will support you) to back off on some of these stringent actions *if* the boy pursues counseling in a serious manner.

Consider joining a TOUGHLOVE group in your area. It is deeply rewarding to share problems and solutions of disruptive teenagers with parents suffering through the same difficulties. Write or call the Community Service Foundation, Sellersville, Pennsylvania 18960, (215) 257-0421, to get information about TOUGHLOVE groups in your part of the country.

Many of you will see my recommendations in this section as 'gutter fighting.' Many of them are probably just that. But I ask you to consider: if your son, whom you deeply love, were lying in the gutter surrounded by vermin of every description and you saw his life oozing away, would you not dive into the gutter and do everything you could possibly think of to save him? I know you would; love demands it.

SUPPORT FROM THE SYSTEM

A PPS victim doesn't embrace a piratical lifestyle simply because his parents made a few mistakes. Other significant people in his environment have contributed to his affliction. Aunts, uncles, cousins, grandparents, teachers, employers, ministers, and well-intentioned neighbors comprise a system of affiliates who have undoubtedly also made mistakes. They probably gave the child pity, special dispensations, and an endless string of second chances which only taught him to be a more effective manipulator. The people who comprise the victim's system must also help him shape up.

The system can have a positive impact on the PPS victim by supporting what you as parents are trying to do. However, the chain of people who comprise the system is only as strong as its weakest link. His cousin must not take him out drinking. His grandparents must not slip him unearned money. His aunt must not give him pity when he calls. His employer must fire him if he deserves it. His counselor must confront him if his self-defeating behavior warrants it. Your friend or neighbor must not give him room and board without your approval. If just one of these things occurs, the program of help is sabotaged.

As parents, your biggest job is to implement the

recommendations outlined above. However, you must also reach out to the people in the young man's system and explain to them how they can help. Ask them *not* to undermine what you're trying to accomplish. Assure them that you are doing what absolutely must be done. Cajole them into supporting your efforts; make sure they know how important those efforts are.

Once you've enlisted the aid of those in the victim's system, you've done all you can do. You must hope that the young man will profit from the lessons of the school of hard knocks. As I pointed out before, the best, and possibly only, remedy for the effects of the magical dust is *reality*.

If you think your son may be becoming a PPS victim, I urge you—for your welfare as well as his—to take action *now* to stop this senseless destruction. If you're a mother with a husband who does not share your concern, persuade your spouse to read this book, especially Chapters 10 and 11. He can't help being afraid of what might lie ahead for his son.

If you face an older victim of the Peter Pan Syndrome, you have my deepest understanding and support. I realize that you'd rather lose your right arm than watch your son destroy his life.

One last bit of advice: don't waste your time feeling guilty. It only makes matters worse. If your son is captured by the legion of lost boys, whatever his age, take action so that he will become a dropout. Your son doesn't need your guilt. He needs your help.

13 For Wives and Lovers

> Wendy leaps out of bed to put her arms round Peter, but he draws back; he does not know why, but he knows he must draw back. Peter is never touched by anyone in the play.

Barrie's narrative suggests that Peter is enslaved by a senseless compulsion. He inexplicably pulls away from Wendy's compassionate outreach. She wanted to comfort him; he wouldn't allow it. If you are in love with a victim of the Peter Pan Syndrome, you know the frustration Wendy experienced. You are baffled by the victim's 'rules of loving':

Keep your distance. Don't share any feelings until I give you permission to. Don't expect me to share feelings in return. Do not challenge my thoughts. Touch me according to my schedule.

These unspoken edicts crush spontaneity, an essential ingredient in a mature love relationship. That they are unspoken makes love difficult; that they are contradictory makes love impossible. You can't possibly offer love when your partner has expectations of you that are hewn in stone. You must behave in a strictly defined manner or you will be rejected. If it weren't for your awareness that he has the potential to be a great love partner, you'd never tolerate his childish manipulations.

But you do tolerate them! And by doing so you are contributing to your own heartache. That's the bad news. The good news is that you can change things. The PPS victim can learn to abandon his flight to Never Never Land, but he needs a place to start. That place is with the woman who loves him. And your place to start is with the blueprint for change developed in Chapter 2.

Love gives you the motivation to help him. The blueprint gives you the direction in which to go. The only other ingredient you need is hope. Will your care make a difference? There's a light beckoning to you from the end of the tunnel that says Yes. The light fades in and out from time to time, but is there nonetheless. Its message endures: come join me and things *will* get better. You don't have to keep doing the same old thing. Life can be much more exciting and fulfilling if only you dare to try. The light even has a name; it's Tinkerbell.

ON BECOMING A 'TINKER'

Two types of women are drawn to the victim of the Peter Pan Syndrome. One is well practiced in taking a back seat to men and is quick to fall into the role of a protective mother figure. She is insecure herself and the victim's dependency makes her feel needed. It even gives her a distorted sense of strength. Her sex with the PPS victim is ritualistic and predictable; it's also very quickly over with. She doesn't recognize that the victim is immature, and she persuades herself to believe that his problems are normal. She sticks with this mate, figuring her love life will improve. It doesn't. I call this type of woman a 'Wendy.'

The other type of woman wants spontaneity, growth, and mutual adaptation in her relationship with a man. She recognizes the PPS victim's immaturity but is drawn to his devil-may-care attitude. She, too, figures the guy will outgrow some of his juvenile behavior. However, when he fails to do so, this woman doesn't stick around. She ends the relationship, disappointed and disillusioned. She never fully understands why the love went sour. I call this woman a 'Tinker.'

If the PPS victim is trapped in Never Never Land, he will usually be 'in love' with a Wendy. He will be addicted to the cuddling, the pity, and the protectiveness. His Wendy will shield him from his own immaturities. When he explodes in rage or drinks himself into alcoholism, she will understand and take him back. She will tolerate him because he needs her so badly. There are a lot of Wendys at AlAnon meetings.

If the PPS victim returns from Never Never Land, he will look for a Tinker to share his life with. He will need her mature love and support as he flexes emotional muscles he never knew he had. Likewise, if a Wendy harnesses the electrical charge that lies dormant within her, she can become a Tinker. If she gets fed up with being a perpetual mother figure, she will challenge her mate to change. If he does not, she will abandon her Peter Pan and look for a man who isn't afraid to be a whole person. This is why many Peter Pans and Wendys end up in a divorce court, while ex-victims and Tinkers are so busy discovering life that you never hear of them.

You may not want to hear this, but if your husband or lover is a PPS victim, there's an excellent chance that you are a Wendy. You may not always have been a Wendy, and there may be a solid sparkle of Tinker in your soul. But if you've invested time and energy in a relationship with a PPS victim, there's some degree of Wendy lurking in your subconscious.

When I help wives and lovers cope with a PPS victim, I first focus on what bad habits they possess that complement those of their mate and/or encourage him to do the things he does. I encourage them to get their own house in order before trying to help their mate.

There's a good chance that you can become a Tinker without necessarily walking away from your present relationship. As I noted above, Tinkers as well as Wendys are attracted to the PPS victim because of the many positive aspects of his personality. You need not automatically give up on the positives in order to deal with the negatives. However, be forewarned: becoming a Tinker will put a stress on you and your current relationship. If the PPS victim had a high score (say, above 25) on the test in Chapter 2 and rejects your help, there is a good chance that you'll ultimately give up on him and break off the relationship. It will come as no surprise when I say that you can't 'make' him change, you can only help.

Your next step in the change process, then, is to examine yourself for Wendy characteristics. You do this to dedicate yourself to *your own* personal growth and maturity. That, in itself, is very beneficial, with many long-range payoffs. The second reason for changing is to lure your husband or lover away from Never Never Land and into the reality of being a caring, fragile human being like the rest of us. This will frighten him and he may resist. It will be difficult and require a lot of work on your part and on his.

If you decide to quit being your mate's mother and become a Tinker, the change will do you good even if you lose the guy in the process. But if you change primarily for the purpose of helping your mate, then you are still doing what you've done in the past—sacrificing yourself for his welfare—which is just what he wants a mother figure to do. You simply jumped out of the frying pan into the fire.

SELF-EXAMINATION

Here's a test for you to take about yourself. It requires that you look into the mirror of self-reflection, examining yourself for Wendy characteristics.

How many of the following statements sound like things you have said either to yourself or to someone else?

1. Your mate has been particularly cruel, leaving you with the realization that he is regularly nasty to you. Do you say to yourself, 'I only hope that I can hang on until he changes'?
2. There's talk of his leaving and you say, 'There's no way I can make it without him.'
3. You consider divorce or breaking off the relationship and think, 'If I leave him, it will be too much for him to handle.'
4. Someone asks you if you work, and you answer, 'No, I'm just a housewife.'

206

5. After reviewing his lack of consideration, his refusal to share feelings with you, and his cold sexual demands, you say, 'But, oh, he loves me so much.'

6. Your mate blows up at you for a messy house he never helps clean, or food that he doesn't like, and you say, 'I know it's my fault.'

7. Your mate includes his buddies in time periods that he says he wants to spend with you, and you say, 'I'm just a bitch for getting upset.'

8. Your mate has plenty of money to buy drinks for his buddies but rebels when you want to spend money on yourself. And you say, 'I'm wrong not to stay within my strict budget.'

9. When someone asks you what you like best about your husband, your first response is 'Oh, he's a great provider; he works fourteen hours a day.'

10. You are victimized by your mate's insensitivity and you say, 'If I tried to be more like him, this wouldn't hurt so much.'

How many of these statements have been in your mind and/or come out of your mouth? Using the old technique, 'on a scale of one to ten . . . ,' you can assign yourself a Wendy score. You don't need categories to evaluate your Wendy score. Suffice it to say that as you move upward from a score of three or four toward a nine or ten, the more you are trapped in Never Never Land with your mate. The lower your score, the more likely that you'll be able to make the conversion to a Tinker and lure your mate away from the legion of lost boys.

Conclude your self-examination by asking yourself three questions, similar to those asked at the end of Chapter 2:

How did I get this way?

What am I thinking about?

What can I do to change it?

Let's briefly consider the last question first. What you can do about it is to combine your motivation with your hope and use the blueprint for change to guide you in giving your relationship your best shot. As soon as we deal with the first two questions, I will outline specific suggestions to help you become a Tinker.

The first two questions are best treated as variations of a more fundamental question: What is it about me that makes me unconsciously support a pattern of behavior that is eventually hurting me and my hopes for a loving relationship?

This question has already been answered in a down-to-earth, well-documented way by a sensitive, insightful woman who must have coped with a PPS victim at one time during her life. Her name is Colette Dowling, and her brilliant book is *The Cinderella Complex* (see page 260). Any Wendy who wishes to become a Tinker must first confront her own Cinderella Complex and resolve to overcome it.

THE CINDERELLA COMPLEX

Although there can be no substitute for a careful reading of Ms. Dowling's book, permit me to summarize the critical points made in the book that relate to the question before us.

The Cinderella Complex is defined as:

> A network of largely repressed attitudes and fears that keeps women in a kind of half-light, retreating from the full use of their minds and creativity. Like Cinderella, women today are still waiting for something external to transform their lives.

Dowling believes that women have been trained to be dependent and to fear independence. It is my belief that many women cope with their fears by retreating into a motherly role (a Wendy) with the hope that being needed will somehow give them security. Therefore, it is my view that *being a Wendy is one way women cope with their Cinderella Complex*.

Here's how Dowling courageously describes her own retreat:

> Now I had land and flowers, a big house with plenty of

rooms, small, comfy window seats, nooks and crannies. Feeling safe for the first time in years, I set about concocting the tranquil domicile that lingers as a kind of 'cover memory' of the most positive aspects of one's childhood. I made a nest, insulating it with the softest bits of fluff and cotton I could find.

And then I hid in it.

What's crucial to remember about Dowling's retreat is that she did it while relating to a man *who wasn't a victim of the Peter Pan Syndrome* (my clinical inference). The lesson is clear: there's a good chance that you might seek the comfort of being a Wendy *regardless* of your husband's or lover's propensity toward the PPS. In fact, you might have been unconsciously looking for a PPS victim whose need for a mommy made you and him a perfect (although neurotic) couple.

If you're willing to look at the blind spot created by your love, then you can see that you have a certain degree of magical thinking that is not significantly different from your mate's. Hence, if it's true that the PPS victim uses magical dust to fly away to Never Never Land, is it not also true that women who love Peter Pan are waiting for a magic wand to transform them into Cinderella, believing that their back-breaking sacrifice will somehow create a fairyland coach that will whisk them away from drudgery and loneliness?

There is an unspoken victim-rescuer arrangement existing between the PPS victim and his Wendy. On the surface it appears that the woman is the victim and the man the rescuer; that the man is strong, the woman weak. I don't believe that this is actually the case. In fact, the power dynamics are just the reverse. The man is weak and the woman is strong. The sad part of this is that she is strong for all the wrong reasons.

First of all, there should be no power dynamics in an egalitarian relationship. The victim-rescuer arrangement is, by definition, destructive to a growth-oriented marriage.

Second, the woman is enduring derision and disrespect that no human being should tolerate. Her own hidden fear of independence pulls her into a Wendy role, where she tolerates more pain than makes rational sense. Certainly, if the roles were reversed, you can be sure that the PPS victim wouldn't put up with such discomfort for even a minute.

Third, the woman is in touch with her emotions and knows how to give voice to her feelings. This makes her considerably stronger than the PPS victim, who's lost touch with his feelings (usually) but covers this weakness by pretending that feelings aren't important.

Finally, the very fact that I address so much of this book to females is evidence that I've concluded that in the case of Peter Pan and Wendy, my best opportunity to help the PPS victim is to help his mate. She may be waiting for a ride in a magical coach, but my experience suggests that she has the courage and determination to admit her mistakes, forgo her pseudo-strength, and work to make things better.

WHAT CAN YOU DO TO CHANGE IT?

This is the question we've been leading up to beginning with the test in Chapter 2 summarizing a blueprint for change (which you should have in hand), and ending with a candid look in the psychological mirror, complete with an admonition concerning the influence of the Cinderella Complex.

You are now going to use that blueprint to make some changes in the way you and your husband or lover interact. As you do, keep two things in mind.

First, one overriding recommendation runs through all the situations I will discuss. That is: *When you confront a PPS behavior, what you do is not nearly as important as what you don't do. STOP SAYING AND DOING WENDY THINGS. Stop giving voice to your hidden fear of independence by hiding behind Wendy.*

Second, use the positive attributes listed on your blueprint to approach the negative ones. And approach the 'sometime' negative ones before tackling the 'always' behaviors. For example, if your blueprint tells you that your mate never flirts with other women but is sometimes shaken by your sexual aggressiveness, thank him for his fidelity and tell him that you are going to give him a back rub that may last for the rest of the night. This gives you the opportunity to desensitize his uneasiness about your sexual aggressiveness as it promotes the possibility that he will rub your back in return.

If your mate had a low PPS score and your Wendy rating was benign, you may think the following list of recommendations doesn't apply to you. But consider: Have you totally overcome your Cinderella Complex? Are you absolutely insulated from falling into the trap offered by the magic of Never Never Land and fairy godmothers? I doubt it. Even if you consider yourself a Tinker, there may be a charming imaginary man wearing a little green suit waiting for you just around the corner.

Okay, let's go to work.

Here's how I recommend that you cope with the twenty PPS behaviors outlined in Chapter 2:

1. *He overreacts, pushing you to excuse him or absolve him from guilt.*

DON'T:
- Try to appease him with motherly comments such as, 'Dear, you did the best you could; it wasn't your fault.'
- Get into any discussion in which you support his unrealistic rationalizations.
- Take away his pain by giving him pity.

DO:
- Ask him how it *feels* to make an error.
- Ask him leading questions; e.g., 'What could you have done differently? Did you learn anything for the future? What could you do next time?'
- Leave the room if he continually batters you with his innocence.
- Relate mistakes you've made.

- Inject some humor ('Oh, honey, it's the first mistake you've made this year.')
- Offer some rational alternatives. 'Anger is okay. Give yourself the right to make mistakes. A mistake is nature's way of reminding you that you're human.'
- If he gets angry at you because you won't feel sorry for him, say, 'I can't take your pain away; that's your responsibility.'

  2. He forgets your anniversary, birthday, or other important dates.

DON'T:

- Drop subtle hints.
- Expect guilt when he sees how upset you are at his omission.
- Shame him by buying him a big gift when you know he's forgotten.
- Plan storybook Christmases or anniversaries.
- Compare him to other men who remember important dates.
- Complain to others about your man's forgetfulness, even jokingly.

DO:

- If you want a gift, you'll probably have to purchase it yourself. Tell him, 'For my birthday, you got me this beautiful sweater.'
- Make not-so-subtle hints like inserting the appropriate dates in big red letters on a prominently displayed calendar.
- To encourage him to remember the day, tell him the night before, 'Let's have a special dinner tomorrow for our special day.'
- Tell him, unemotionally and preferably not near any date of importance, how much his remembering your birthday and other days means to you. Tell him *why* it's important.

212

- Ask him to talk with you about his happiest childhood memory as it relates to his birthday or holidays. Share good feelings about giving love to others.
- Ask yourself which is more important, the gift or the thought.

   3. *He tries to impress other people at parties, especially other women..*

DON'T:

- Flirt with other men to show him how bad it feels.
- Try to compete with him for becoming the life of the party; he'll only try harder and blame you if people ignore him.
- Hang onto his arm and complain, 'You're ignoring me.'
- Give him a blow-by-blow account of his cruelty in the car on the way home.
- Make apologies to others for his behavior.
- Make an idle threat ('I'll never go to another party with you.').
- Compare him to other men at the party. ('Harold got Marge a drink and brought her a sweater when she was cold.') Your PPS victim will only resent Harold.
- Make vague complaints ('You don't pay attention to me.').

DO:

- Consider not even going to the party if your mate hasn't dealt with your concerns.
- Ask someone else (not another man) for a ride home from the party if he does things that hurt you.
- Realize that you don't need to be 'attached' to your mate at a party. Go off by yourself and have your own fun.
- Forge your own way when it comes to getting a drink or meeting new people.
- At an appropriate time (possibly the next day), confront him by saying, 'When you kiss another woman in my

presence, I feel———. Do not do this in front of me again.'

- Be specific and factual when confronting him about the things he said that you didn't like. For example, 'I will not listen to you bad-mouthing my mother in order to impress your boss. If you do it again, I will leave the party.'

   4. He finds it almost impossible to say 'I'm sorry.'

DON'T:

- Try to goad or pull an apology from him.
- Point out each time that he should apologize.
- Bring up past mistakes and keep reminding him of his constant errors.
- Psychologize his weakness by analyzing why he can't say it. For example, 'The reason you don't admit mistakes is that you have an overblown ego.'
- Make fun of him because he's not up to 'normal' standards.

DO:

- Accept apologies in other forms. For example, 'I wish I hadn't yelled at you.'
- Say 'I'm sorry' when you are, to both him and others.
- Thank him for any attempt he makes to be honestly remorseful.

   5. He is insensitive to your need for sexual foreplay.

DON'T:

- Submit to intercourse just to please him.
- Pretend you enjoy it.
- Falsely praise his prowess and skills.
- Begin a heated discussion of sexual problems in bed.

DO:

- Be sexually adventuresome by trying new techniques. If

you need guidance, Alex Comfort's *The Joy of Sex* is quite helpful (see page 276).

- Initiate sex yourself sometimes in a seductive and subtle manner. Sit on his lap and stroke him lovingly. Don't get up until *you* want to.
- Tell him both verbally and with gestures what would feel good to you during lovemaking. As you instruct him, do it gently, focusing on what you want him *to do*, not what he does wrong.

    6. He always helps buddies but rarely gives you the same consideration.

DON'T:

- Make comparisons. 'You spend all day washing your buddies' cars and never wash mine.'
- Expect your guy to do things that he's not good at.
- Belittle his friends; you'll be seen as the bad one.
- Set yourself up for failure. For example, asking him to run an errand for you when you know he's planning to pick up his friend at the airport.

DO:

- Expect completion of a task you asked him to do. For example, 'I'll get you some lunch as soon as you finish washing the car.'
- Make plans to do a job together. Make cleaning the garage a project for both of you on a Saturday morning.
- Be generous with your praise and approval when he does something that you requested.
- Give him plenty of time to complete the requested task.

    7. He expresses concern about your problems only after you've complained.

DON'T:

- Expect him to show concern over your problems; he considers that he has more problems than you do.
- Whine or complain that he doesn't care about you.

- Continue a discussion if it deteriorates into an argument about which one of you has the biggest problems.
- Make every situation a monstrous problem. Save your concern for a problem that is very high on your personal list.

DO:

- Expect your mate to listen to you. If he doesn't, ask him when he will have time to give you his undivided attention.
- Tell your mate, 'This is important. Listen to my feelings and concerns and don't abuse them.'
- Make a positive comment any time you see a male and female sharing their concerns. For example, 'I really like that character (on TV). He got into the woman's life and tried to help.'
- Praise or thank him whenever he notices your moods.
- Teach him by example. Be open with your concern about another person's problems. Show him how to listen.

8. *He initiates an activity only if he wants to do it:*

DON'T:

- Go with him if it's an activity in which you have no interest.
- Wait for him to organize an outing you'll like. You'll wait forever.
- Expect that you and he will always share the same interests.
- Complain about never getting to do what you want; that's your fault.

DO:

- Take the initiative yourself. For example, 'I bought tickets for a show. We'll go next Friday night.'
- Compromise. For example, 'I'll go to the hockey game and then we'll eat at that new French restaurant.'

216

- Become comfortable going places without him. Go to a movie by yourself or with another friend.
- Introduce him to new experiences. Many a football freak has discovered the beauty of the symphony or the art museum. If it doesn't work, forget it and try something else.

9. He finds it difficult to express feelings.

DON'T:

- Belittle this inability, either to him or, especially, in front of others.
- Pounce on any small attempt, however inept. You'll scare him off.
- Make fun of him as compared to other men who know how to express feelings. He'll only feel more incompetent.
- *Ever* use a feeling he expressed against him. He'll only retreat more.

DO:

- Share your feelings freely and without fear, with him and others.
- Use 'I feel,' 'I'm concerned about,' 'I wonder,' 'I'm scared of' in showing him that it's okay to feel and share those feelings.
- Comment favorably about another man who expresses his feelings, *without* comparing your mate to that man.
- When he tries to express a feeling by saying, 'I feel that . . .,' *gently* confront him by reflecting on the word 'that.' 'That' isn't a feeling; it's your mate's way of avoiding a feeling by talking *about* thoughts or opinions. So, you might say, 'I know you have opinions and thoughts about that situation, but how do you *feel?*'
- Praise his attempts to get in touch with his feelings, no matter how feeble.
- Get a copy of Dr. Eugene Gendlin's book *Focusing* (see

page 262) and both of you practice getting in touch with your feelings together.

10. He wants to be close to his father, but isn't.

DON'T:

- Converse with his father while your mate sits silently by; you can't make up for his shortcomings.
- Talk with his dad about him. 'Yes, John is having trouble with his job.'
- Become their go-between. If they talk through you, bow out of the situation.
- Tell his father how bad his son feels. Your mate must do that for himself.

DO:

- Draw your mate into a conversation with his father. You can be a catalyst without being a go-between.
- Suggest outings for your mate and his father. You could even arrange the first activity to get the ball rolling. Do it as a surprise present.
- Suggest that he send his father a birthday or Father's Day card, without doing it for him.
- Initiate discussions regarding your mate's father. 'Where did he go to school?' is a beginning. Move toward the expression of your mate's feelings about his father, without trying to be your mate's therapist.

11. He doesn't listen well to differing opinions.

DON'T:

- Bait him. If you know he's opposed to something, steer clear of that topic in your discussions.
- Apologize to friends about your opinionated mate.
- Yell at him for being a thick-headed dope.

DO:

- Ask him to repeat what he heard you say at any given point in a discussion. For example, 'Could you tell me what you just heard me say?'
- Introduce new ideas regularly, using a newscaster's format without offering your opinion. Once he responds, give your opinion and then ask him if he heard you.
- Take an example from a conversation that your mate had with one of his buddies in which he didn't listen well. Then comment, 'Did you hear what your friend said about his troubles at work? I think he wanted some help from you and you somehow missed his request.'
- If and when he complains about not getting along well with his boss or co-workers, suggest that when others are talking, he should take a deep breath, hold it for a moment, and then let it out slowly. This relaxation technique may help him reduce his nervousness and listen more effectively. (See *The Relaxation Response*, page 259.)

12. He has unrealistic flashes of rage.

DON'T:

- Feel as if you have to save him from his rage or talk him out of his anger.
- Choose this time to talk about anything that is important.
- Add fuel to the fire by trying to outdo his anger with your own.

DO:

- Control your own anger, even if that means removing yourself to the bathroom and counting to 100.
- Leave the house if you feel in any danger whatsoever.
- If you're ever struck during this flash of rage, *get help*. If you can't find a local help number in the phone book, dial the toll-free operator (1-800-555-1212) and ask for

any hotline, especially for abused women, that is available to you. Then *call!*

13. *He's intimidated by his mother, and you get mad at her.*

DON'T:

- Belittle his mother.
- Describe your mate with words like 'wimp' or 'mommy's boy.'
- Try to keep his mother away from him. For example, 'Oh, Mom, I'm sure he'd like to run you to the store but he's sleeping right now.' You can't save him from his own hang-up.
- Get mad at his mom because *he* has a problem with her.

DO:

- Be a stimulus rather than a go-between by reminding him of how he kowtows to his mother. For example, 'You worked until 1 A.M. and then got up at 5 A.M. to shovel your mother's walk.'
- Praise his mother's good points. 'She's a fantastic cook.'
- Confront your husband or lover about the way in which he permits his mother to run his life. Your best bet is to stick with this confrontation rather than talking to his mother about a problem that is really his.

14. *He feels underemployed.*

DON'T:

- Play his fantasy game with him. Refuse to discuss any dreams of future jobs until he makes a concrete move.
- Try to find a better job for him.
- Complain about your work unless you're ready to make some specific changes.

DO:

- Show well-thought-through and aggressive career choices for your own work goals. If you elect to be a homemaker, become a regular reader of *Consumer Reports, Prevention,* and other periodicals that provide the solid information you need.
- Help in any way you can if he seeks career information, redesigns his resumé, or schedules interviews.
- Point out capabilities that he hasn't seen. 'You're good with your hands,' 'You have a good way with the public,' and 'You're good with numbers' are ways you can support his career development.
- When he complains about his job, say, 'I suppose that's true; what are you going to do about it?'

    15. *He is devoid of honesty and warmth in relating to others.*

DON'T:

- Cover for him. If he doesn't show warmth toward others, let them discover it and react in their own way. Don't protect him from the natural consequences.
- Speak for him, especially when he's there. For example, don't tell the children, 'Your father is very proud of you.'
- Complain about what a cold, indifferent man he is.

DO:

- Be as warm and honest toward him as you can be.
- Prompt him in ways of sharing. For example, 'I'm sure your boss would like to know that you appreciate his help.'
- Build on any inkling of honesty and warmth he expresses. For example, 'It made me glow inside to see how you hugged your grandmother. It was absolutely beautiful.'
- Go slow in touching the warmth inside of him. It took him years to build the defenses and it will take time for him to dismantle them.

16. He has a problem with alcohol; it changes his personality.

DON'T:

- Ever take a drink out of his hand; you're assuming a mother role.
- Tell him how cute he is when he's drinking.
- Beat around the bush when confronting him about his drinking. For example, 'Joe seems to drink as much as you and he doesn't get hostile.'

DO:

- Arrange parties where the focus is on something other than drinking. For example, bridge, trivia games, etc.
- Give him specifics about his personality change and express exactly what you don't like.
- Control your own liquor intake.
- Leave a party where he is drunk and obnoxious after making sure that one of his buddies will take care of him.
- Offer to get him a club soda and lime (or other such nonalcoholic drink).
- Attend AlAnon meetings and, if you have teenagers, encourage them to go to AlAteen meetings.

17. He goes beyond limits to have fun.

DON'T:

- Complain about his pushing himself to have fun.
- Try to stick with him stride-for-stride when you're tired.
- Drag him away from an event with his friends. He'll only protest and want to stay longer.
- Feel sorry for yourself by saying something like, 'Why don't you have fun with me like you do with your buddies?'

DO:

- Help him project outcomes of overextending himself.

For example, 'If you stay up till 4 A.M., you'll have a terrible time with your sales presentation tomorrow.'
- Be willing to be a party-pooper. For example, tell him privately, 'I'm dead tired. Let's continue this next week.'
- Lure him away from some of his buddies by seducing him with some private fun at home.

18. He has clouded chauvinistic attitudes.

DON'T:

- Challenge his attitudes with blatant feminism, hoping to badger him into respecting you.
- Make fun of his chauvinism in front of other people.

DO:

- Express your opinions without sounding apologetic. Become acquainted with rational writings about the problems of women's liberation.
- Quietly assert yourself, complete with the necessary follow-through on issues that you judge to be important.
- Give him material that will help him look at his own sexist attitudes. *The Male Machine* (See page 261) is a good book for this purpose.
- Praise and thank him for trying to promote egalitarian attitudes.
- Arrange for the sharing of chores and other household duties as well as child care (if applicable). Take a firm stand on this.

19. He appears to be afraid and won't discuss it.

DON'T:

- Badger him for self-confession. He'll only withdraw more.
- Analyze him or try to read his mind. For example, 'You wouldn't have so many problems if you didn't lack self-confidence.'

- Employ nasty comments or name-calling ('wimp,' 'gutless wonder').

DO:

- Discuss situations in which you are fearful, without pressuring him to reciprocate.
- Offer to role-play work situations to develop his assertiveness.
- Reflect on his fear and suggest alternatives. For example, 'You sound frightened about tomorrow. You know, it's okay for a wonderful man like you to be afraid.'

20. *He seems above it all and often sits there like a stone.*

DON'T:

- Scream in order to make him react.
- Get defensive about your emotions. For example, 'I am not emotional.'
- Push your emotions beyond your real feelings, hoping to finally get a rise out of him.

DO:

- Curb grandiose attention-getters. Be emotional without flaunting it.
- Admit your emotions without shame. For example, 'Sure, I'm emotional because this is an emotional situation.'
- Examine what kind of emotional reaction you expect from him and specifically share this with him.
- Set a regular time and place for sharing feelings and talking about problems.
- Confront his withdrawal as a sign that he doesn't care. For example, 'When you just sit there I get the idea that you don't care.'
- Let him know that he doesn't have to react emotionally to the same degree that you do. In fact, you don't have a blueprint for how he should feel. Tell him that.

These dos and don'ts give you plenty of guidance in the art of becoming a Tinker. As I said before, the only way to help your husband or lover drop out of the legion of lost boys is to *lure* him away from Never Never Land. You will face certain failure if you stick with Wendy characteristics believing that you can eventually *make* him return to reality.

The above recommendations and the reading list at the back of this book will help you develop the risk-taking, assertiveness, discussion techniques, rational thinking, relaxation, and self-control you need to become the best you can be. *That* is the way you give your relationship its best chance for success.

WHEN TO WALK AWAY?

There is a limit to what a Tinker will endure. If you are becoming a Tinker, there's a chance that your man may reject your changes and refuse to return from Never Never Land. As you may recall from Chapter 7, Peter rejected Tinkerbell and stayed with Wendy (provided she cleaned his house). If your Peter doesn't respond to his Tinker (the new you), you have only one practical option left—to walk away from the relationship. But when?

The simple answer to the question of when to walk away is this: walk *after* you've tried all possible Tinker solutions and *before* you've lost all hope. Let me explain.

Walking away gives you one last chance at the relationship. If you move gradually toward this drastic step, then you will have given your mate plenty of time to hear your dissatisfaction and learn how to respond to the new you. However, he may not take you seriously. Your walking away may change that. You may shock him into trying to save the relationship.

As you walk away you should have two things in mind. First, if he comes running after you, do you want him to catch you? If you do, walk away while there is at least a glimmer of love left in you for him. Second, he may stay in

Never Never Land and *not* run after you. Then you are left with the fact that he doesn't want you if you won't be his mother. In that case, you will keep on walking. The relationship is over.

In most cases, the decision to walk away isn't as simple as I make it sound. Women react differently to the suggestion of walking away. Here are the major ways:

Some women threaten to walk away but don't really mean it. Such an idle threat is something a Wendy does to shame her 'little boy' into being good. He might shape up for a few days, but he will stockpile even more disrespect for her over the long run.

Other women want to walk away, but fear stops them. 'I don't have any money.' 'I can't work full time and raise the kids.' 'I don't have anywhere to go.' If you give in to these fears, forgo being a Tinker and stick with Wendy; *that's okay too!* I know this comes as a surprise after all I've said above. But understand. *I'm not suggesting that all women must become a Tinker or be miserable forever.*

Maybe you say, 'I'd rather be a mother to my man than not have him at all.' If that's the truth, then admit it. You may not have the greatest relationship in the world, but you need not suffer horribly either. Just don't lie about the relationship, especially to yourself. If you accept the truth, then you can be a little more of a Tinker from time to time, doing the best with what you've got. Just having the freedom to accept things the way they are can improve your life immediately.

Other women think of walking away and have an instant guilt trip. 'I made him treat me this way.' 'I didn't follow our marriage vows.' 'I'm just being selfish and running away.' The guilt sounds like a result of the woman's weaknesses. Maybe some of it is. But most of it comes from the fact that the woman knows her man is weak and is protecting him by shouldering the blame. I call this 'stray dog' guilt.

You can imagine how you might feel if you ignored the whimpers of a lost and hungry stray dog. Who could turn Benjy away without at least feeding him? Is not this guilt the same kind of reaction? I suggest that it comes from a feeling akin to that of turning a helpless stray dog out into the cold, cruel world.

The 'stray dog' guilt is really saying, 'My man is too helpless to make it without me, and I'm cruel to turn my back on him. Why, he can't even cook for himself!'

Maybe he can't cook or sew; maybe he doesn't even know where the washing machine is. But does that mean he can't learn? It's possible that you have contributed to his dependence (that's why I suggest you give him time to gradually get used to the Tinker in you), but is he helpless? I doubt it. He just needs to learn.

Before considering the last major reaction to the thought of walking away, I want to share with you one small incident in the life of a woman who contributed to the helplessness of her PPS mate.

Cindy had been married to Ken for ten years. During that time she had never failed to prepare his meals, do his laundry, set out his clothes, buy his beer, make his barber appointments, and do all the other little self-care things he asked her to do. When she got a job, she still took time to make certain these things were done. And, like most Wendys, she did not receive little considerations in return. She was the giver; Ken was the taker.

When her work took her away in the evenings, she always prepared the food ahead of time, leaving instructions for Ken on when to take the food out of the oven. One night she returned home around 9 P.M. Ken was sitting anxiously in the family room. When she walked in, he just stared at her dejectedly.

She was immediately concerned. 'What's wrong, honey?'

He gave her a look of self-pity. 'Oh, I just haven't eaten yet, that's all.'

Cindy was perplexed. 'What do you mean? I left chili in the crock pot and a note telling you that it would be ready by six at the latest. Why didn't you eat?'

With a look of total helplessness on his face, he replied, 'I couldn't find the ladle.'

Knowing that the lady wasn't lying to me, I asked in amazement, 'What did you do?'

She answered honestly. 'I got the ladle and gave him his dinner.'

Deal with this 'stray dog' guilt by not doing so many things for him. If you wait long enough, he'll learn. Then you've eliminated one reason for being afraid to walk away, and possibly you'll find more reasons to stay!

Finally, there are many women who just don't know whether or not to walk away. They are confused. There is good and bad in the man they think they love. These women have said, 'I wish he wasn't so nice sometimes. I almost wish he would beat me. It would make it easier to leave.'

For these women, a decision about walking away is excruciating. The negatives and positives get all mixed together. If you are one of these confused women, then you know the agony of vacillation. One the one hand is his good side; on the other, his bad side. What can you do when the good and bad seem equal? Obviously I can't make the decision for you, but I can give you some help in clarifying the confusion.

First, get a piece of paper. Divide it into two columns and write 'Negative' at the top of one column, 'Positive' at the top of the other.

Next, list the things that are negative about your mate. You can take most of these off the blueprint you used earlier and add any behaviour, attitudes, or habits that I haven't mentioned.

Now rate each of these negatives using that informal measuring tool, 'a scale from one to ten.' Rate them according to how these negatives affect you. Since the measurement is not a perfect tool, think about the negative for a moment and assign a number that reflects how bad you feel when he does this thing. The higher the number, the worse you feel. For example, excessive drinking might feel like a 10, while his flirting feels like a 6.

Once you've written down all the negatives and given them a subjective rating, add up all the numbers and you will have one number that reflects how *bad* you feel being around this guy.

Next, write down the positive things that he does. You may have to think about it for a moment. Here are a few hints: makes good money, is nice to sleep with, is familiar lover (not necessarily a good one), enjoys mutual friends, likes to go to parties, plays a sport with me, is nice to the kids, and talks with me about the news. The fact that he is just there can be a positive thing. Add to these suggestions using this rule: a positive thing is something you would miss if you walked out the door right now *without* another man waiting for you.

Once you have a list of positives, assign each one of them a number from one to ten, reflecting how good you feel when he does or says the positive thing. Add all of these numbers up and you will have one number that reflects how *good* you feel being around this guy.

Finally, compare the two numbers. Which one is larger? How much larger? If the positive number is larger than the negative, then you have to reevaluate your complaints. If the negative number is only slightly larger (5 or 6 points), then maybe you ought to hang in there and work at becoming more of a Tinker. But if the negative number puts the positive number to shame (50 or 60 points), then maybe you ought to reread most of this chapter and answer the question, 'What is it about *me* that keeps me hanging on?' Or, better yet, find a trustworthy counselor to help you find the answer.

The thirty-three-year-old woman whose blueprint was used for instructional purposes in this book completed this piece of homework and reached the following conclusion: the negative score was 117 and the positive score was 84, indicating a lot of feelings in both directions, the negative outweighing positive by a hefty 33 points. Because of the positive things, she wasn't ready to simply walk away; because of the persistence of the negative things, she wasn't content to just 'hang in there.' She took the next step.

She found a lawyer who would talk with her the first time about a divorce without charging her. As she left, she took his card and gave it to her husband, telling him what she had done.

The threat of divorce shocked him. He overreacted, begging and pleading for another chance. The woman used her new-found Tinker skills to confront his begging and pleading. She didn't want either of his extremes—his indifference or his guilt. She wanted some changes. She got one, probably the most important. Now he was listening. Together they found a competent marriage counselor who helped them reconstruct a healthy relationship.

When I last saw her, she was optimistic about the future. She retook the test in Chapter 2 (which I encourage you to do whenever you wish to evaluate any progress or lack thereof). She was able to admit honestly that there were no longer any 'always' behaviors.

The exciting flash of Tinkerbell beamed from her eyes as she told me how their marriage counselor had guided them in improving their sex life. I guess her closing statement says it all.

'I've always complained about how slow he's been in getting things done. But not any more. I finally found one thing he does real slow that I love.'

14   For Friends and Siblings

> Hunkering on the ground or peeping out of their holes, the boys are not unlike village gossips gathered round the pump.

> The boys clear away with dispatch, washing dishes they don't have in a non-existent sink and stowing them in a cupboard that isn't there.

If you think your friend is a PPS victim, you might be able to help. If your brother refuses to grow up, your sibling relationship might give you an inside track to offering aid. Whatever your status, don't follow the example set by the boys in Peter's legion.

Barrie's description suggests that the lost boys couldn't resist talking about Peter's immaturity behind his back. In his presence they patronized his silliness by going along with his pretense. It's easy to make fun of a PPS victim; it's tough to help him. If you find yourself 'hunkering,' 'peeping,' 'gossiping,' or otherwise supporting unrealistic behavior, I recommend that you suspend any attempt to help the victim and take a long look at yourself. Are you living with a strong reliance upon magic wands and Never Never Land?

DEGREE OF DISABILITY

All men have a little magic dust sprinkled somewhere on their soul. If they control it rather than let it control them, they can maintain a youthful outlook on life and be forever growing up. So when you think about helping a potential

PPS victim, you have to be careful in determining just how much magical dust covers the guy's psyche. In other words, you have to assess his degree of disability.

You won't know a man the way his mother, wife, or lover does. But in some ways you might know him better. If he is a PPS victim, you'll see or hear behavior that he won't show the women he loves. (As a sister, you're apt to have a unique position of influence. More below.)

Before offering help, you must answer the question, What right do I have sticking my nose into his business? An assessment of his potential disability gives the answer. If the guy you call friend or brother behaves in most of the following ways, I believe you have not so much a *right* as a *responsibility* to lend a helping hand. That's what being a friend or family is all about.

Does he exhibit:

chauvinistic attitudes? 'I don't know why women think they have to act like men.'

sex role conflict? 'If we ever let those fags out of the closet, we're all in serious trouble.'

rape talk? 'I'll just teach the bitch what a man can do to her.'

excessive drinking? Drinks to get drunk and then becomes nasty and/or cruel to others. Or, simply has a drinking problem.

rowdy and obnoxious behavior? The best example of this is the guy who goes to a sporting event and becomes boisterous, disruptive, and spoils the enjoyment for everyone around him. This is usually associated with excessive drinking.

wild driving habits? He drives as if he owns the road and gets angry if other people make the slightest mistake.

selfishness? He demands to be the center of attention; won't listen to conflicting opinions; likes to feel sorry for himself.

prejudice? Feels compelled to tell racist jokes; regularly refers to minorities in degrading ways.

AVOIDING THE PITFALLS

If you face the social/personal insensitivities of the PPS victim, you must, first of all, refuse to support his attitudes and behavior. In fact, if you face a stone wall when trying to give him positive help, you can offer support by refusing to go along with his pretense, false gaiety, and obnoxious behavior.

Avoid the pitfalls of inadvertently reinforcing the PPS victim's problems by following these don'ts:

DON'T:

- Giggle when he acts like an ass.
- Laugh at his racist jokes.
- Criticize him behind his back.
- Agree with his chauvinistic attitudes.
- Ride with him when he drives like a maniac.
- Support his sex role conflict by responding to his intolerance.
- Buy him drinks when he's had enough.
- Continue to sit with him at a public function where he's boisterous and obnoxious.
- Give him any indication that you support his rape talk.
- Pay attention to him when he's forcing himself on other people.
- Give him pity.
- Compete with him when he has to win.
- Hang around him when he's cruel to other people.

When you do any of these things, you may think you're being a friend, but you're only making things worse.

ACTIVE IGNORING

The first step toward helping the PPS victim is attempting to change a situation without directly confronting the victim's behavior. You do this with a technique I call 'active ignoring.' You ignore what the guy is doing or saying and simply change the direction in which the particular behavior is headed.

To implement active ignoring, try these suggestions.

DO:

- Make a comment about the importance of women becoming persons, suggesting that everyone, including men, will be better off.
- Order coffee, tea, or soda water instead of another beer.
- Say, 'Homosexuals have a right to find happiness just as much as you do.'
- Say calmly, 'I'd like to get there in one piece' when he's driving like a maniac.
- Change the subject when he spouts his racist or sexist views.
- Contradict his rape talk with a comment like, 'Personally, I like someone who *wants* to share sex with me, not someone I have to force to do it.'
- Respond to his obnoxious public behavior by remarking, 'I really enjoy watching this event.'
- Ask somebody else a question when he's trying to monopolize a conversation, pretending that he didn't even make his last comment.

If you take any of these mildly aggressive steps, be prepared for caustic comebacks. The PPS victim won't like his comment ignored or you taking his audience away from him. The greater his degree of disability, the more likely he is to use your action as a stimulant for increasing his own behavior.

HUMOR

The next helpful step involves a lighthearted confrontation. You might be able to help your friend or brother by encouraging him to take himself or the situation less seriously. If you use humor to lighten the load, follow these suggestions.

DO:

- Say, 'The booze is baking your brain, buddy.'
- Say, 'Sure, you're going to rule the women of the world, aren't you?'
- Say, 'You'd better calm down if you don't want a dentist bill' when he's using prejudicial remarks to make fun of others.
- At a public event, say in a good-natured way, 'I remember the first time I had a beer; I acted like an idiot, too.'
- Say, 'Are you trying out for the Indy 500?' when he's driving recklessly.
- Say to another member of a group, 'Old Joe here is practicing to be a politician' when he tries to monopolize the conversation.
- At the golf club or on the tennis court, say, 'If you keep trying to beat up on me, I'm going to start crying.'
- Upon hearing rape talk, you might say, 'You might show her what a man can do, but then she'll show you what a woman can do and she won't kiss you in the process.'
- Hearing the antihomosexual talk, you might try this daring response: 'Are you afraid that some gay guy might get into your pants?'

Humor may help break the spell that the PPS victim casts on a gathering or event. It may also be seen as very hostile (for example, the last suggestion above). If you try to add light to a stormy situation and it only gets worse, back off immediately.

MILD CONFRONTATION

The next step toward helpfulness moves you into a new arena. It calls for mild confrontation. You now say something to the victim that is aimed directly at his behavior. You also find the best possible time to confront him; that means you do it in private. The confrontation is mild because of the spirit that motivates it: 'I really care about you, but I don't like what you do sometimes.'

If you decide to take this giant step toward offering assistance to the PPS victim, follow these suggestions.

DO SAY:
- 'You don't have to throw your manhood around.
  Women would like you a whole lot more if you didn't pretend to be so macho.'
- 'That hard-nosed, screw-'em-good talk hurts your chances for good sex. Go for the gentle routine; I know you've got it in you.'
- 'You know, I've seen you be very helpful to people who have less than you do. I just can't believe that you are really so callous.'
- 'Showing off doesn't become you. You're too nice.'
- 'You're not as mean as you pretend to be. You're just a pussycat. You'll get farther with your soft fur than with your sharp claws.'
- 'I don't think you realize how other people turn away from you when you brag so much. And I know you want people to like you. Slow down, you have friends. But you have to give them a chance to talk.'
- 'You know, sometimes I think you don't like yourself very much.'
- 'I worry about your drinking. I think you're in over your head and don't realize it.'
- 'I get embarrassed for you when you get so wild; like the other night at the hockey game. I just don't believe you really want to spoil other people's good times.'
- 'Sometimes I get scared for you. Like when you drive; it almost looks as if you're flirting with suicide.'

As you can see, mild confrontation includes an element of support and care. There is hope in what you say. You stroke the guy gently as you confront him.

Mild confrontation is especially effective for a sister to use with her brother. When you use it, add a reference to how nice he was when he was growing up. Even if he was rebellious, find something positive to say about him, possibly from his pre-teen days. A sister using mild confrontation

236

has to count on the fact that a family bond still exists. An older sister will probably have more luck with this approach than a younger one.

If mild confrontation backfires (The guy says, 'My problems are none of your business'), you have two choices: proceed to the next and final step, or just forget about trying to help. As you make this decision, keep in mind that the PPS victim may have retreated so far into narcissistic Never Never Land that he doesn't listen to anyone. At that point, he becomes just plain mean.

DIRECT CONFRONTATION

The last step toward helping the PPS victim involves a do-or-die statement. If you've tried everything else with no results, consider direct confrontation. If you do reach the stage of direct confrontation, you will most likely feel some anger against your friend or brother. Give this anger a voice but do your best to make it sound positive. However, you won't be able to avoid the implication contained in the confrontation. That is, 'If you persist in this behavior, you will lose me as a friend.'

DO SAY:

- 'Any decent woman who is worth loving just won't put up with your macho routine for very long.'
- 'I know that sex can be fantastic with mutual respect and sharing. Your rape talk really turns me off.'
- 'If you keep driving like a maniac, I'll stop riding with you. I don't want to have an accident.'
- 'I come out here [tennis, golf, etc.] to have fun. But the way you play, you make it painful. Let's lighten up or this will be our last outing.'
- 'If you don't calm down, I'm leaving' at the outset of a boisterous public display.
- 'You're going to have to go drinking by yourself. I already have enough problems without seeing my friend turn into a drunk.'

237

- 'I know a really great counselor. Why don't you talk to him once or twice? It wouldn't hurt and it might help.'
- 'Do you know how your wife and kids feel when you act as if you don't care about them? Start showing people that you love them.'
- 'If you're going to keep acting like an ass, I really don't want to be around you.'
- 'You've changed since I first met you. What's going on with you? I'm listening.'
- 'Can I help you? You obviously have some problems and I don't think you even know it.'

These direct confrontations should first be made in private. If they are ignored or rejected, you have only one more chance—to say them publicly. I rarely advise anyone to take this extremely harsh approach. It might shame the guy into admitting he needs help, but more than likely it will cause even more rebellion.

In the final analysis, you have to know that you did everything within your power to try to help the PPS victim you call friend or brother. The steps outlined in this chapter guide you in doing the best you can for him. It may take a day, a week, or a month before you know whether or not your help paid off.

If all your attempts fail, you are left with only one option. You say, 'I won't call myself your friend and sit idly by while you destroy your life. If you want my help, you know where to find me.'

As you walk away, keep in mind that your final act may be just what's needed to blow away the magical dust of Never Never Land.

15 For the Victims

> In a sort of way Peter understands why he must not be
> touched, but in most sorts of ways he doesn't. It has
> something to do with the riddle of his being. If he could
> get the hang of the thing his cry might become 'To live
> would be an awfully big adventure!'

I have a very good friend named Larry. As a psychologist
and a psychotherapist, I've learned to cope quite well with
not being asked to parties. Most people don't want a shrink
for a personal friend. Larry is the exception. He's mature
enought to know that I can't spend all my time analyzing
people.

Larry is an absolutely beautiful human being. He's kind,
loving, gentle, and honest. He has a thriving law practice in
a major metropolitan city, two lively, well-behaved kids,
and a very special wife—his own Tinker—whom I admire
and love. Larry is the kind of person whose very presence
makes the world a better place.

But Larry wasn't always so full of life and love. He once
pledged allegiance to Peter and the legion of lost boys. As
with Peter, there were many times that the riddle of his
existence left Larry lost and lonely. Larry figured out the
riddle. It was a difficult struggle. There were many casual-
ties, regrets, and sadnesses as Larry made his way back
from Never Never Land. But he made it.

One night he told me of his journey and shared with me
the solution to the riddle. It was easy being his friend. Not
once did I think about therapy or saying the 'correct' thing; I
just listened. When he finished, we cried. When he left my

house, we hugged. I love Larry. This is his story.

The Early Years

Larry was a simple-minded, strong-willed farm boy. He was raised in the rural Midwest in a small house so remote that the old joke fit like a glove: you just can't get there from here. Associating with dogs, cows, ducks, pigs, horses, and chickens for so many years gave Larry the idea that all of life was as peaceful and tranquil as the barnyard that he shared with the animals.

The serenity of the barnyard was a stark contrast to the horror that possessed Larry's family. To this day he doesn't understand what was happening. But whatever it was, he first became aware of it at the age of five. The tortured screams of his mother woke Larry out of a deep sleep, but for a long time he thought he had been awakened by nightmares. Slowly he discovered that his mom and dad were fighting. He was afraid to leave his room; he feared going to sleep. He sat frozen in terror, his heart pounding.

During the day, Larry's imagined nightmares were always on his mind. He learned how to concentrate on schoolwork despite the continual fear. He says that even today he has the ability to concentrate when opposing attorneys try to rattle him. But the price he had to pay hasn't ever been worth it.

Larry dedicated himself to uncovering the cause of his terror. It wasn't long before he discovered that he could listen to what his parents said by sitting quietly on the stairs when they thought he was asleep.

Strangely enough, he never heard his father utter a word. His mother's lamentations filled his tiny head. 'You abuse me and treat me like one of your animals. You take that horrible tool between your legs and use it to hurt me. Why can't you find your relief with a pig and leave me alone?'

Larry sat there with his head cocked in confusion. What was Mom talking about? Dad was hurting her. And he didn't say a thing. Larry believed his mom; why shouldn't he?

The verbal attack continued. 'You don't take Larry with you. You ignore him. I see his little eyes looking to you for something, anything. But you act as if he isn't there. Your oldest son is a bother, a bother. And you forced yourself on me to bring him into the world. He didn't ask to be born.'

Larry remembered returning to bed on many nights formulating an answer to the problem. In his own simple-minded, childlike way, he reached a conclusion. His mother was in terrible pain and she blamed his dad for it; his dad and his 'tool.' But that couldn't be. His dad *did* like him. After all, Larry reasoned, Dad shows me how to milk cows and feed the chickens. He helps me and talks to me. It's not Dad's fault. There was only one other possibility: *he* was to blame for Mom's pain. Larry was the problem.

Larry's conclusion that he was a bad boy didn't hurt too much. In fact, it gave him the answer. He would simply learn how to be a good boy. He would do everything he was told, never talk back, and thereby never cause his mother any more trouble.

Larry had no way of knowing that he had reached a disastrous conclusion. Neither of his parents told him that he was not the cause of their troubles. Thus, the more he tried to please his mother, the more she showered him with affection. Larry was so good at behaving himself that his mother made a catastrophic move. She started praising him for being nicer to her than her own husband. The covert message came through loud and clear.

Larry's pity for his mother soon became coupled with his mistaken notion that he could save her from pain. As he grew toward adolescence he was forced to choose between his parents. The distance between Larry and his father grew steadily. His mother lived off Larry's pity and was buoyed by his allegiance. The more he ignored his father, the more his mother praised him for being the 'only bright spot' in her life. Larry was proud of himself; he also lived in constant fear. His whole world would collapse if his mother *ever* got angry at him. He was panic-stricken at the thought of Mom's rejection.

Larry's religious training sealed his fate. As a pre-ecumenical Catholic, Larry was exposed to the threatening rigors of the confessional and the fear tactics of the brides of

241

Christ—the nuns. Larry remembers fearing two things most—dishonoring his mother and masturbation, which in those days was called self-abuse. These two things, more than anything else, Larry believed, would send him to hell, where he would burn forever. He now knew what his 'tool' was and why it was so horrible. He vowed never to touch it.

One particularly 'enlightened' bride of Christ confirmed Larry's unrealistic desire to save his mother. She told him, 'When you are bad to your mother, it's like shooting an arrow full of poison into her heart. When her heart is full, she will die.'

One thing saved Larry from certain destruction. He was a hard worker. His labors around the barnyard and in the garden produced a work ethic that would have put Calvin to shame. Because his work pleased his mother, Larry was a workaholic by the time he was twelve. Although he often labored for the wrong reasons, work gave him a source of honest pride that was to be his comfort in the challenging years that lay ahead.

Two major conflicts emerged during Larry's freshman year in high school. He endured daily rejection from most of the kids, and he discovered the pain and pleasure of his 'tool.'

Upperclassmen made fun of him because he was a freshman. The freshman boys belittled him for studying like a girl. The girls giggled openly at his personal interests. Rock 'n roll was in; Larry liked the fox trot. Elvis was king; Larry bought Andy Williams records. Ducktails and grease was the look; Larry had curls. In the language of the late fifties, Larry was a nerd.

Masturbation put Larry on a staggering guilt trip. Boy, did it feel good! But the pain that followed! Thoughts of burning flesh pierced his consciousness at all times of the day and night. For Larry, hell began the day he started playing with his 'tool.'

In addition to pledging contrition and absolute abstinence to God, Larry worried constantly about his mother finding out. She would reject him for enjoying his tool. He remembered her words; he thought of using it on a pig. The fear of Mom's rejection had now become a cause of panic. The thought of her disapproval turned his guts to stone.

One day Larry was sitting idly in his bedroom. He doesn't remember the exact date; the pain of being a teenager has turned those days into a pitch-black hall of horrors—memories occasionally stab him, but he doesn't know where they come from.

As he often did, he started rubbing his penis, pretending that it didn't feel good. He thought not liking it would protect him from the guilt. It never worked. Just as he was giving in to the pleasure of reality, his dad walked into the room. Larry was frozen in panic. His father hesitated and then said, 'I won't tell your mother.' He walked out and it was never discussed again.

Larry's worst fears were reinforced. If Mom finds out, she'll hate me for my tool just like she did Dad. But Dad won't tell her. Hold on! In Larry's mind, there was something terribly wrong with what his dad did. To this day, Larry gets angry everytime he remembers how his father abandoned him when he needed him the most.

Larry is convinced that his rich and boundless fantasy life saved him from psychological suffocation. He was a bright kid, and it was easy for him to jump off from reality and take a trip into the world of imagination. There were no limits. There was no imperfection, no disapproval. Most important, there was no guilt. The sense of freedom kept bringing him back to his make-believe world.

Larry's fantasies always provided a refuge. He could hide in his head just as he had run to hide in the attic when he was younger. He never understood that he was running away from reality. He didn't know that he was addicted to the allure of daydreaming. He just wanted relief and he had found it.

Laughter and hard work brought Larry out of his attic of reverie and back to reality. Grandpa had taught him to laugh; nature had taught him to work. (Not surprisingly, whenever Larry talks about the barnyard or his grandfather he sheds a glow of warmth and a sense of security.)

243

Now Larry would need all the help he could get. He was about to leave home.

Leaving Home

Larry had excelled at high school sports, especially base-ball. He had been offered several scholarships to play ball at fine universities. But his mom didn't want him to associate with the big city kids. She wanted him near the priests. It doesn't take much of a guess to figure out where Larry went to college.

When Larry entered a small Catholic college his person-ality was skewed to the negative. Laughter, hard work, and an active imagination were clearly outweighed by a general fear of social disapproval, a burning desire to be close to a father figure, an ever-deepening guilt about masturbation, and a now phobic reaction to the possibility of rejection by Mom. Needless to say, Larry's college days weren't much of an improvement over his early years.

Larry's fears grew. Daily letters from Mom made his hands tremble. Does she still love me? Once he read them, he breathed a sigh of relief. Yes, she does. Mom was using the United States Post Office to keep Larry in bondage.

Larry tried to close the gap with his father by pleasing the priests. But he was shoved into another vicious double bind. He served the priests every way he could think of, frantic for approval. Yet as his masturbation continued he was forced into the confessional to beg these 'fathers' for deliverance from eternal damnation. He hated them for their cold and calculated indifference to his pain. He envied them, believing that they had no trouble ignoring their tool. It was logical that thoughts of becoming a priest invaded this nebulous career planning.

There were bright spots in his undergraduate days: his A average, a few friends who seemed to suffer just as he did, his top-rank standing as a baseball player, and his special buddy. It was this buddy, several years older than Larry, who introduced him to the brightest spot of all.

Her name was Jackie. She was so real and so sexy that

she put Larry's *Playboy* fantasies to shame. His buddy was dating Jackie's sister, so weekend visits to his buddy's home put Larry and Jackie in the back seat together.

Larry learned how to neck, pet, and come in his pants. Strangely enough, he didn't mind confessing these 'sins of the flesh.' Somehow, Larry used his intellect to conclude that enjoying Jackie just couldn't send him to hell. His new-found freedom brought him face to face with his lack of sex education. It also dampened his enthusiasm for the priesthood.

Larry looks back on May of 1962 with embarrassment and delight. He can laugh about it now, but then he almost died. He calls it 'the cottage incident of '62.'

Jackie's parents had a cottage on a lake that they used as a summer home. On the second weekend in May, Jackie suggested that she and Larry go up to the cottage on Saturday and officially open it for the season. Larry quickly agreed. There was every indication that they would spend the night by themselves. Larry's fantasies were alive with thoughts of playing house with Jackie. He was a virgin. Unfortunately, he didn't know what that meant.

Soon after their arrival, Jackie suggested that they have a drink. Larry didn't know much about alcohol. He had had a beer at his cousin's wedding the summer before. He was about to be introduced to a pitcher full of sloe gin fizz.

They sat on the couch with the pitcher on the table in front of them. It wasn't long before the booze was forgotten in the heat of passion. Larry's pornographic reading and his rich imagination had made him proficient in foreplay. Jackie loved it. Her breathing quickened as did the tension with which her fingers stroked Larry's back. She and Larry shifted clumsily so that they were lying side-by-side on a narrow couch. Larry moved to the next level of lovemaking.

Jackie's blouse was thrown on the table in front of them and Larry almost screamed with delight as he unsnapped her bra with one hand. He had read about 'studs' who could do that. He was a stud. It wasn't long before his bubble burst. Literally and figuratively.

245

Jackie had obviously been in this position before. But that never crossed Larry's mind as he gently nuzzled her breasts. She moaned; that he had expected. She whimpered; that he had also expected. She clutched him tighter; he didn't expect that but it felt good, so why not enjoy it? Then she did the unexpected. She whispered, 'I need you.'

Larry was dumfounded. He didn't know what she meant. Being an honest country boy, he replied, 'For what?'

Undaunted, Jackie continued. 'I'm tense. I need you inside of me for release.' His penis was harder than he could ever remember. As her hands moved below his waist, it suddenly dawned on him what studs did when they 'made it' with a woman.

Larry panicked. He pressed against Jackie's breasts, hoping his fear would subside. She responded by unzipping his pants and grabbing his penis. Larry erupted. His semen spurted forth, past Jackie's hands and onto her pink panties. He tried to pretend that it hadn't happened. His embarrassment was overwhelming. He held Jackie, trying to think of something to say. Little did he realize that he was about to be saved by the sloe gin fizz.

He grappled for his handkerchief in a desperate attempt to clean up the mess his 'tool' had made. He was so nervous that he paid no attention to what he was doing. In his bumbling way he managed to kick the table and knock the pitcher of booze onto the floor. An ugly red stain seemed to form instantly.

Larry had an out from his embarrassment. He pulled his pants up and rushed to the kitchen to get some towels. When he returned, Jackie was dressing and had a look of disbelief on her face. Larry's innocence was gone. It wouldn't return for thirteen years.

Larry returned to school from that weekend filled with guilt and determination. He washed some of the guilt away in the confessional. He channeled his determination to avoid future guilt by keeping his mind on the books and off sex.

He petted with girls in the future but always managed to

246

avoid letting things get out of hand. Or, as he jokingly put it, 'I made sure nothing got into anybody's hands except my own.'

Larry's worry about his mother's rejection continued unabated. So did his retreat into his fantasies. He couldn't help thinking about all the fabulous things he could have done with Jackie. His imagination was so strong that at times he almost believed he wasn't virgin any more.

Larry entered graduate school with the mind of a thirty-year-old and the maturity of a child. His perfect record made transition from the undergraduate classroom to the graduate seminar seem like a snap. Four weeks after settling into a new routine, the winds of misfortune once again blew Larry out of his attic of isolation and into reality. He met the woman who would become his first wife.

The First Marriage

Marilyn was beautiful in a subdued sort of way. She had raven-black hair, captivating brown eyes, and a statuesque figure that both beckoned and forbade. She was indeed cautious. It was she who refused to let things get out of hand; Larry was grateful and filled with admiration. It was she who admonished him to study; Larry worked even harder. It was she who suggested that they be serious; Larry proposed.

Marilyn warned that they must confess their impure petting and resist it until they were married. She excused Larry's fervor, saying she understood his manly needs. Larry knew that his mother would approve of Marilyn. He was right. Mom was pleased, which pleased Larry. Both women seemed to be cut from the same womanly cloth.

The wedding night was a disappointment. Marilyn appeared to endure Larry's foreplay. There was no moaning, whimpering, or clutching. Her body was sensuous but not alive. Her flesh felt tender but her spirit was flat. She took no pleasure from sex save that of seeing Larry pleased. Larry was almost ashamed of enjoying himself. But he knew he'd improve. He would please Marilyn. He was good at pleasing people. He went to sleep that first night with a gnaw of familiar pain in his guts. He was afraid.

Larry's fear of rejection had not disappeared. It had doubled. He now had two women to please. It would take him years to recognize that on that blustery November day, with winter's despair just around the corner, he had married his mother.

Married life grew steadily worse. Instead of enjoying sex, Marilyn performed a service. Rather than supporting Larry's studies, she complained about his lack of attention. She seemed to have no purpose or direction. None, that is, until she became pregnant. To this day, Larry's memory about the birth of his son is a haze. He remembers balancing the final year of law school with a part-time job and taking care of his son. Marilyn hid from motherhood just as she had hidden from other things she didn't understand.

Larry's fantasies once again proved his salvation. Work, study, and childcare occupied only half of his mind. The other half was absorbed in seeking refuge in perfection. He became the perfect lover, companion, and confidant. He paid little attention to Marilyn except to notice that she was slowly becoming a competent mother. The only time that life felt real was when he held his son. The more he experienced a father's love, the more his anger toward his own father turned to regret.

By the time he got his first job in a law firm, Larry's fantasies were working overtime. But something was wrong. They didn't give him the peace and contentment he had come to know and expect. Irritation and indifference crept into his marriage. Feelings of artificiality plagued him. Wherever he was, it seemed like the wrong place. He belonged somewhere else. Not knowing where that was, he just kept going.

Larry never talked with anyone about his problems. He barely admitted them to himself. However, Marilyn didn't have that trouble. She talked with her mother about Larry's indifference; she got pity. She confided in a girlfriend; she got sympathy. She told Larry's mother; she got action.

For four months, Larry was bombarded with phone calls

and letters from his mother. She belittled him for not growing up. She warned him that she was starting to disapprove of his attitude. She intimated that her health was deteriorating as she worried about her son.

The guilt was working. Larry tried harder to pretend he loved his wife. He promised his mother that he wasn't getting a 'big head' as she had surmised. He let his work slide in an effort to appease Marilyn. The only way he could please her was to apologize profusely for alleged transgressions. He did, hating every minute of it.

The tension was mounting. Larry's physician told him that he had an ulcer. Larry thought: I'm only twenty-seven and already my stomach is going bad! He still didn't know where he belonged, but one thing was evident—he didn't want to be with Marilyn.

Larry had to pretend that he was back in the cottage with Jackie in order to maintain an erection during intercourse. Marilyn seemed to enjoy sex more. Larry didn't care. He felt terrible. He was a sitting duck when Terry came storming into his life.

She was a secretary in a neighboring law firm. Business regularly took him to her office. Her eyes devoured him. Her smile made him feel as if he were the only man in the world. He contrived endless excuses to go to her office. They talked about everything. They flirted with each other for months. One night he met her in a bar. She was with a girlfriend but immediately joined Larry at his table.

Larry had come a long way since the fiasco of the sloe gin fizz. He prided himself as a connoisseur of fine scotch. His fantasies had given him the image of the perfect woman for him. He was in shock when perfection sat next to him. They both drank Johnnie Walker Black, flirted unashamedly, and suddenly were holding hands. It seemed natural. With his guilt and fear dissolved in good booze, Larry told Terry how much he liked her. Without hesitation, she replied, 'I've wanted you since the first time I saw you.' This time Larry didn't ask 'For what?'

Lovemaking with Terry was phenomenal. He stayed hard for an hour. Terry did more than moan and whimper.

She talked to him about how good he made her feel and how she wanted to share that feeling with him. Once, he started thinking about Marilyn; Terry sensed his uneasiness. Without a word, she stroked the worry away. Their passion steadily grew and the talk turned to heated words of encouragement. As Larry entered the hallway of inevitability, Terry started writhing in ecstasy. The next ten seconds taught him the meaning of the word 'climax.'

Their simultaneous orgasm was Larry's symbolic release from bondage. He could never again use his fantasies to escape reality. He didn't want to, not if this is what reality could offer.

Larry knew what he had to do. He was absolutely terrified, but come what may he was going to do it. He told Marilyn that he was moving out. Amid her tears and screams of recrimination, he did just that. For the first few days, he drank almost continuously and cried like a baby. But Terry was there. She supported him, loved him, and took him to bed, giving him lesson after lesson in reality. Their explorations into oral sex erased from Larry's mind all thoughts about 'sins of the flesh.' He no longer saw his penis as a 'tool,' but as an extension of his mind.

From Virgin to Vagabond

Larry encapsulates the next four years of his life this way: 'I was bound and determined to make up for lost time. The cottage incident of '62 stuck in my memory. I was going to investigate every body I could lay my hands on. I started with Terry. It's a wonder my penis didn't fall off.'

Terry's litany of hedonism describes Larry's journey from virgin to vagabond. It became their private joke. When asked what she wanted out of life, Terry would always answer, 'Clothes, furs, money, sex, booze, and you.' Terry and Larry lived together for three years.

Terry was a party girl with principles. She believed in using men to attain the 'good life,' but was faithful to one man at a time. Provided he didn't get a disease and kept his conquests to himself, Terry accepted the polygamy of her new roommate.

Larry appreciated Terry and spent weekends with her. But during the week, Larry was 'on the make.' His narcissistic tendencies led him to believe that every woman in a room wanted to sleep with him. His ability to say the right thing in order to please people often gave him the chance to prove it. Larry had his cake and was eating it too. But he wasn't cut out to be a hedonistic party boy. Several experiences taught him that reality might be delightful, but is not always kind.

There was Joy. Larry met her in a bar and she quite bluntly said that she wanted to sleep with him. However, when Larry took Joy to her apartment, they were accosted by Joy's ex-boyfriend, who pulled a gun and threatened to kill both of them. Larry was lucky to be proficient in contrition. He ran quickly away, not worrying about Joy's welfare. He was embarrassed at being a living coward.

There was Peg. Larry met her at a convention and they spent the night together without much forethought or fanfare. They parted as unceremoniously as they had met. Two days later, Peg started calling Larry at the office. He told her it was best to forget their night together. Then she started calling at his home. Terry felt the infringement and accused Larry of violating one of their agreements. Only when Larry fabricated a story of possible gonorrhea did Peg leave him alone.

There was Ann. She was twenty years old and determined to have an affair with an older man before she got married. It sounded as if she was using Larry as a proving ground to test her sexuality. No matter how much or how often Larry had sex with her, she kept demanding more. It was evident that she had not had an orgasm and was going to keep on working at it until she *made* it happen. Larry finally had to lie by telling her that he was married and his wife was getting suspicious.

There was Sally. She was an attractive young woman, recently divorced and terribly lonely. She knew Larry's favorite bar and boldly sought him out. She didn't really

251

appeal to him but she was, in Larry's vagabond lexicon, 'hot to trot.' He took her to her apartment, relaxed her with comforting words, undressed her with tact and verve, and moved her gently to the bedroom. The more she spoke of needing him, the softer his penis became. By the time she was begging him to take her, his penis had shriveled. He covered his embarassment by doing his Humphrey Bogart routine: telling her how he couldn't possibly take advantage of her loneliness and still like himself in the morning. He got dressed and, despite her protests, loudly cursed himself for being so cruel. He vaguely admitted the truth to himself; Sally didn't turn him on.

There were other women. Larry remembers most of their names but few of their faces. The more he pursued them, the more dissatisfied he became with himself. He thought back to the empty years with Marilyn and once again reached the same conclusion: I don't know where I belong, but this isn't it either.

Another piece of reality invaded Larry's pursuit of pleasure. He missed his son. Although the boy lived nearby and Larry actively participated in his life, Larry just didn't feel content not raising his son. The sadness of that realization, combined with the futility of his vagabond lifestyle, thrust Larry right back where he had started; he was lost and afraid. He had run away from being a frightened little boy only to discover that now he was a frightened big boy.

The ghost of his mother's rejection lived on in Larry's soul. It seemed to gather energy now that he was purposeless and depressed. Mom didn't write or call much any more. She did, however, send missives of emotional blackmail via Larry's sister. Sis would say, 'Mom is worried sick that you're living in sin. It's just killing her.'

Larry experienced a new response to his mother's latest attack. He was angry. He grew more irascible every day. He clobbered Terry with cruel innuendos about how she prostituted herself for a rich cock, though he didn't fit the description. He ridiculed their private joke. She was a safe target for his rage.

The day Terry moved out, she dared him to make an

appointment with a therapist. He called her a 'spiteful bitch' and went drinking. He wasn't interested in meeting any new women and the last thing on his mind was having sex. He didn't have sex but he met a woman. Her name was Connie. He didn't know it then, but Connie was the woman who would teach Larry the meaning of love.

Finding His Tinker

They talked for hours. For the first time in his life, Larry closed the bar. All the times before, he had either hurried out in pursuit of a 'good screw' or staggered out hoping that he could drive home before the scotch put his brain to sleep. He can't recall what they talked about. But he does remember that it was easy and comfortable. He felt no pressure to perform. Wherever his mind wandered, Connie was right there listening. When neither had anything to say, there was a peaceful silence.

He decided he would shock her with his worldly ways. He said, 'Do you like oral sex?' As if he had asked her whether she liked fine wine, she responded, 'Sure. Do you?' Well, so much for that pretense.

Larry drove slowly home, amazed at the sights and sounds of early-morning America. He had never seen them before. His head was spinning with words. Lies. Truth. Sex. Love. Fear. Serenity. Honesty. Belonging. Where do I place my money? Which one is the key to the payoff? I've had fear and that isn't it. I've had plenty of sex and that isn't it. Love? I don't even know what that means. I want the answer and I want it now. I'm not waiting any longer.

Larry's therapist was a silver-haired man of fifty with a well-trimmed gray beard, half-moon glasses, and a kindly smile. He was known as a no-nonsense kind of man who cared about people but didn't like neuroses. Larry had come to the right place. This guy even *looked* like a shrink.

The therapist simply waited for Larry to begin. Larry wanted to know where he should start. 'Wherever you want to,' was the reply. Because his fear and anger about his mother dominated his feelings, Larry started there. He filled the therapy room with thoughts, feelings, and memories. His 'tool,' Mom, Dad, the cottage incident of '62, Marilyn, his son, embarrassment, fear, masturbation (that was difficult), and, for some reason, Connie, who stood out in his mind although he didn't really know her. He apologized for not making sense. But he *was* making sense. A lot of sense.

'You really feel as if you're bad, don't you?' The doctor waited.

Larry recalled his confusion. 'Sure I feel bad. That's why I'm here. I feel terrible.'

'That's not what I mean. I mean you feel bad *here*.' The doctor pointed to his heart. 'In your soul, you feel bad. Unworthy. As if you had to earn the right to be alive.'

The session ended without Larry totally understanding what the doctor had said. Unworthy? Bad? He hated to admit it, but there was something to that idea. He tried to get it out of his mind. He couldn't. He had to keep thinking about it. He couldn't sleep. He called Connie. She was a breath of fresh air. They shared some silliness; then he was left with the sounds of silence.

Suddenly he was deathly afraid. He even thought he heard voices. He looked around his house, but there was nothing. He listened intently. Something was happening. But it wasn't coming from outside his head. He thought: am I hallucinating? Have I finally cracked? He concentrated on what he was feeling. Certain words came into his mind: Doom. Explosion. Terror. Cease to exist. Nothingness.

The silence closed in on him. He was scared to death. He wanted to run. He waited. Nothing happened. He waited again. Then a feeling of euphoria passed through him. Fear and euphoria? He *was* losing his mind. It made no sense.

In the next few weeks, Larry dedicated his time and energies to two goals: getting to know Connie and working at his therapy. His ability to carry out his duties while concentrating on other matters really paid off. He had the same strange experience twice in three short weeks. Each time, it followed his therapy and occurred as he encountered the loud silence. His understanding slowly unfolded.

Connie proved to be another kind of therapy. Her maturity, strength, and sanity drew Larry closer to her each time they talked. One night it suddenly occurred to him that they had never made love. He finally asked why they hadn't. In that same peaceful tone she replied, 'I figured you'd say something when you got around to it. You have other things on your mind.'

In Larry's best estimate, they made love for two days. After sex, they would talk. Then they would eat and sip a little wine. And they'd talk some more. And love some more. Larry never felt that old urge to get dressed and leave. He felt totally comfortable just being naked and talking. He saw Connie every day.

He also felt full of energy. Not only could he engage in intercourse for as long as he wanted, but he also had a renewed zeal to reinstitute his jogging program. It had died somewhere along the road to hedonism. Larry was excited. It had been many years since he felt this way—thirteen, to be exact. He was back in the cottage with Jackie. He was still clumsy, concerned about approval and, despite his vagabound years, naïve. Only this time it was different. This time he *wanted* to be young and silly.

As Larry realized that he was learning what love meant, he came to understand what the therapist was saying about his strange experiences.

The sounds of silence and his willingness to confront the truth brought him face to face with the reality he had been avoiding for most of his life. He had mistakenly believed that reality would destroy him. When it did not, he was euphoric.

Lary stopped talking. I waited for him to continue. He didn't. I had been walking in his shoes for hours, listening to an unbelievable story. And now, he just stopped.

I pressured him. 'You're not going to stop now, are you?'

'I've told you the whole story. You know Connie and I got married and had a child, and that my other son is living with us now. You know how much I'm learning about love. And each day is a new adventure in living. What else is there?'

'Well, for one thing, what do your mom and dad think of all this?'

His smile evaporated. 'I still struggle with that. They disapprove of me now more than ever. Mom has done her big rejection number and I've survived it quite well. Dad just sits there and listens to her. What else can he do?' He was hurting, but he continued. 'The biggest problem is the anger. They abused me. Emotionally. I'll never get over that. I can live with it, but I'll never get over it.'

'Ever hear from Terry?'

His smile returned. 'Last time I heard, she was living with another guy. Good old Terry, she'll never change.'

'Whatever happened to you two? Sounds like you had a good thing going.'

'It was doomed from the start. I was running around trying to prove I was a tough, macho man, and she was sitting home waiting for me to pay attention to her. She stockpiled a lot of resentment. I didn't make much money in those days, either. I was so busy partying and trying to get laid that I ignored my law practice. She never admitted it, but she didn't want me screwing around on her. She was right about my seeing a shrink, but it was her version of a cheap shot.'

'So what's the answer to the riddle?'

'Huh?' My question had obviously interrupted a bit of reverie. 'Oh, the riddle. You're the shrink; solve it yourself.'

'C'mon, man, get serious.'

He did. 'It sounds simple, but it's not. When I was a little boy, I sat on the stairs and decided that I was bad. Not that I did bad things, but that *I* was bad. Nobody told me that I was wrong. All my life, I ran from that lie. I didn't let myself grow up inside. I didn't let myself feel anything that I thought might be bad. I did everything I could to prove that I was good.

'I worked myself like a crazed animal. I did everything within my power and then some, to squeeze the devil out of my soul. I spent so much time trying to prove that I was good, I never learned how to be me. Just to be me.

'It took the sounds of silence to shock me. With no noise

around me, I found the courage to face the truth. The devil is not in my soul. I'm good. I spent all those years trying to prove something I didn't have to prove. I am good and the things I feel are good. I've done some stupid things, but *I am good.*' Larry was crying.

My heart was with him and I cried, too. 'What a waste of precious time. That's sad.'

There was no self-pity in his eyes, only tears of remorse. 'It certainly is.'

'What about the fear?'

'Oh, it's still there. I still feel afraid. Connie knows it. Sometimes, when she wants to touch me, I get tight inside. I don't want her hand anywhere near me. I'm afraid to let her love me, afraid of the price I might have to pay. But there's no price; it's just a vicious flashback. Back to the stairs and the decision that I was bad and had to pay. The fear is there, all right. I guess it always will be. The memories burn too deeply. But we handle it. We even get closer together because of the fear. *That's* the answer to the riddle.'

I was caught up in his soul's struggle. 'What is?'

'Don't you see? It's simple. I don't have to be afraid of fear any more. I have someone who loves me just the way I am. She wants to share my pain just the way it is. Now I'm free. I can be young forever.'

This is Larry's story. It's a tale of emotional paralysis, social impotence, parental rejection, sexual hang-ups, and a belief in mental magic. Larry jumped from one extreme to the other in searching for the truth. But he found it, and the story has a happy ending. Larry accepts his manhood and the reality that love has no price tag. He now knows that it's okay to be hard on the outside and soft on the inside.

Larry overcame the Peter Pan Syndrome and returned from Never Never Land. If he could do it, anybody can.

Helpful Reading

The following books are relevant to the causes and cure of the Peter Pan Syndrome. Though the list is not exhaustive, these books will add depth to your understanding of the development of the PPS and, in many cases, provide you with creative solutions not covered in this book.

Bach, George, and Peter Wyden. *The Intimate Enemy*. New York: Avon, 1970.

> An accomplished psychotherapist teaches couples to 'fight fair.' 'Fight' actually means to have a constructive discussion no matter how heated it might become. It is difficult to 'fight fair' with a PPS victim. Dr. Bach gives the reader many specific things to do or say to achieve the goal.

Baer, Jean. *How to Be an Assertive (Not Aggressive) Woman in Life, in Love and on the Job*. New York: Signet, 1976.

> Countless suggestions for socially appropriate assertions make this a very helpful book for the woman struggling to become a Tinker. The author's recommendations are graded so that, no matter how skilled you are in assertiveness, you will find help. This is an excellent companion to *Risk-Taking for Women* (see Morscher and Jones).

Benson, Herbert, with Miriam Klipper. *The Relaxation Response*. New York: Avon, 1976.

> This book teaches you the many ways to relax. Relaxation is an excellent medium within which to practice new thoughts. A PPS victim can use relaxation

as the first step in regaining control over his life.

Burns, David. *Feeling Good: The New Mood Therapy*. New York: Signet, 1981.

Perhaps the best book on the innovations in cognitive therapy, an approach that can be very beneficial to PPS victims' magical thinking. Dr. Burns takes the 'power of positive thinking' beyond the inspirational and into the scientific.

Comfort, Alex. *The Joy of Sex*. New York: Crown, 1972.

This is a highly popular book that graphically instructs the sensitive adult in the science and art of lovemaking.

Dowling, Colette. *The Cinderella Complex*. New York: Pocket Books, 1982.

This is must reading for anyone interested in the Peter Pan Syndrome. Women's hidden fear of independence is the motivating force behind the emergence of Wendy traits. You don't need psychoanalysis, however, to cope with the Cinderella Complex.

Elkind, David. *The Hurried Child*. Reading, Mass.: Addison-Wesley, 1981.

Pushing our children to grow up too fast may have many negative side effects, one of which is a retreat into Never Never Land. This is excellent reading for parents.

Ellis, Albert, and Robert A. Harper. *A New Guide to Rational Living*. North Hollywood, Ca.: Wilshire Book Co., 1975.

One of my all-time favorite books and a work that I regularly recommend to all my therapy clients. Dr. Ellis is the dean of cognitive therapists. I would call him my hero, but he would quickly label my idolization as irrational.

Ellis, Albert, and William J. Knaus. *Overcoming Procrastination*. New York: Signet, 1979.

As one might suspect, procrastination spotlights a deeper problem than simple laziness. A pessimistic, 'I'm-no-good' attitude often lies at the heart of procrastination. The PPS victim can delve into a supposedly simple problem in order to get at the underlying truth. Although the book is very confrontative in style, Dr. Ellis is a therapist filled with concern and love.

Fasteau, Marc. *The Male Machine*. New York: McGraw-Hill, 1974.

Never outdated for the man who wants to take the pressure off himself by learning how males have been shoved onto the relentless treadmill of constantly proving their toughness. Although a bit overstated at times, *The Male Machine* gives men a breath of fresh air.

Fensterhaim, Herbert, and Jean Baer. *Don't Say Yes When You Want to Say No*. New York: Dell, 1975.

This book will help a woman to become a Tinker. The emphasis may be on saying 'No,' but the book is loaded with positive suggestions, especially for overcoming sexual uncertainties. The authors present an invaluable script for learning the ABCs of self-induced relaxation.

Frankl, Viktor. *Man's Search for Meaning: An Introduction to Logotherapy*. New York: Pocket Books, 1980.

Existential psychology offers great hope for anyone journeying through life searching for meaning. The PPS victim will learn that all emotional experiences are good, and that authenticity can be had by simply listening to one's soul. This book will be a powerful influence on even the casual reader's life.

Friday, Nancy. *My Mother/My Self*. New York: Dell, 1981.

A warm and candid look at a woman's struggle to own her life. The author deals with sexual awakening in such a tender fashion that any woman should be proud of her sexuality.

Fromm, Erich. *The Art of Loving*. New York: Harper and Row, 1974.

PPS victims may have forgotten what love is, or may never have known true love. Careful reading of this classic work can help correct that deficit. The book lends itself to soul-searching discussions.

261

Gendlin, Eugene T. *Focusing*. New York: Bantam, 1981.

Step-by-step instruction in Focusing, a technique to help you identify thoughts and feelings as well as 'focus' on solutions to key problems.

Glasser, William. *Reality Therapy: A New Approach to Psychiatry*. New York: Perennial Library (Harper and Row), 1975.

All of us must eventually cope with the dictates of reality. Dr. Glasser gives the reader an indispensable guide for organizing real experiences and profiting from them.

Janus, Sam. *The Death of Innocence*. New York: Morrow, 1981.

A masterful book that looks at the horrors of children who have an abbreviated childhood. This could be considered a companion to Dr. Elkind's *The Hurried Child*. Janus examines the lifestyle of children whose innocence dies abruptly.

Jourard, Sidney. *The Transparent Self: Self-disclosure and Well-being*. Second Edition. Princeton, N.J.: D. Van Nostrand Reinhold, 1971.

This book will help the PPS victim cope with emotional paralysis. The author introduces his topic by saying: 'We conceal and camouflage our true being before others to foster a sense of safety, to protect ourselves against unwanted but expected criticism, hurt, or rejection. This protection is purchased at a steep price.' To take full ownership of his emotions, the PPS victim must choose to become transparent to himself and those who love him.

Kiley, Dan. *Keeping Kids Out of Trouble*. New York: Warner, 1979.

The first of my three child-rearing books in which parents learn that children are quite capable of manipulation. Over 100 case histories are analyzed, and innovative solutions proposed. I take a strong stand against permissiveness throughout the book.

Kiley, Dan, *Keeping Parents Out of Trouble*. New York: Warner, 1982.

The second of my child-rearing books, in which the reader will learn how to implement a back-to-basics approach in the home. Strategies for coping with chores, curfew, school, peer pressure, drug abuse, and other frequent problems are outlined and explained.

Kiley, Dan. *Dr. Dan's Prescriptions: 1001 Nonmedical Hints for Solving Parenting Problems.* New York: Coward, McCann & Geoghegan, 1982.

The third book in my three-part child-care series. It is a compilation of workable solutions to daily parenting problems. I offer no theories or explanations, only answers.

Kopp, Sheldon B. *If You Meet the Buddha On the Road, Kill Him!* New York: Bantam, 1976.

A very serious and eye-opening look at the pilgrimage of being a therapy patient. It is must reading for anyone investing time and money in psychotherapy. Although alarming, the title reflects the theme of the book; that is, eliminate (by no returning) any therapist who acts as if he or she has all the answers to your problems.

Lasch, Christopher. *The Culture of Narcissism.* New York: Warner, 1980.

A challenging analysis of the social, political, historical, and psychological aspects of narcissism makes this important reading. Although a bit difficult to understand at times, the book is very clear on one important point: narcissism is *not* a fun-filled, happy-go-lucky lifestyle.

Machlowitz, Marilyn. *Workaholics: Living with Them, Working with Them.* New York: Mentor, 1981.

The PPS victim may try to compensate for past procrastination and avoid rejection by working beyond all rational limits. This book provides understanding and help for the victim and those who love him.

Marks, Burton, and Gerald Goldfarb. *Winning with Your Lawyer.* New York: McGraw-Hill, 1980.

If you're seriously considering walking away from your marriage, you'll want to speak with an attorney.

This book offers candid advice that gives you confidence in seeking one. Chapters I through 4 and 7 are especially applicable.

Masters, William H., and Virginia E. Johnson in association with Robert J. Levin. *The Pleasure Bond.* New York: Bantam, 1976.

The psychology of sex within a marriage has never been dealt with better. The following statement introduces the book as it provides a lesson in itself: '[A husband and wife's] sexual relationship mirrors their personal relationship, in which each is responsive to the other's wishes, each takes pleasure in pleasing the other and each values having the respect of the other.'

Mayle, Peter. *'What's Happening to Me?'* Secaucus, N.J.: Lyle Stuart, 1975.

Another delightful book in an important series of sex education works. This gem helps kids cope with puberty and understand the biological and emotional changes. The information is honest and refreshing. It will help parents prepare their children for any sexual conflicts that may arise in later adolescence.

Meichenbaum, Donald. *Cognitive Behavior Modification: An Integrative Approach.* New York: Plenum Press, 1977.

This is a textbook that will be understandable to the informed layperson. It adds considerable substance to the popular books written by Burns, Ellis, and Peale. Excellent reading for all those who wish to understand how and why our thoughts can be reprogrammed.

Money, John, and Patricia Tacken. *Sexual Signatures: On Being a Man or a Woman.* Boston: Little Brown, 1975.

An excellent primer on how we are a man or a woman socially, biologically, and psychologically. A good reference for any adult who wishes to understand the background of modern-day conflicts.

Morscher, Betsy, and Barbara Schindler Jones. *Risk-Taking for Women.* New York: Everest House, 1982.

Becoming a Tinker, confronting a PPS victim, and considering divorce are risky ventures. This primer on infantile attitudes. It is a thorough background study and prepares you to profit from the cognitive therapy of Burns and Ellis.

Tillich, Paul. *The Courage to Be*. New Haven, Conn.: Yale University Press, 1952.

PPS victims suffer great anxiety about just being who they are. They often lack courage to discover themselves. This classic work provides insightful answers to perplexing philosophical questions. If you or your loved one is trapped in Never Never Land and don't have the courage to be, this book will give your soul a pathway to life. The reader should be prepared to reflect on each page, since complicated topics are discussed in depth.

risk-taking is occasionally oversimplified, but it guides the female reader with specific suggestions, empathy, and humor.

Peale, Norman Vincent. *The Power of Positive Thinking.* New York: Fawcett Crest, 1963.

Dr. Peale uses quotes from scripture and general theological references to support his inspirational message. You need not be a Christian or even a theist to profit from this classic work, especially the recommendations for building self-confidence. Not only are his suggestions given in a folksy way, but they also have substance in light of recent developments in cognitive behavior modification.

Phillips, Debora, and Robert Judd. *How to Fall Out of Love.* New York: Popular Library, 1980.

This is a warm and witty self-help book that covers much more than the title indicates. It provides excellent help in the areas of thought control, relaxation, and sexual problems. Any woman considering walking away will find tremendous help in this book.

Reuben, David. *Everything You Always Wanted to Know About Sex But Were Afraid to Ask.* New York: Bantam, 1971.

This is an excellent source for both older children and adults. The title says it all, except that Dr. Reuben writes with a wit and charm that take away all guilt and embarrassment from this critical topic.

Russianoff, Penelope. *Why Do I Think I Am Nothing Without a Man?* New York: Bantam, 1982.

This book will help you cope with the Wendy inside of you. The author inspires you to become a whole person and to own your life. The book could have been subtitled 'On Becoming a Tinker.'

Serban, George. *The Tyranny of Magical Thinking.* New York: Dutton, 1982.

This book helps you understand the complicated nature of magical thinking, one of the seven major personality traits of the Peter Pan Syndrome. You will also realize that change necessitates challenging

265